THE ALL NEW ATOM

Future/Past

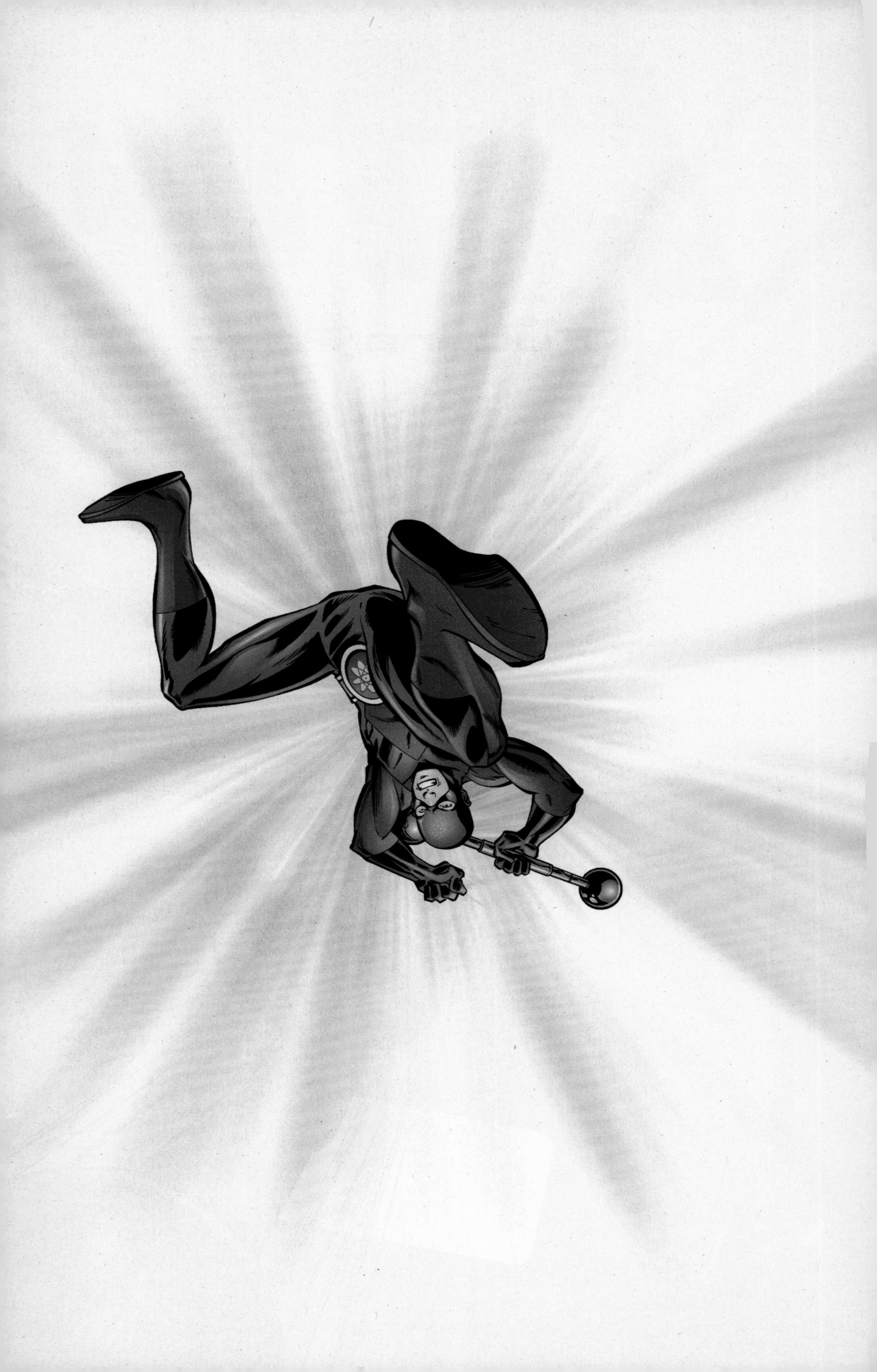

Future/Past

Gail Simone Writer

"THE MAN WHO SWALLOWED ETERNITY"
Mike Norton Pencils **Andy Owens** Inks

"JIA"
Eddy Barrows Pencils **Trevor Scott** Inks

Pat Brosseau Travis Lanham Letters

Alex Bleyaert Colors

Original Covers by **Ladrönn**

Dan DiDio
Senior VP-Executive Editor

Mike Carlin
Editor-original series

Tom Palmer Jr.
Associate Editor-original series

Bob Joy
Editor-collected edition

Robbin Brosterman
Senior Art Director

Paul Levitz
President & Publisher

Georg Brewer
VP-Design & DC Direct Creative

Richard Bruning
Senior VP-Creative Director

Patrick Caldon
Executive VP-Finance & Operations

Chris Caramalis
VP-Finance

John Cunningham
VP-Marketing

Terri Cunningham
VP-Managing Editor

Alison Gill
VP-Manufacturing

David Hyde
VP-Publicity

Hank Kanalz
VP-General Manager, WildStorm

Jim Lee
Editorial Director-WildStorm

Paula Lowitt
Senior VP-Business & Legal Affairs

MaryEllen McLaughlin
VP-Advertising & Custom Publishing

John Nee
Senior VP-Business Development

Gregory Noveck
Senior VP-Creative Affairs

Sue Pohja
VP-Book Trade Sales

Steve Rotterdam
Senior VP-Sales & Marketing

Cheryl Rubin
Senior VP-Brand Management

Jeff Trojan
VP-Business Development, DC Direct

Bob Wayne
VP-Sales

Cover art by Ladrönn
Logo design by Rian Hughes

**THE ALL NEW ATOM:
FUTURE / PAST**

DC Comics, 1700 Broadway,
New York, NY 10019
A Warner Bros. Entertainment Company
Printed in Canada. First Printing.

ISBN: 978-1-4012-1568-2

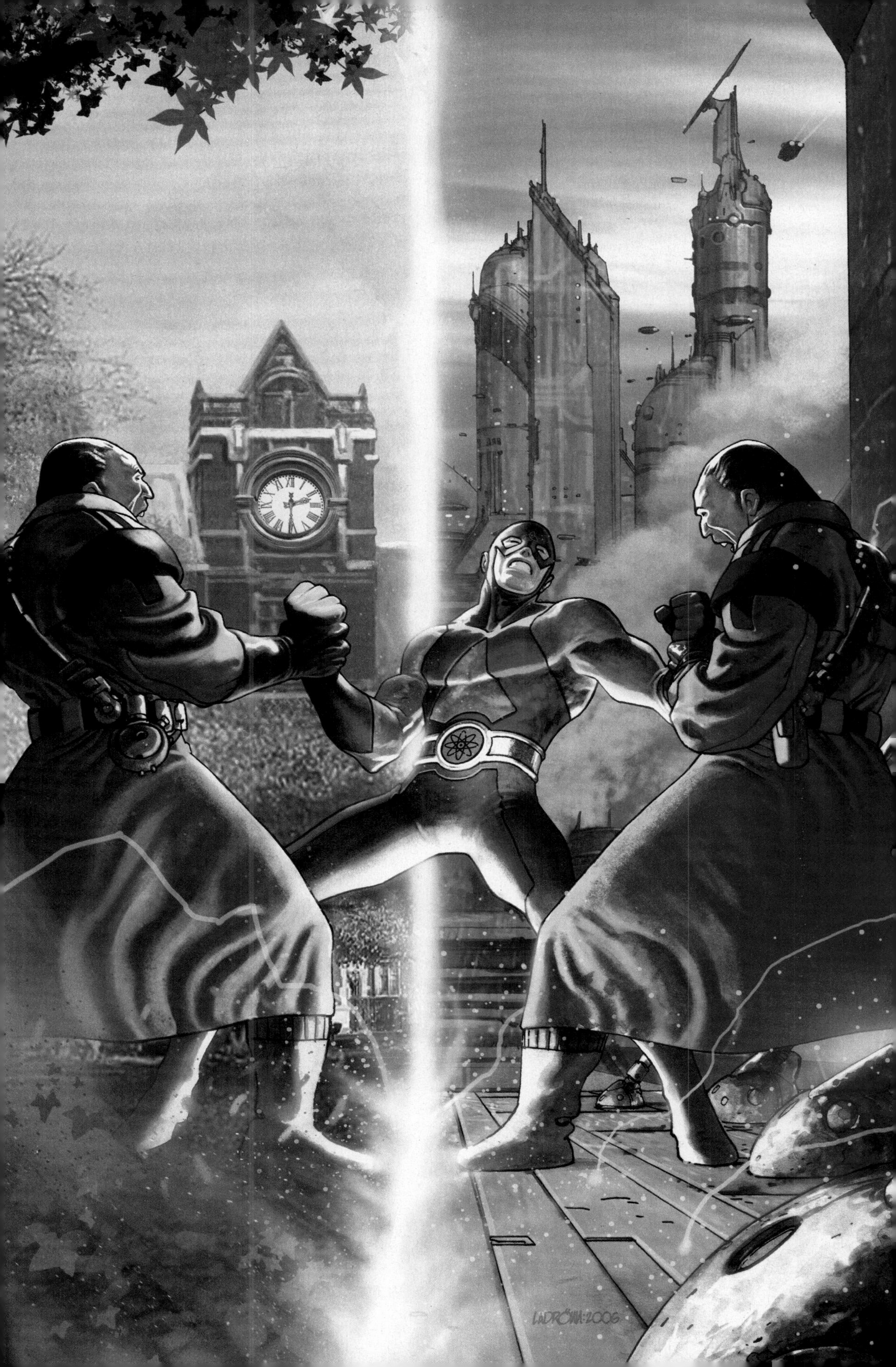
LADRÖNN:2006

THE MAN WHO SWALLOWED ETERNITY: PART ONE
THE ENERGY OF THE UNIVERSE IS CONSTANT

from **THE ALL NEW ATOM #7**

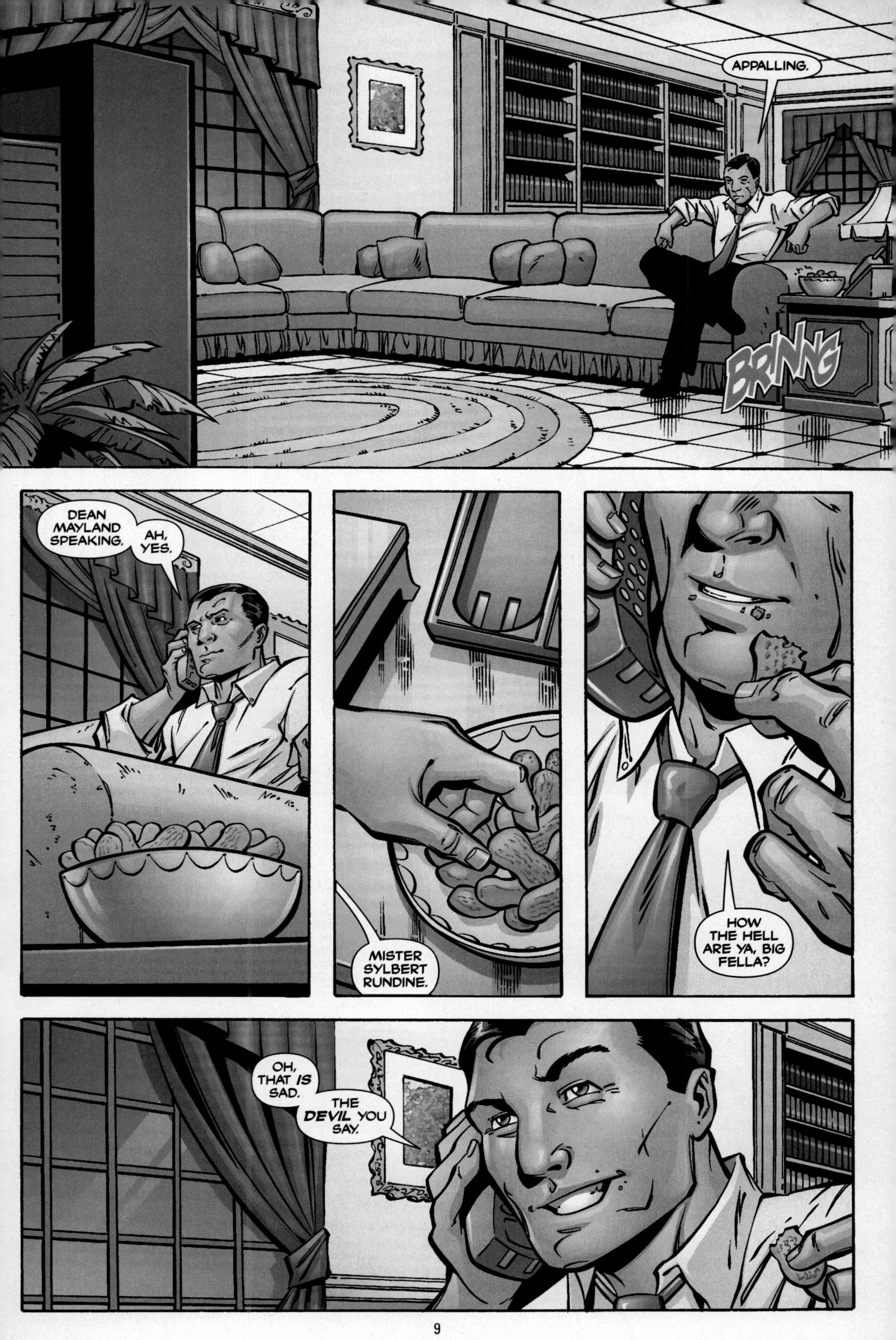
APPALLING.
BRINNG
DEAN MAYLAND SPEAKING.
AH, YES.
MISTER SYLBERT RUNDINE.
HOW THE HELL ARE YA, BIG FELLA?
OH, THAT *IS* SAD.
THE *DEVIL* YOU SAY.

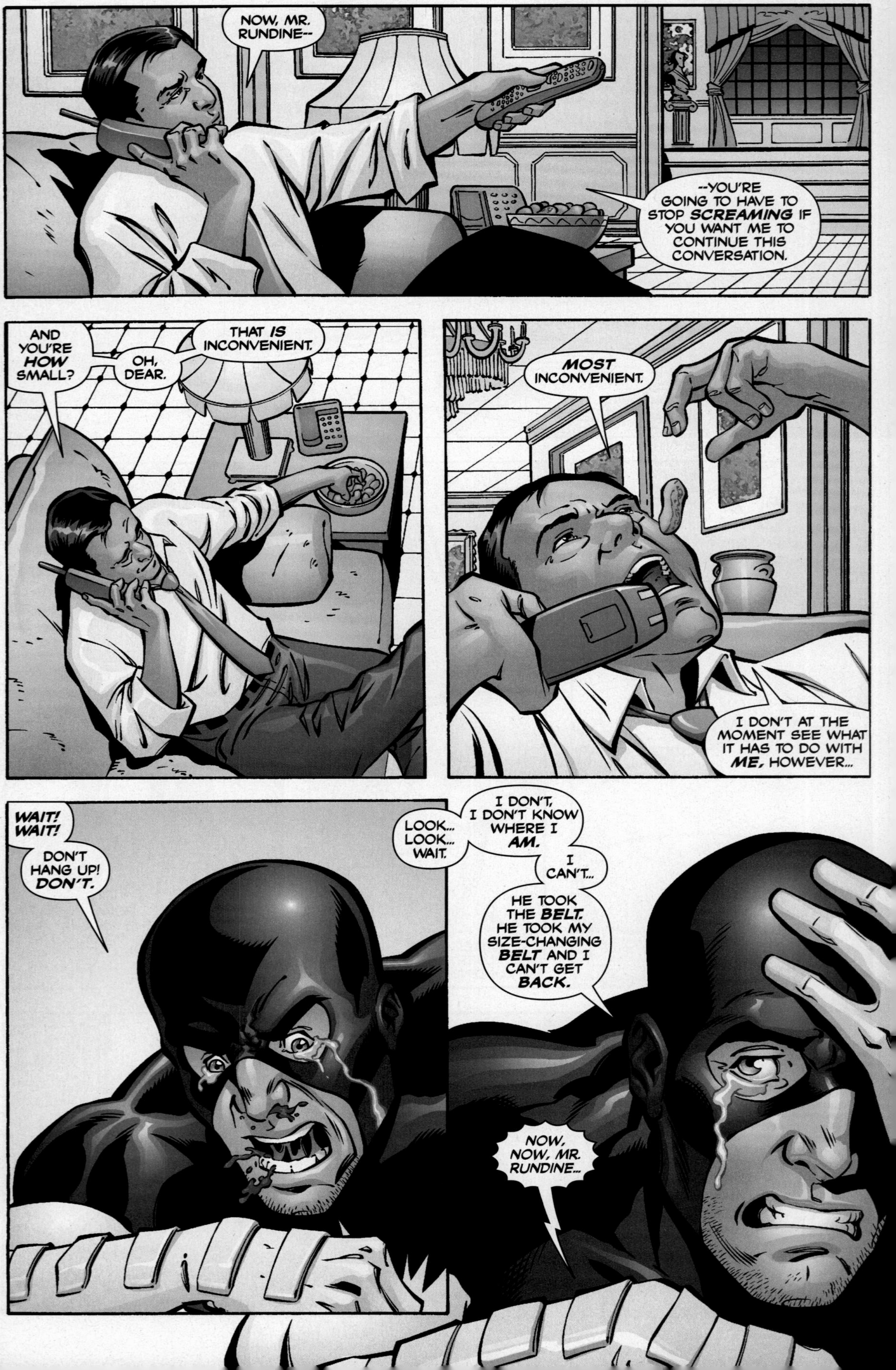
NOW, MR. RUNDINE--
--YOU'RE GOING TO HAVE TO STOP SCREAMING IF YOU WANT ME TO CONTINUE THIS CONVERSATION.
AND YOU'RE HOW SMALL?
OH, DEAR.
THAT IS INCONVENIENT.
MOST INCONVENIENT.
I DON'T AT THE MOMENT SEE WHAT IT HAS TO DO WITH ME, HOWEVER...
WAIT! WAIT!
DON'T HANG UP! DON'T.
LOOK... LOOK... WAIT.
I DON'T, I DON'T KNOW WHERE I AM.
I CAN'T...
HE TOOK THE BELT. HE TOOK MY SIZE-CHANGING BELT AND I CAN'T GET BACK.
NOW, NOW, MR. RUNDINE...

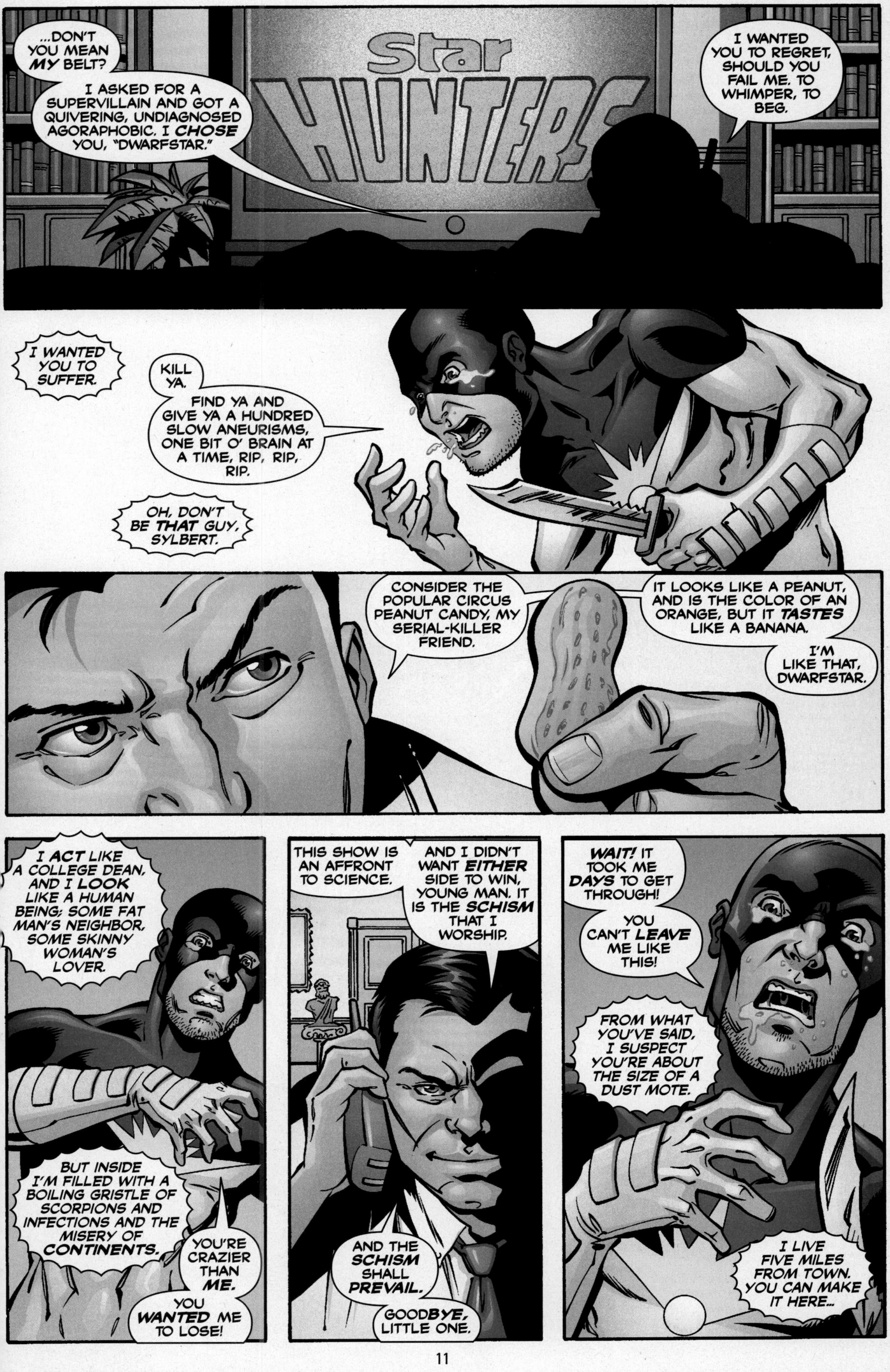
Star HUNTERS
...DON'T YOU MEAN MY BELT?
I ASKED FOR A SUPERVILLAIN AND GOT A QUIVERING, UNDIAGNOSED AGORAPHOBIC. I CHOSE YOU, "DWARFSTAR."
I WANTED YOU TO REGRET, SHOULD YOU FAIL ME. TO WHIMPER, TO BEG.
I WANTED YOU TO SUFFER.
KILL YA.
FIND YA AND GIVE YA A HUNDRED SLOW ANEURISMS, ONE BIT O' BRAIN AT A TIME, RIP, RIP, RIP.
OH, DON'T BE THAT GUY, SYLBERT.
CONSIDER THE POPULAR CIRCUS PEANUT CANDY, MY SERIAL-KILLER FRIEND.
IT LOOKS LIKE A PEANUT, AND IS THE COLOR OF AN ORANGE, BUT IT TASTES LIKE A BANANA.
I'M LIKE THAT, DWARFSTAR.
I ACT LIKE A COLLEGE DEAN, AND I LOOK LIKE A HUMAN BEING; SOME FAT MAN'S NEIGHBOR, SOME SKINNY WOMAN'S LOVER.
BUT INSIDE I'M FILLED WITH A BOILING GRISTLE OF SCORPIONS AND INFECTIONS AND THE MISERY OF CONTINENTS.
YOU'RE CRAZIER THAN ME.
YOU WANTED ME TO LOSE!
THIS SHOW IS AN AFFRONT TO SCIENCE.
AND I DIDN'T WANT EITHER SIDE TO WIN, YOUNG MAN. IT IS THE SCHISM THAT I WORSHIP.
AND THE SCHISM SHALL PREVAIL.
GOODBYE, LITTLE ONE.
WAIT! IT TOOK ME DAYS TO GET THROUGH!
YOU CAN'T LEAVE ME LIKE THIS!
FROM WHAT YOU'VE SAID, I SUSPECT YOU'RE ABOUT THE SIZE OF A DUST MOTE.
I LIVE FIVE MILES FROM TOWN. YOU CAN MAKE IT HERE...

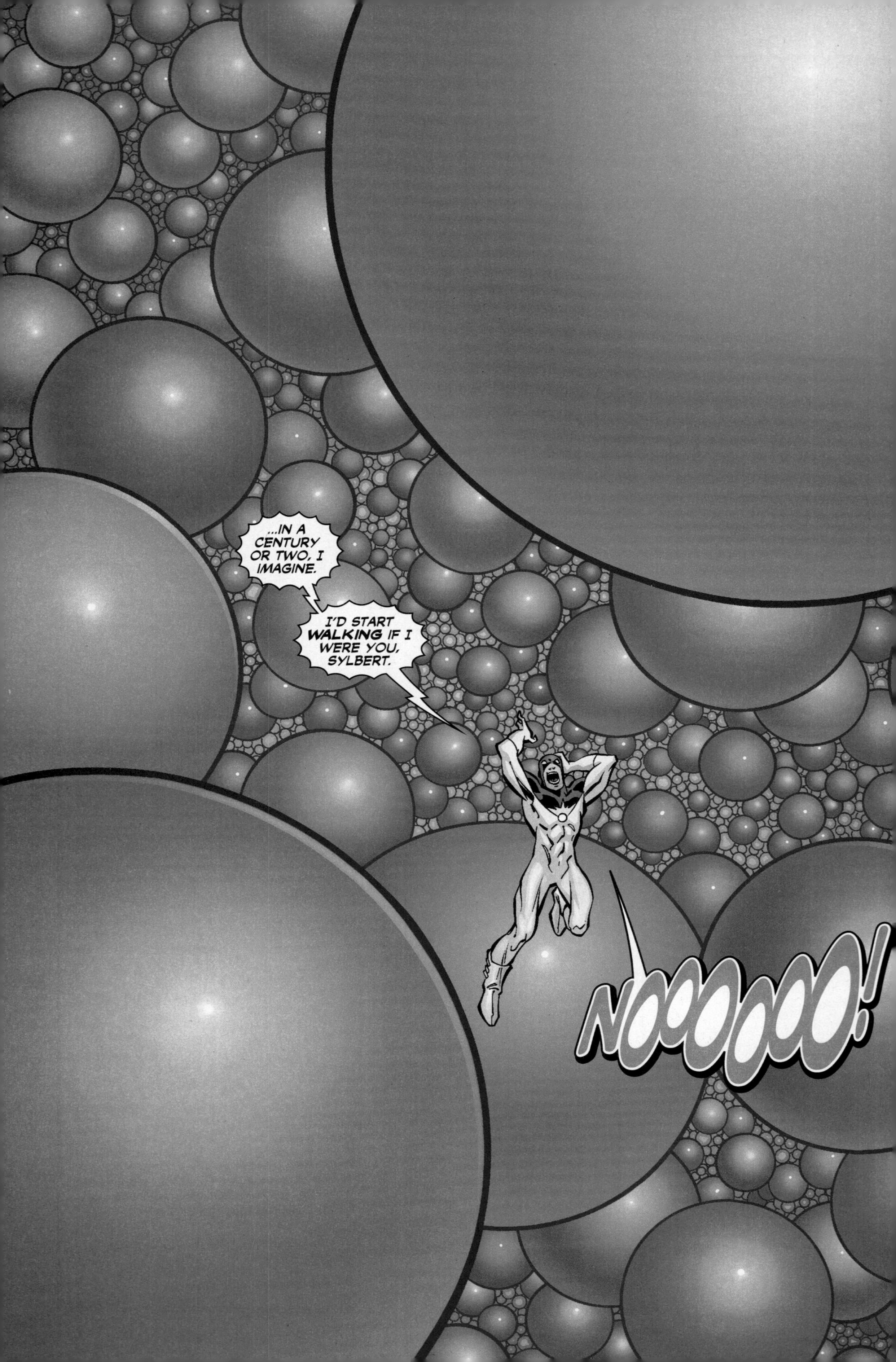
...IN A CENTURY OR TWO, I IMAGINE.
I'D START **WALKING** IF I WERE YOU, SYLBERT.
NOOOOOOO!

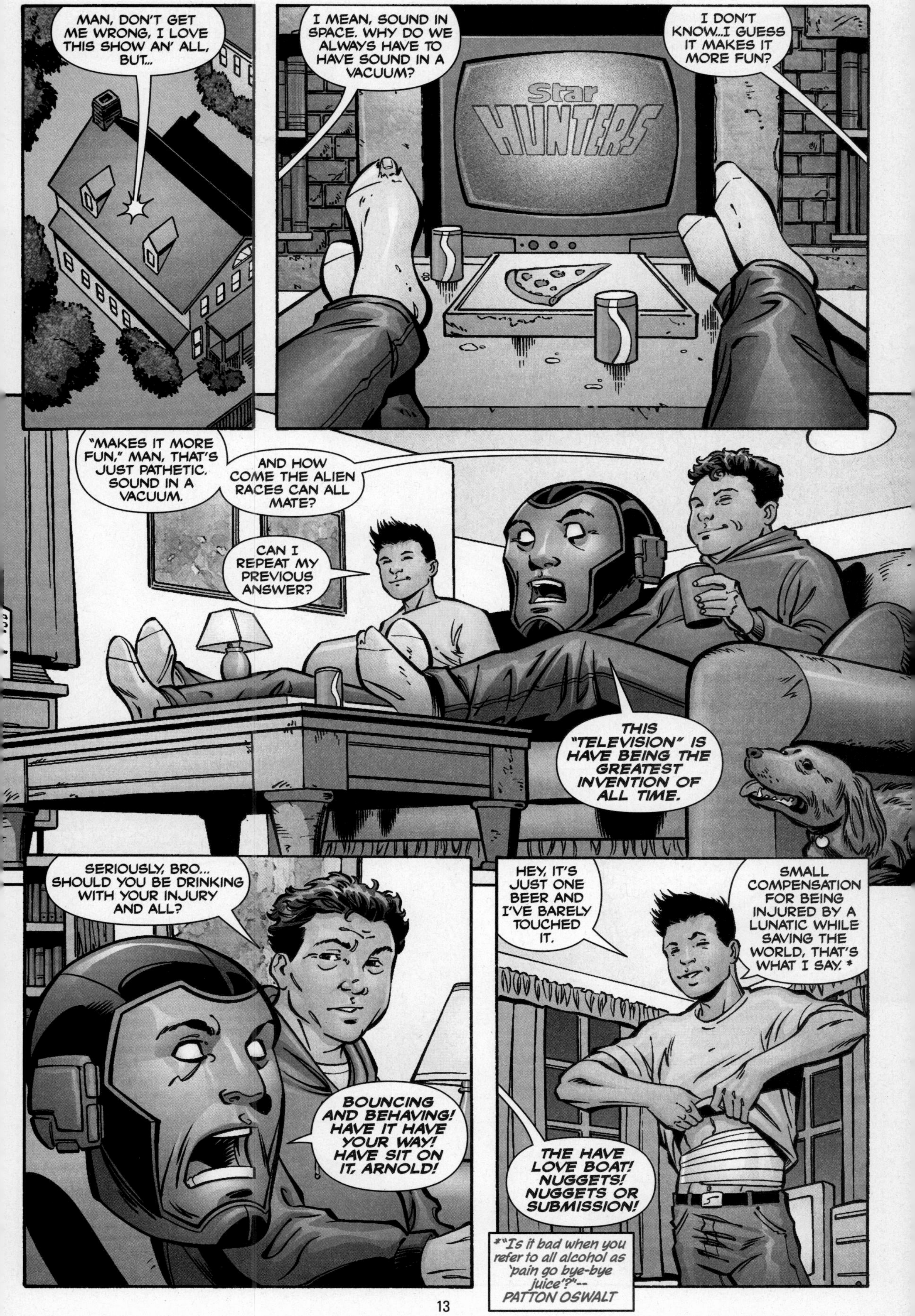
MAN, DON'T GET ME WRONG, I LOVE THIS SHOW AN' ALL, BUT...
I MEAN, SOUND IN SPACE. WHY DO WE ALWAYS HAVE TO HAVE SOUND IN A VACUUM?
I DON'T KNOW...I GUESS IT MAKES IT MORE FUN?
Star HUNTERS
"MAKES IT MORE FUN," MAN, THAT'S JUST PATHETIC. SOUND IN A VACUUM.
AND HOW COME THE ALIEN RACES CAN ALL MATE?
CAN I REPEAT MY PREVIOUS ANSWER?
THIS "TELEVISION" IS HAVE BEING THE GREATEST INVENTION OF ALL TIME.
SERIOUSLY, BRO... SHOULD YOU BE DRINKING WITH YOUR INJURY AND ALL?
BOUNCING AND BEHAVING! HAVE IT HAVE YOUR WAY! HAVE SIT ON IT, ARNOLD!
HEY, IT'S JUST ONE BEER AND I'VE BARELY TOUCHED IT.
SMALL COMPENSATION FOR BEING INJURED BY A LUNATIC WHILE SAVING THE WORLD, THAT'S WHAT I SAY. *
THE HAVE LOVE BOAT! NUGGETS! NUGGETS OR SUBMISSION!
*"Is it bad when you refer to all alcohol as 'pain go bye-bye juice'?"-- PATTON OSWALT

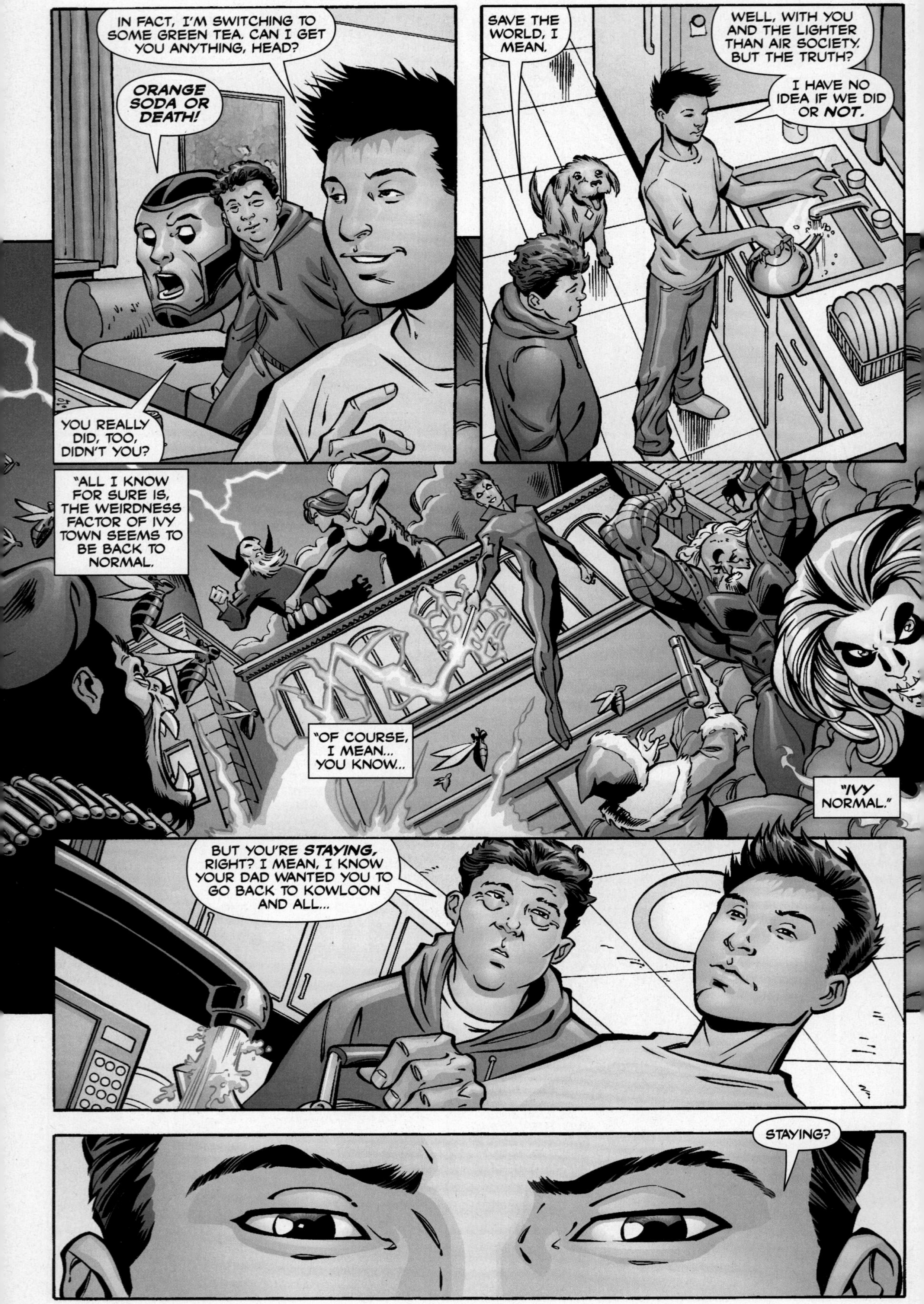
IN FACT, I'M SWITCHING TO SOME GREEN TEA. CAN I GET YOU ANYTHING, HEAD?
ORANGE SODA OR DEATH!
YOU REALLY DID, TOO, DIDN'T YOU?
SAVE THE WORLD, I MEAN.
WELL, WITH YOU AND THE LIGHTER THAN AIR SOCIETY. BUT THE TRUTH?
I HAVE NO IDEA IF WE DID OR NOT.
"ALL I KNOW FOR SURE IS, THE WEIRDNESS FACTOR OF IVY TOWN SEEMS TO BE BACK TO NORMAL.
"OF COURSE, I MEAN... YOU KNOW...
"IVY NORMAL."
BUT YOU'RE STAYING, RIGHT? I MEAN, I KNOW YOUR DAD WANTED YOU TO GO BACK TO KOWLOON AND ALL...
STAYING?

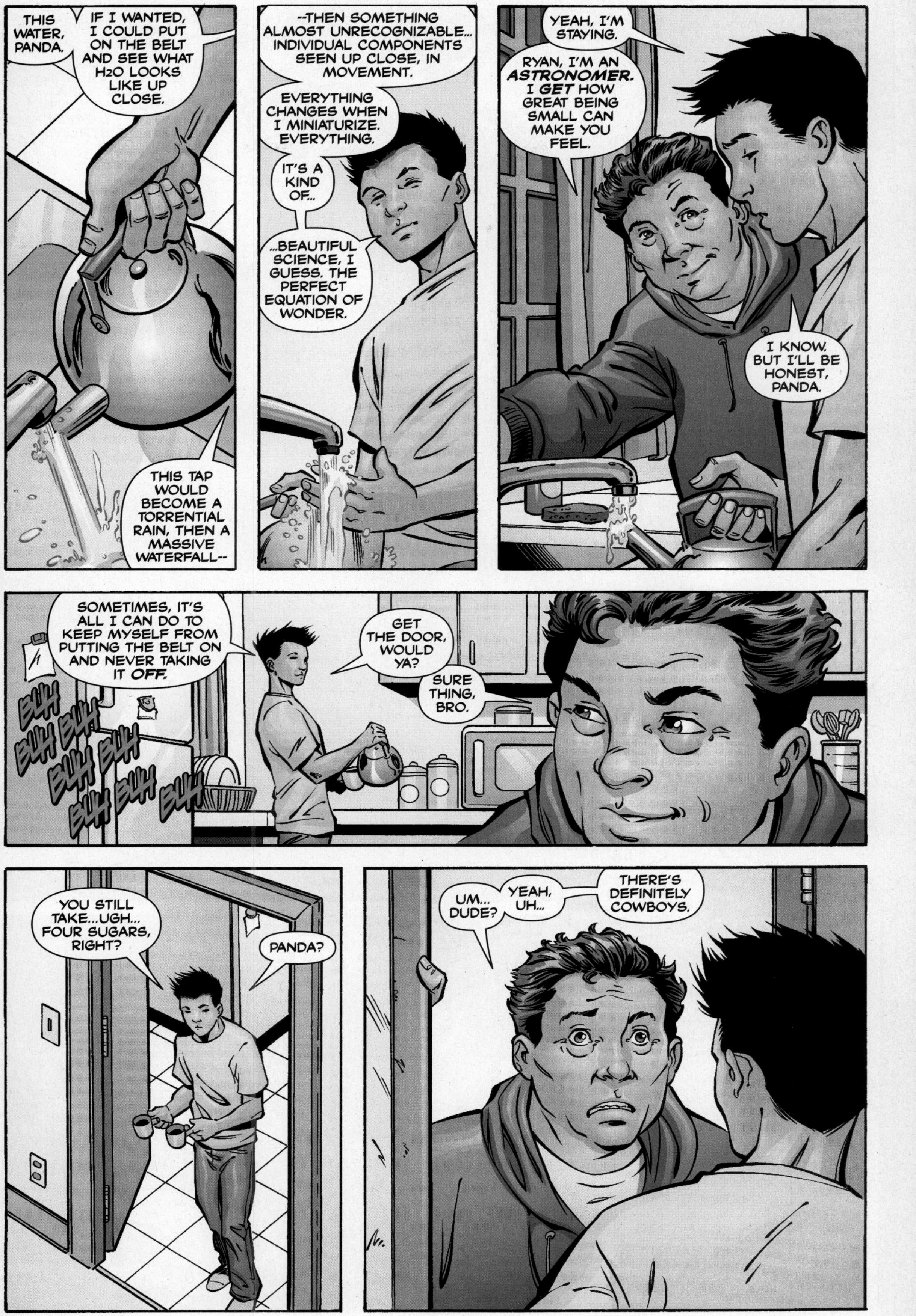
THIS WATER, PANDA.
IF I WANTED, I COULD PUT ON THE BELT AND SEE WHAT H2O LOOKS LIKE UP CLOSE.
THIS TAP WOULD BECOME A TORRENTIAL RAIN, THEN A MASSIVE WATERFALL--
--THEN SOMETHING ALMOST UNRECOGNIZABLE... INDIVIDUAL COMPONENTS SEEN UP CLOSE, IN MOVEMENT.
EVERYTHING CHANGES WHEN I MINIATURIZE. EVERYTHING.
IT'S A KIND OF...
...BEAUTIFUL SCIENCE, I GUESS. THE PERFECT EQUATION OF WONDER.
YEAH, I'M STAYING.
RYAN, I'M AN ASTRONOMER. I GET HOW GREAT BEING SMALL CAN MAKE YOU FEEL.
I KNOW. BUT I'LL BE HONEST, PANDA.
SOMETIMES, IT'S ALL I CAN DO TO KEEP MYSELF FROM PUTTING THE BELT ON AND NEVER TAKING IT OFF.
BUH BUH BUH BUH BUH BUH BUH BUH BUH BUH
GET THE DOOR, WOULD YA?
SURE THING, BRO.
YOU STILL TAKE...UGH... FOUR SUGARS, RIGHT?
PANDA?
UM... DUDE?
YEAH, UH...
THERE'S DEFINITELY COWBOYS.

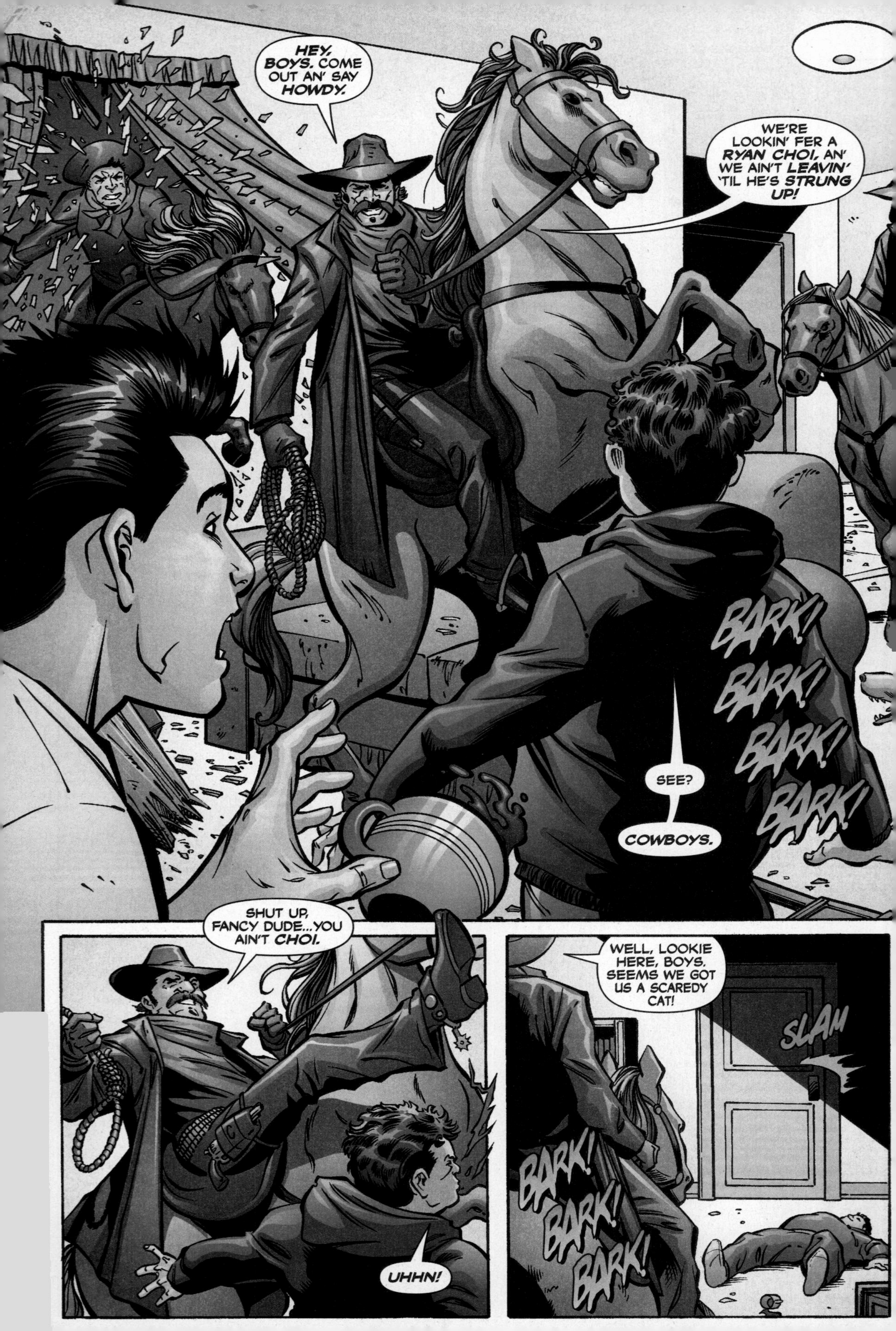
HEY, BOYS. COME OUT AN' SAY HOWDY.
WE'RE LOOKIN' FER A RYAN CHOI, AN' WE AIN'T LEAVIN' 'TIL HE'S STRUNG UP!
BARK! BARK! BARK! BARK!
SEE?
COWBOYS.
SHUT UP, FANCY DUDE...YOU AIN'T CHOI.
UHHN!
WELL, LOOKIE HERE, BOYS. SEEMS WE GOT US A SCAREDY CAT!
SLAM
BARK! BARK! BARK!

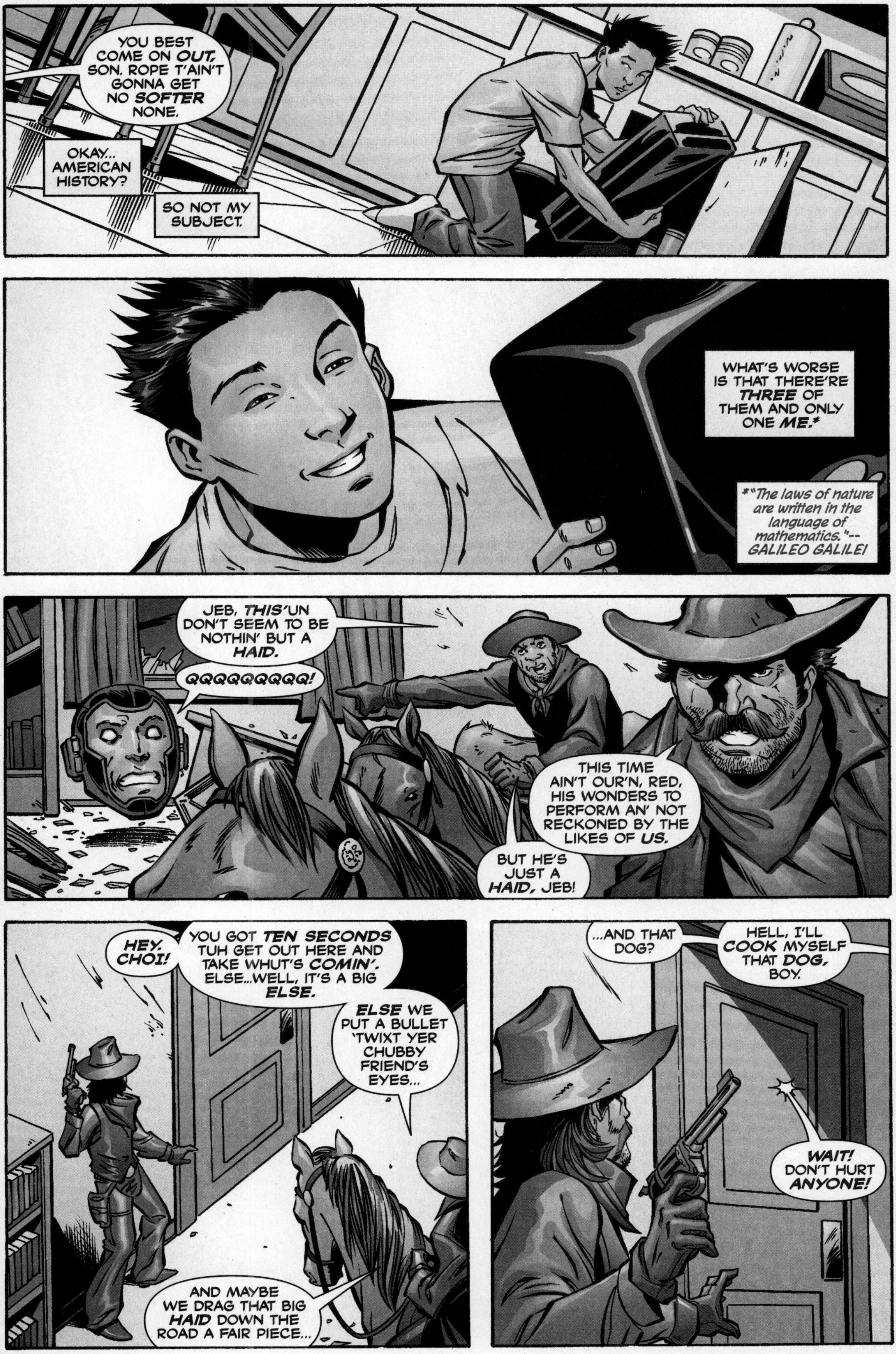
YOU BEST COME ON OUT, SON. ROPE T'AIN'T GONNA GET NO SOFTER NONE.
OKAY... AMERICAN HISTORY?
SO NOT MY SUBJECT.
WHAT'S WORSE IS THAT THERE'RE THREE OF THEM AND ONLY ONE ME.*
*"The laws of nature are written in the language of mathematics."-- GALILEO GALILEI
JEB, THIS'UN DON'T SEEM TO BE NOTHIN' BUT A HAID.
QQQQQQQQQ!
THIS TIME AIN'T OUR'N, RED, HIS WONDERS TO PERFORM AN' NOT RECKONED BY THE LIKES OF US.
BUT HE'S JUST A HAID, JEB!
HEY. CHOI!
YOU GOT TEN SECONDS TUH GET OUT HERE AND TAKE WHUT'S COMIN'. ELSE...WELL, IT'S A BIG ELSE.
ELSE WE PUT A BULLET 'TWIXT YER CHUBBY FRIEND'S EYES...
AND MAYBE WE DRAG THAT BIG HAID DOWN THE ROAD A FAIR PIECE...
...AND THAT DOG?
HELL, I'LL COOK MYSELF THAT DOG, BOY.
WAIT! DON'T HURT ANYONE!

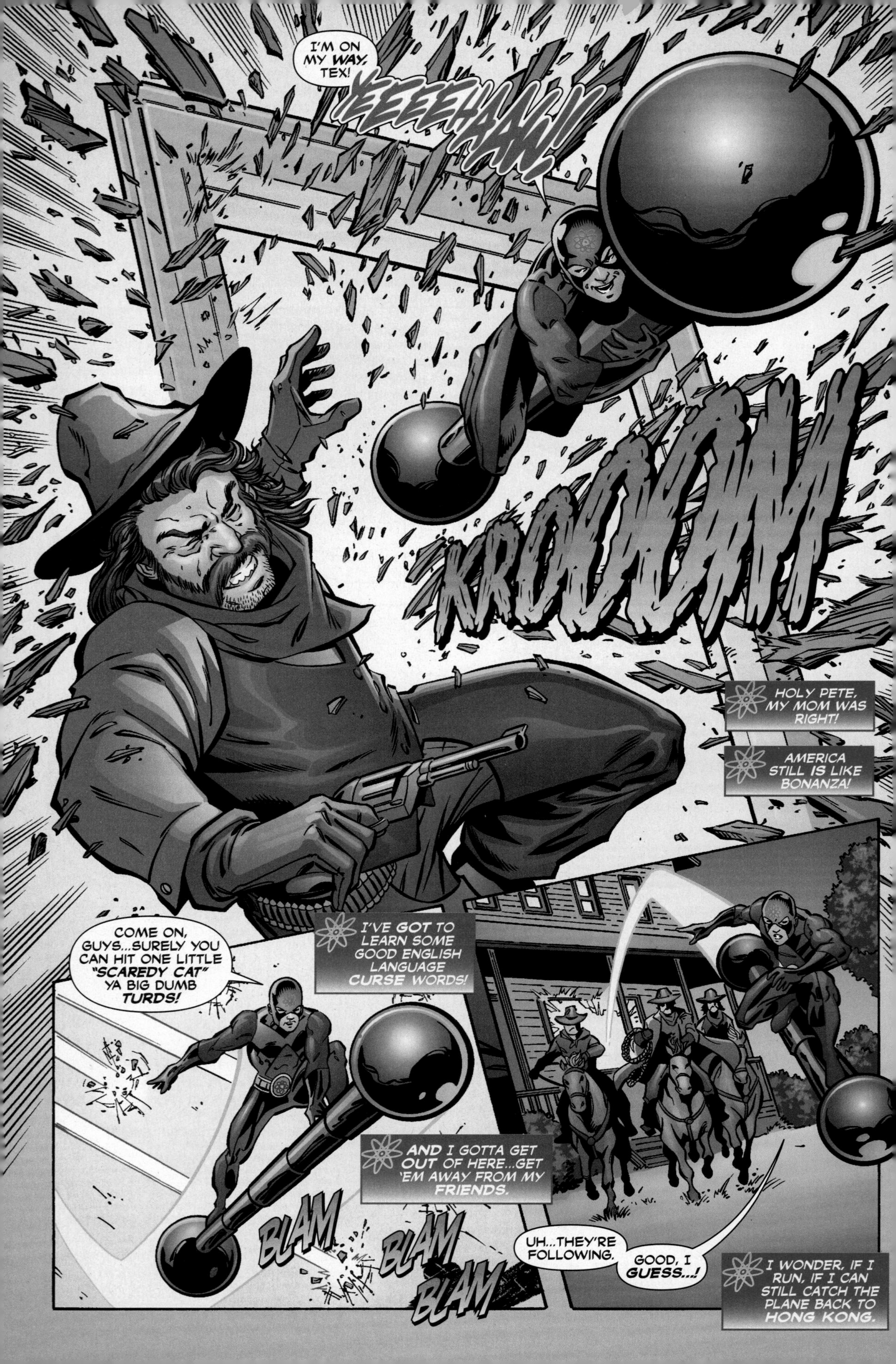
I'M ON MY WAY, TEX!
YEEEEHAAA!!
KROOOM
HOLY PETE, MY MOM WAS RIGHT!
AMERICA STILL IS LIKE BONANZA!
COME ON, GUYS...SURELY YOU CAN HIT ONE LITTLE "SCAREDY CAT" YA BIG DUMB TURDS!
I'VE GOT TO LEARN SOME GOOD ENGLISH LANGUAGE CURSE WORDS!
AND I GOTTA GET OUT OF HERE...GET 'EM AWAY FROM MY FRIENDS.
BLAM
BLAM
BLAM
UH...THEY'RE FOLLOWING.
GOOD, I GUESS...!
I WONDER, IF I RUN, IF I CAN STILL CATCH THE PLANE BACK TO HONG KONG.

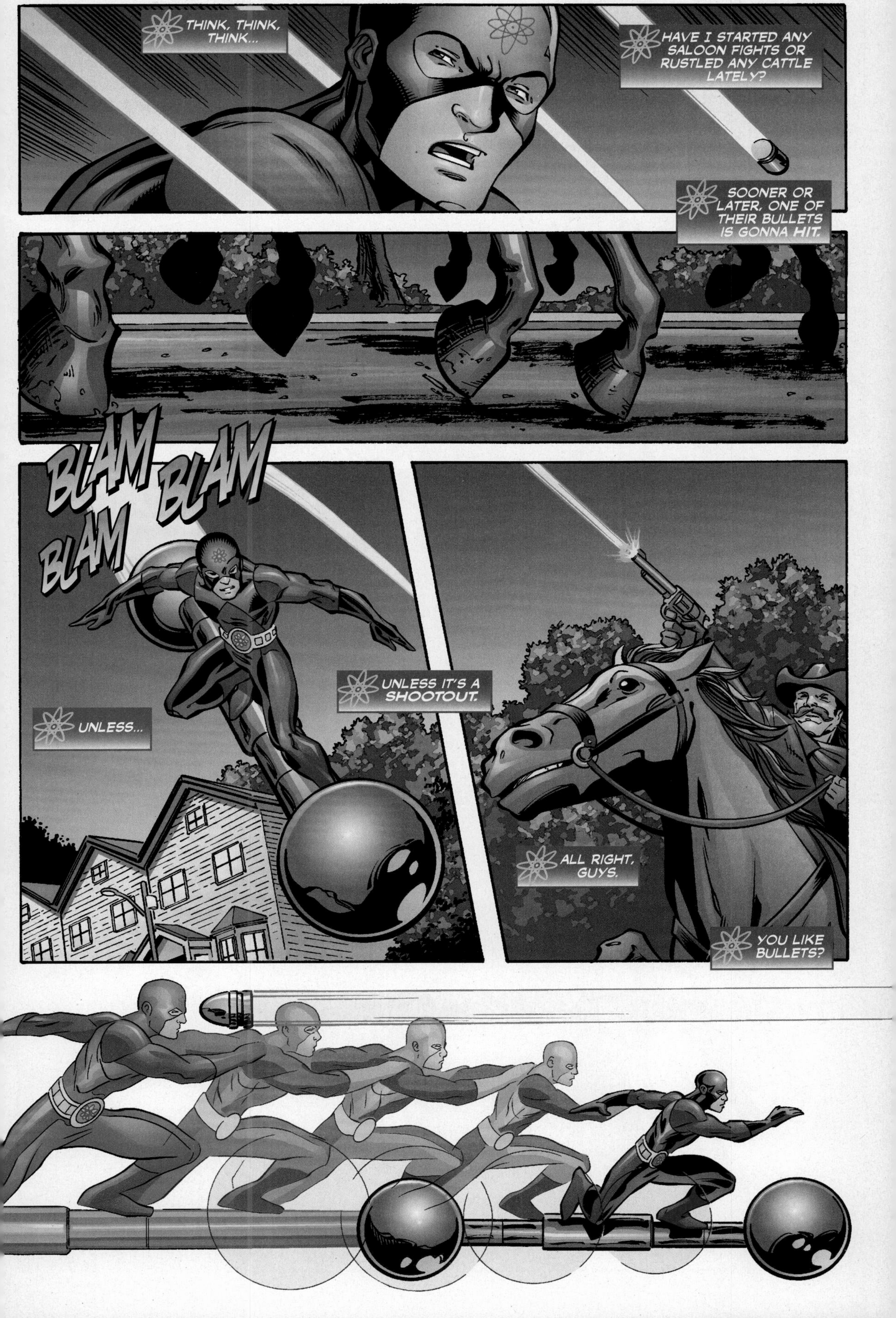
THINK, THINK, THINK...
HAVE I STARTED ANY SALOON FIGHTS OR RUSTLED ANY CATTLE LATELY?
SOONER OR LATER, ONE OF THEIR BULLETS IS GONNA HIT.
BLAM
BLAM
BLAM
UNLESS...
UNLESS IT'S A SHOOTOUT.
ALL RIGHT, GUYS.
YOU LIKE BULLETS?

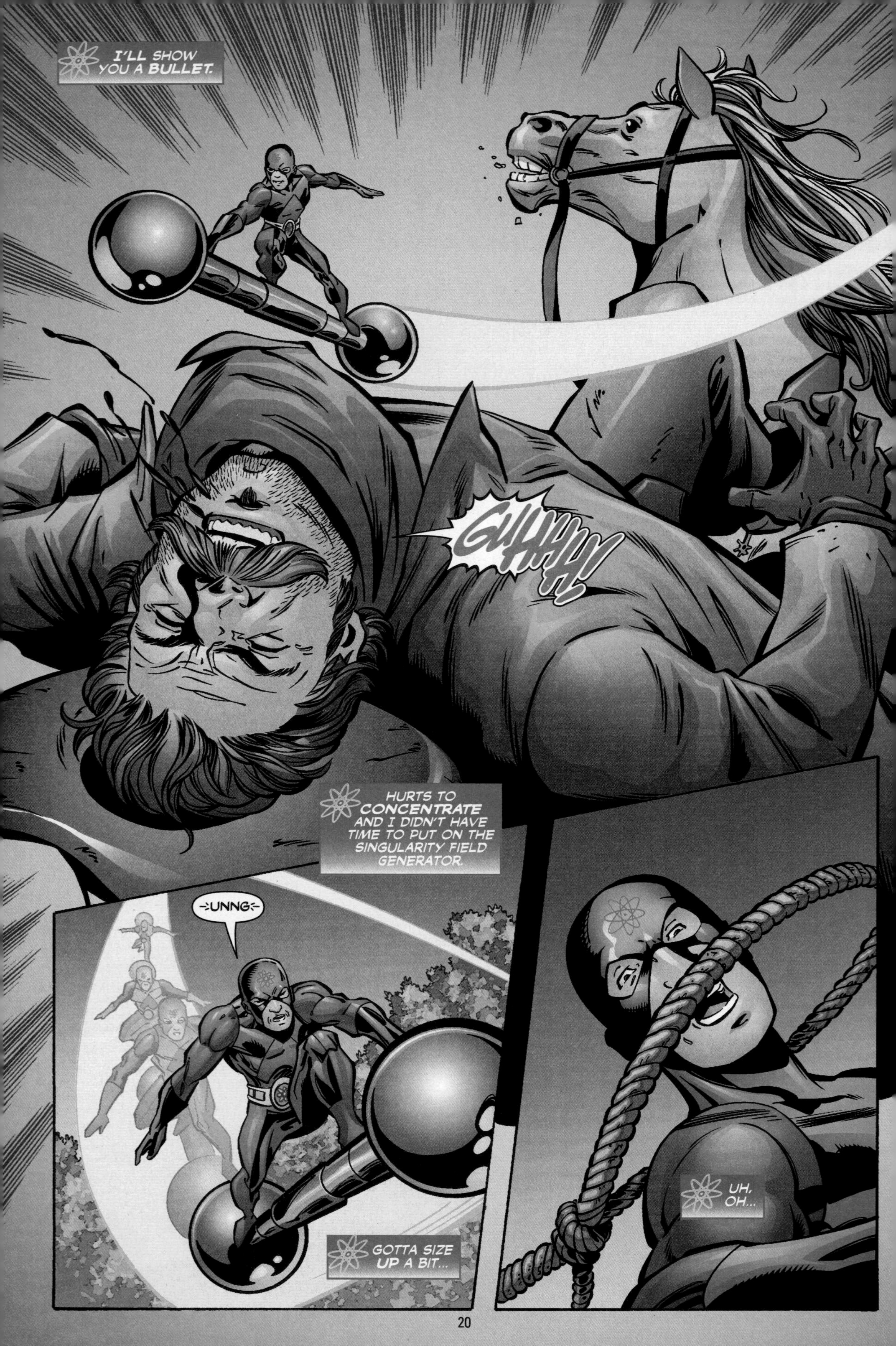
I'LL SHOW YOU A BULLET.
GUHHHH!
HURTS TO CONCENTRATE AND I DIDN'T HAVE TIME TO PUT ON THE SINGULARITY FIELD GENERATOR.
-UNNG-
GOTTA SIZE UP A BIT...
UH, OH...

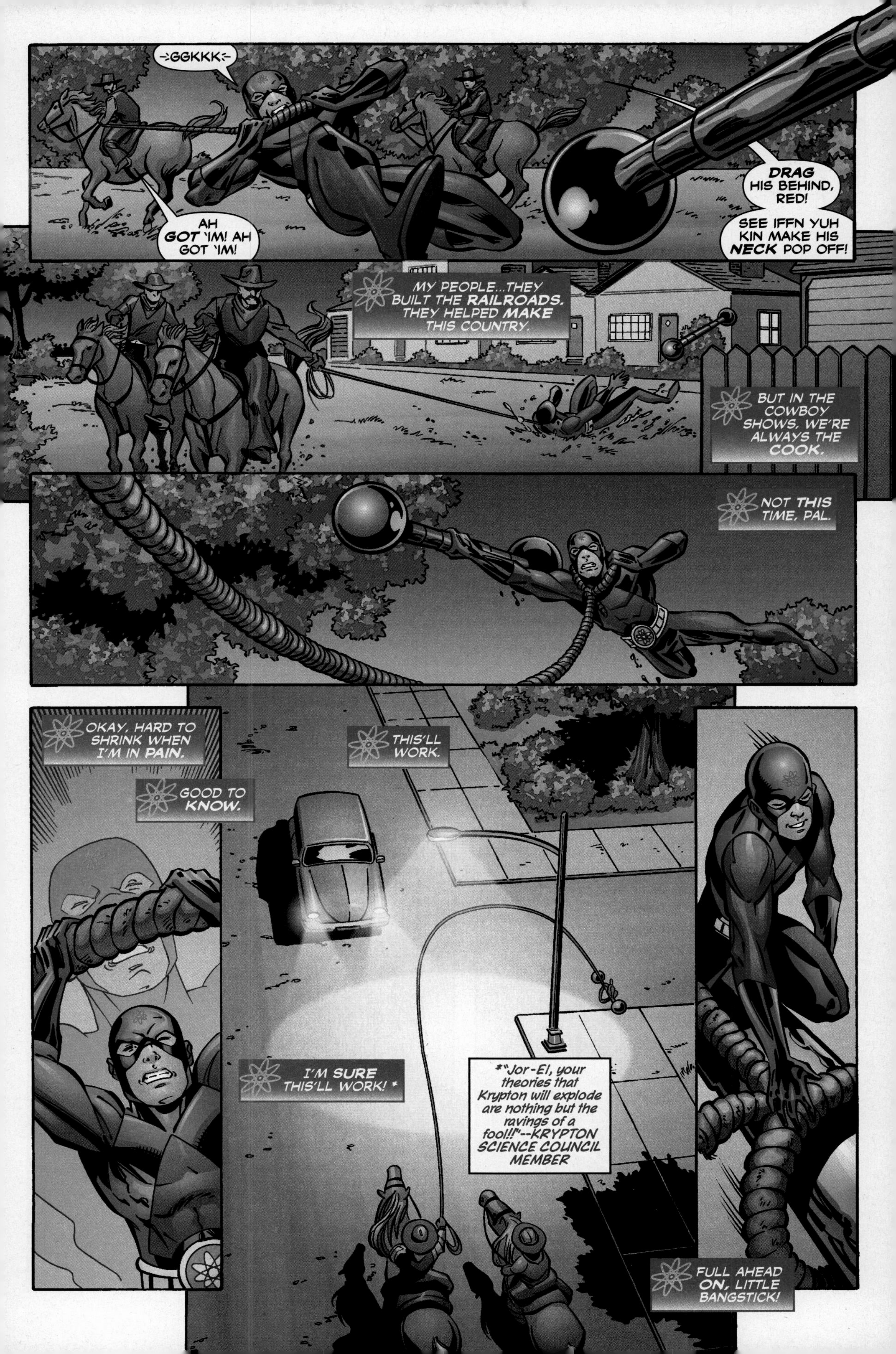
-GGKKK-
AH GOT 'IM! AH GOT 'IM!
DRAG HIS BEHIND, RED!
SEE IFFN YUH KIN MAKE HIS NECK POP OFF!
MY PEOPLE...THEY BUILT THE RAILROADS. THEY HELPED MAKE THIS COUNTRY.
BUT IN THE COWBOY SHOWS, WE'RE ALWAYS THE COOK.
NOT THIS TIME, PAL.
OKAY, HARD TO SHRINK WHEN I'M IN PAIN.
GOOD TO KNOW.
THIS'LL WORK.
I'M SURE THIS'LL WORK! *
*"Jor-El, your theories that Krypton will explode are nothing but the ravings of a fool!!"--KRYPTON SCIENCE COUNCIL MEMBER
FULL AHEAD ON, LITTLE BANGSTICK!

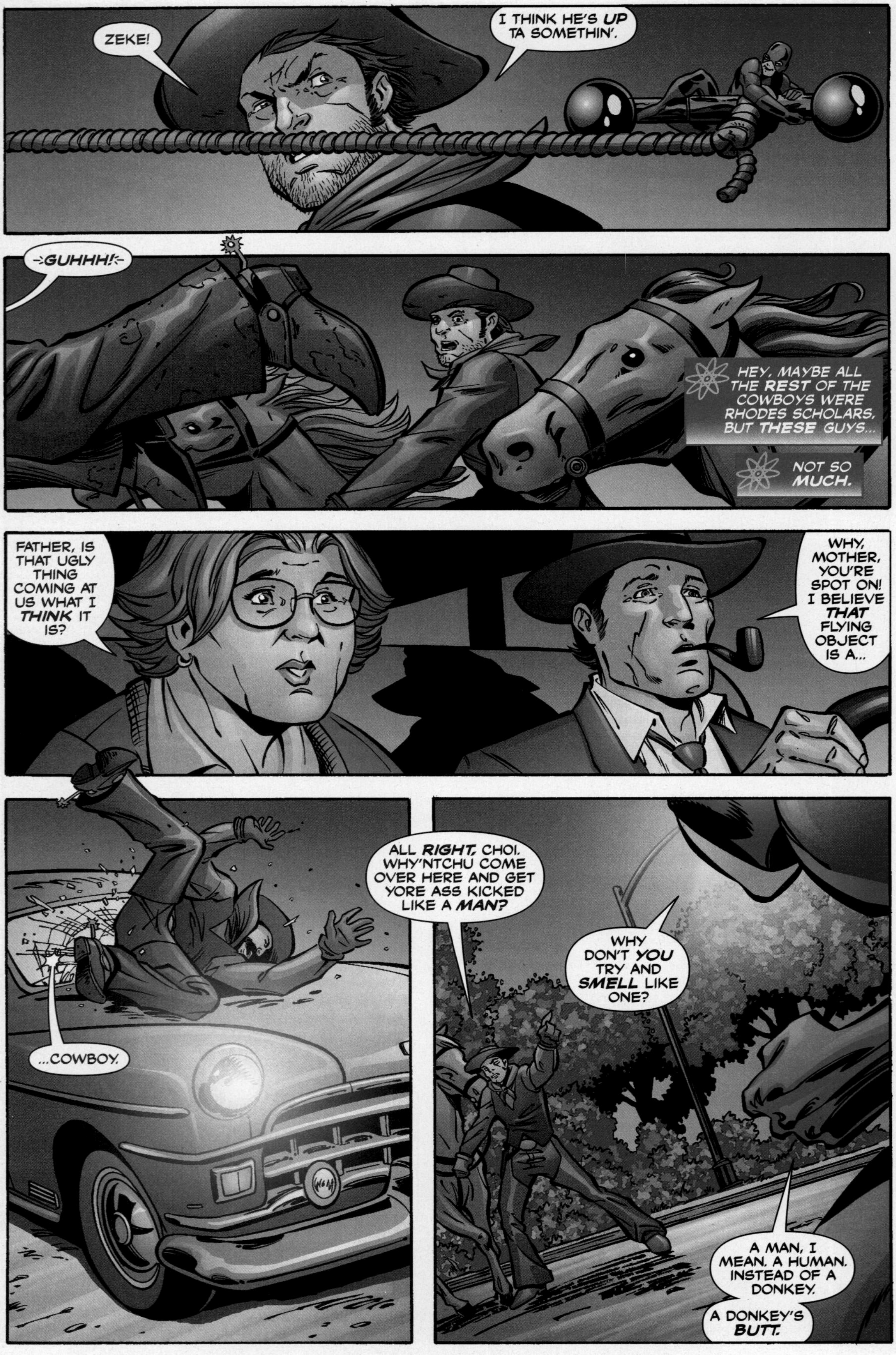
ZEKE!
I THINK HE'S UP TA SOMETHIN'.
-GUHHH!-
HEY, MAYBE ALL THE REST OF THE COWBOYS WERE RHODES SCHOLARS, BUT THESE GUYS...
NOT SO MUCH.
FATHER, IS THAT UGLY THING COMING AT US WHAT I THINK IT IS?
WHY, MOTHER, YOU'RE SPOT ON! I BELIEVE THAT FLYING OBJECT IS A...
...COWBOY.
ALL RIGHT, CHOI. WHY'NTCHU COME OVER HERE AND GET YORE ASS KICKED LIKE A MAN?
WHY DON'T YOU TRY AND SMELL LIKE ONE?
A MAN, I MEAN. A HUMAN. INSTEAD OF A DONKEY.
A DONKEY'S BUTT.

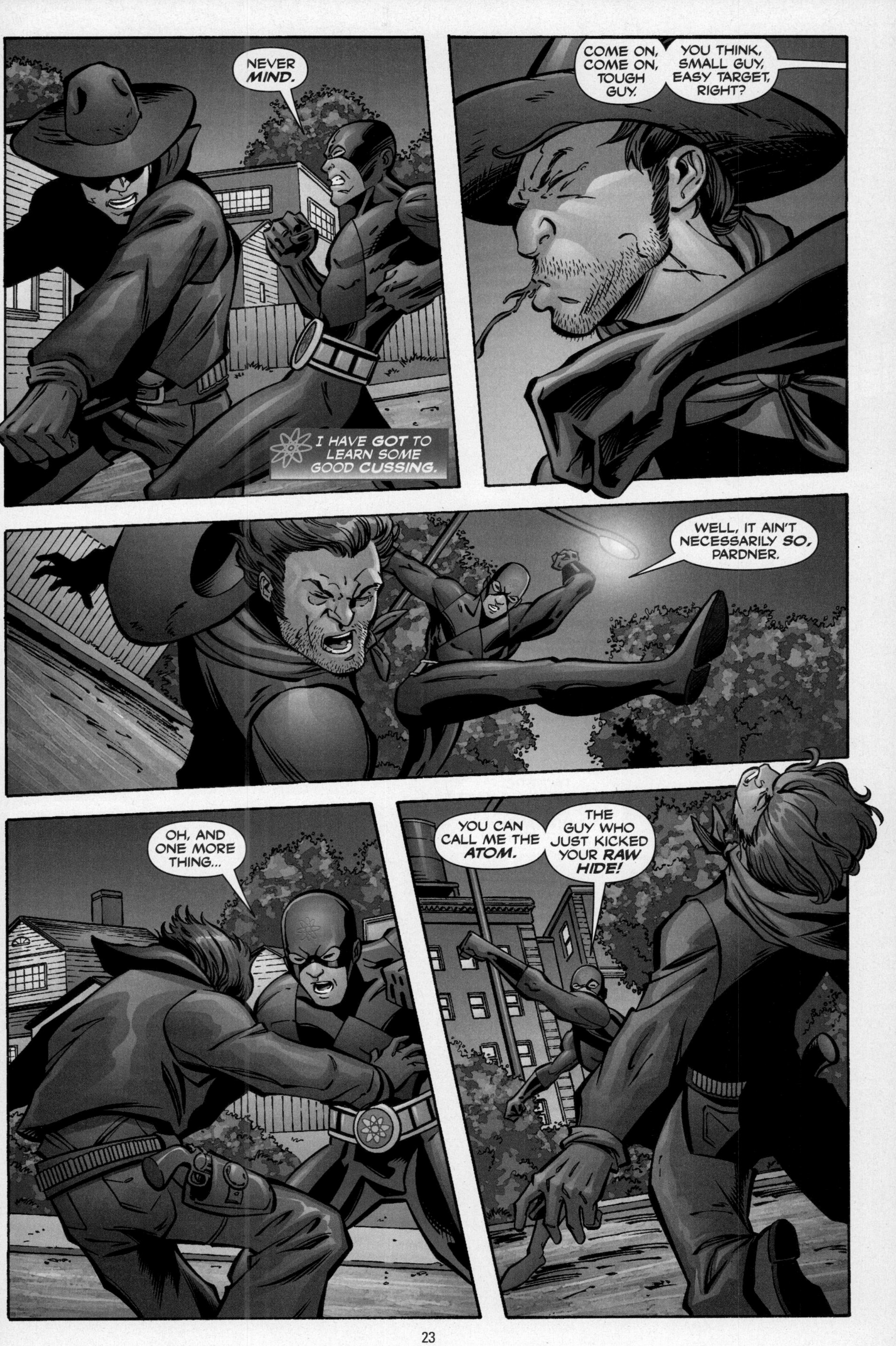
NEVER MIND.
I HAVE GOT TO LEARN SOME GOOD CUSSING.
COME ON, COME ON, TOUGH GUY.
YOU THINK, SMALL GUY, EASY TARGET, RIGHT?
WELL, IT AIN'T NECESSARILY SO, PARDNER.
OH, AND ONE MORE THING...
YOU CAN CALL ME THE ATOM.
THE GUY WHO JUST KICKED YOUR RAW HIDE!

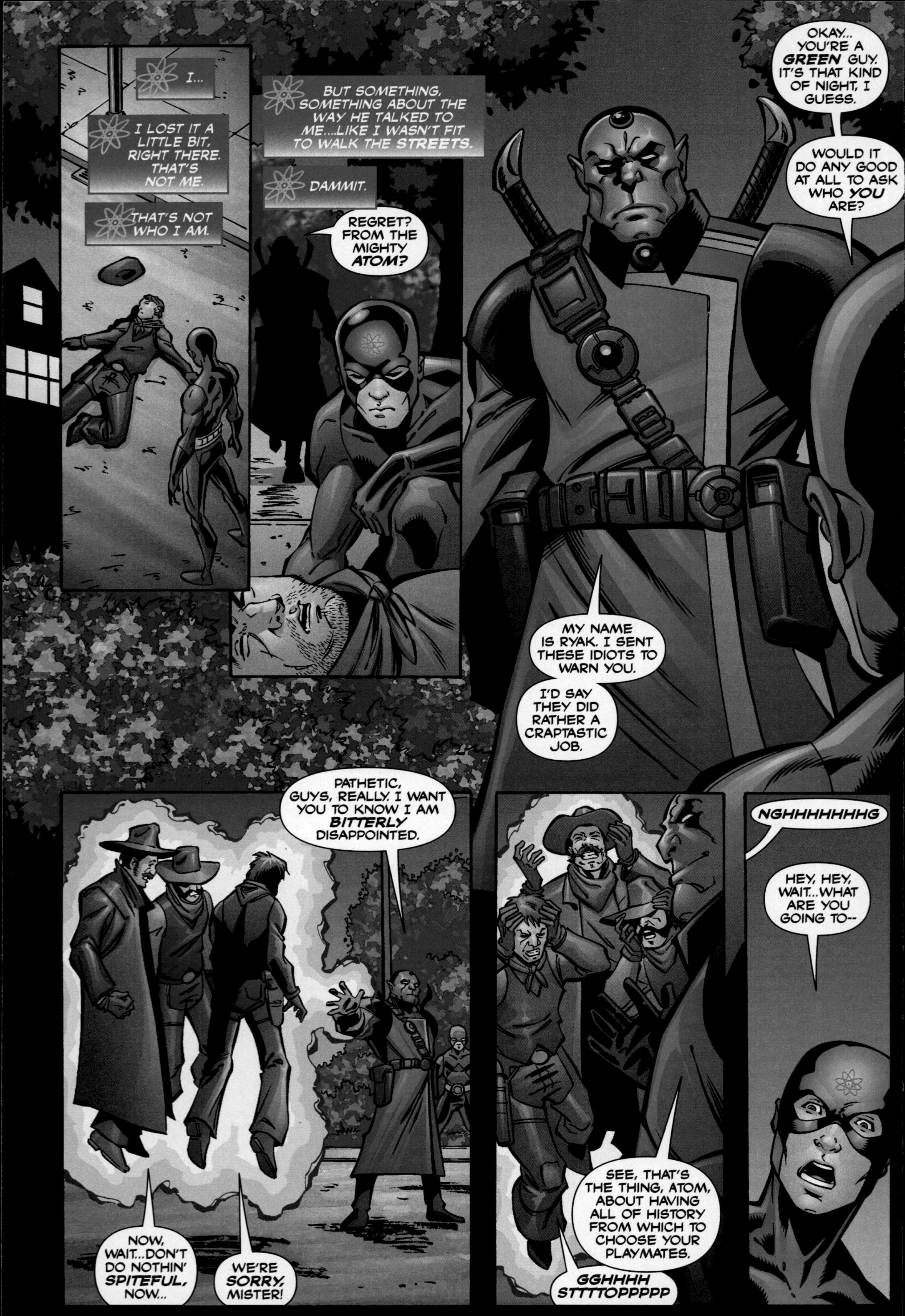
I...
I LOST IT A LITTLE BIT, RIGHT THERE. THAT'S NOT ME.
THAT'S NOT WHO I AM.
BUT SOMETHING, SOMETHING ABOUT THE WAY HE TALKED TO ME...LIKE I WASN'T FIT TO WALK THE STREETS.
DAMMIT.
REGRET? FROM THE MIGHTY ATOM?
OKAY... YOU'RE A GREEN GUY. IT'S THAT KIND OF NIGHT, I GUESS.
WOULD IT DO ANY GOOD AT ALL TO ASK WHO YOU ARE?
MY NAME IS RYAK. I SENT THESE IDIOTS TO WARN YOU.
I'D SAY THEY DID RATHER A CRAPTASTIC JOB.
PATHETIC, GUYS, REALLY. I WANT YOU TO KNOW I AM BITTERLY DISAPPOINTED.
NOW, WAIT...DON'T DO NOTHIN' SPITEFUL, NOW...
WE'RE SORRY, MISTER!
SEE, THAT'S THE THING, ATOM, ABOUT HAVING ALL OF HISTORY FROM WHICH TO CHOOSE YOUR PLAYMATES.
GGHHHH STTTTOPPPPP
NGHHHHHHHG
HEY, HEY, WAIT...WHAT ARE YOU GOING TO--

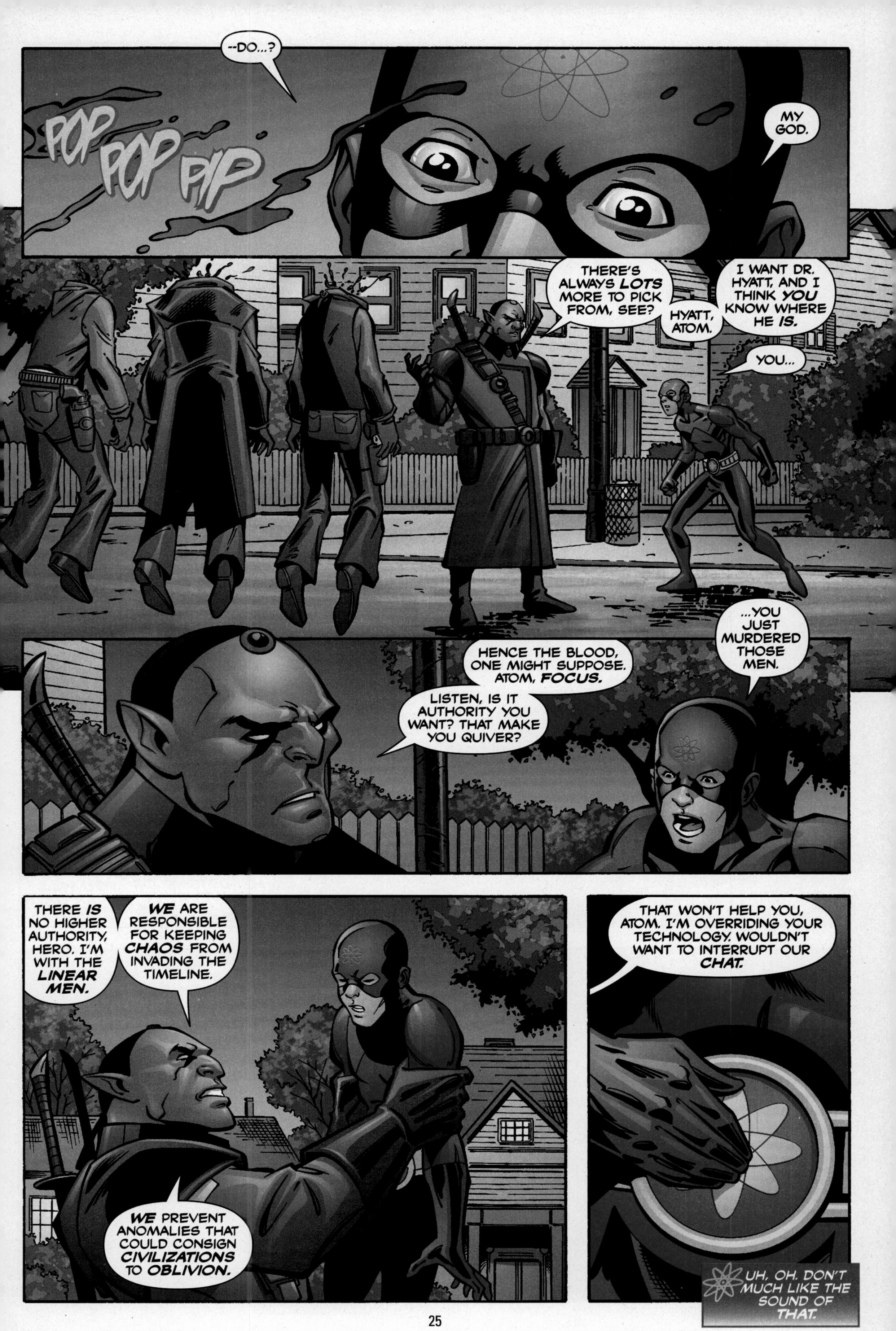
--DO...?
POP POP PIP
MY GOD.
THERE'S ALWAYS LOTS MORE TO PICK FROM, SEE?
HYATT, ATOM.
I WANT DR. HYATT, AND I THINK YOU KNOW WHERE HE IS.
YOU...
...YOU JUST MURDERED THOSE MEN.
HENCE THE BLOOD, ONE MIGHT SUPPOSE. ATOM, FOCUS.
LISTEN, IS IT AUTHORITY YOU WANT? THAT MAKE YOU QUIVER?
THERE IS NO HIGHER AUTHORITY, HERO. I'M WITH THE LINEAR MEN.
WE ARE RESPONSIBLE FOR KEEPING CHAOS FROM INVADING THE TIMELINE.
WE PREVENT ANOMALIES THAT COULD CONSIGN CIVILIZATIONS TO OBLIVION.
THAT WON'T HELP YOU, ATOM. I'M OVERRIDING YOUR TECHNOLOGY. WOULDN'T WANT TO INTERRUPT OUR CHAT.
UH, OH. DON'T MUCH LIKE THE SOUND OF THAT.

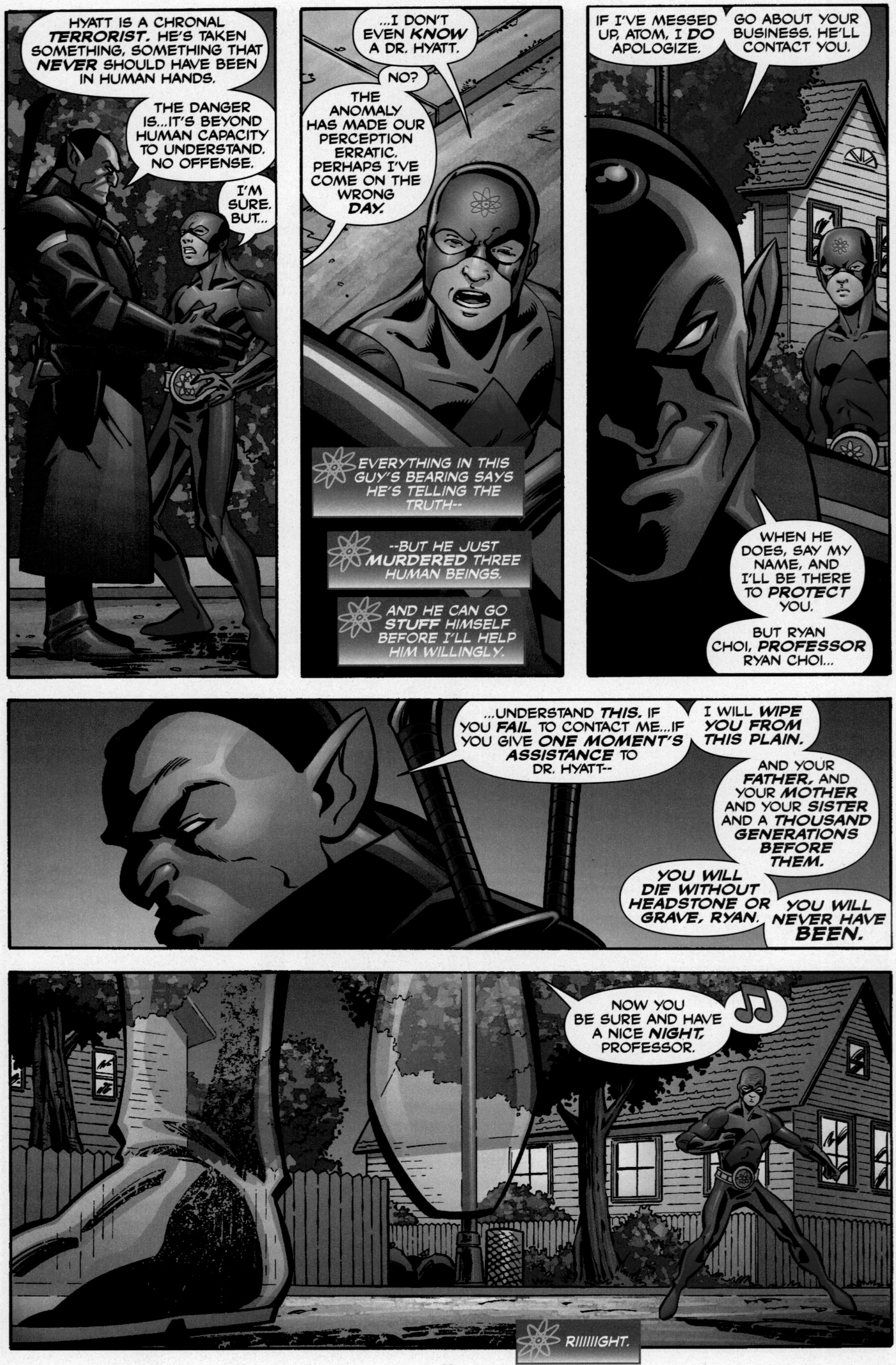
HYATT IS A CHRONAL TERRORIST. HE'S TAKEN SOMETHING, SOMETHING THAT NEVER SHOULD HAVE BEEN IN HUMAN HANDS.
THE DANGER IS...IT'S BEYOND HUMAN CAPACITY TO UNDERSTAND. NO OFFENSE.
I'M SURE. BUT...
...I DON'T EVEN KNOW A DR. HYATT.
NO?
THE ANOMALY HAS MADE OUR PERCEPTION ERRATIC. PERHAPS I'VE COME ON THE WRONG DAY.
EVERYTHING IN THIS GUY'S BEARING SAYS HE'S TELLING THE TRUTH--
--BUT HE JUST MURDERED THREE HUMAN BEINGS.
AND HE CAN GO STUFF HIMSELF BEFORE I'LL HELP HIM WILLINGLY.
IF I'VE MESSED UP, ATOM, I DO APOLOGIZE.
GO ABOUT YOUR BUSINESS. HE'LL CONTACT YOU.
WHEN HE DOES, SAY MY NAME, AND I'LL BE THERE TO PROTECT YOU.
BUT RYAN CHOI, PROFESSOR RYAN CHOI...
...UNDERSTAND THIS. IF YOU FAIL TO CONTACT ME...IF YOU GIVE ONE MOMENT'S ASSISTANCE TO DR. HYATT--
I WILL WIPE YOU FROM THIS PLAIN.
AND YOUR FATHER, AND YOUR MOTHER AND YOUR SISTER AND A THOUSAND GENERATIONS BEFORE THEM.
YOU WILL DIE WITHOUT HEADSTONE OR GRAVE, RYAN.
YOU WILL NEVER HAVE BEEN.
NOW YOU BE SURE AND HAVE A NICE NIGHT, PROFESSOR.
RIIIIIGHT.

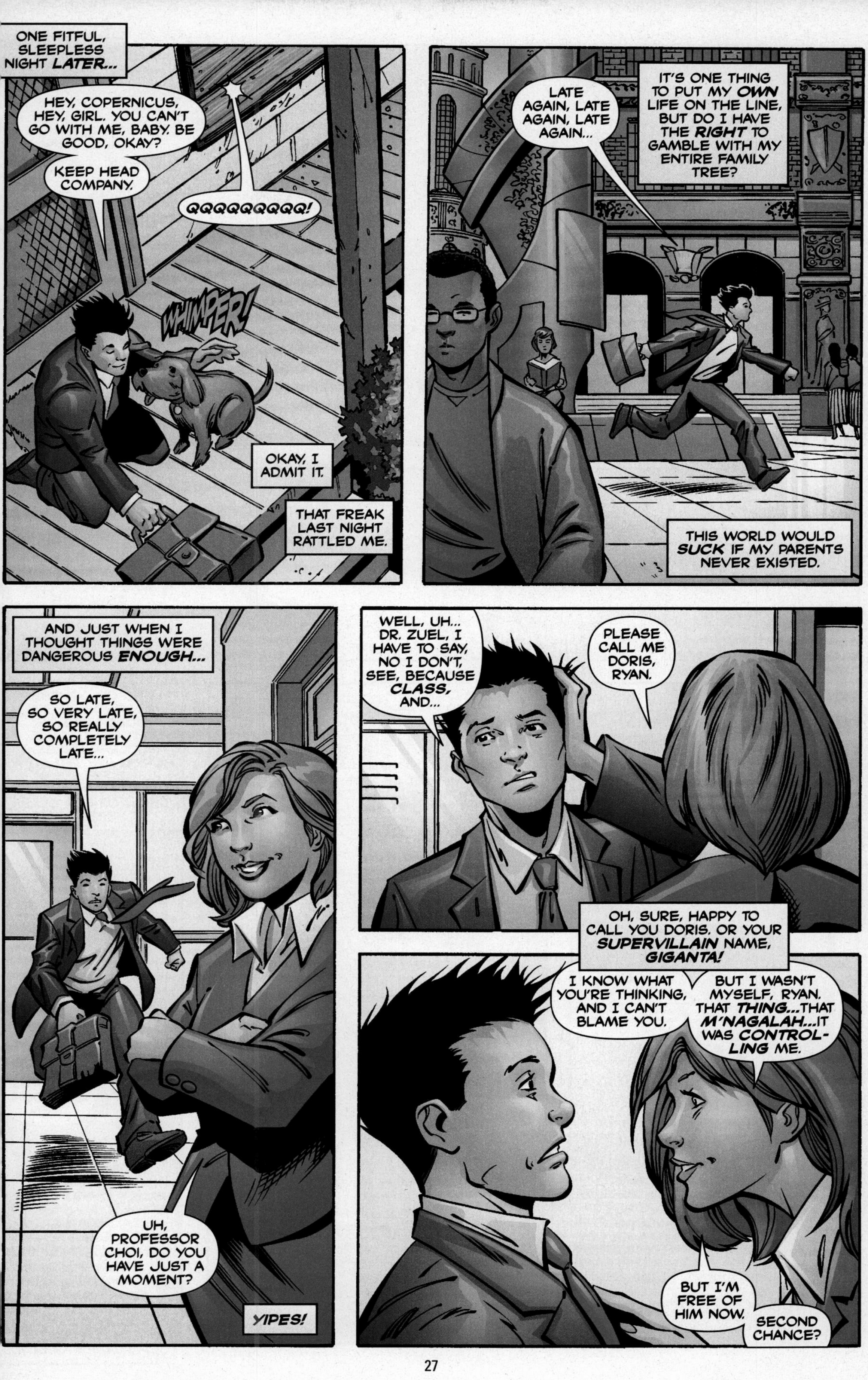
ONE FITFUL, SLEEPLESS NIGHT LATER...
HEY, COPERNICUS, HEY, GIRL. YOU CAN'T GO WITH ME, BABY. BE GOOD, OKAY?
KEEP HEAD COMPANY.
QQQQQQQQQ!
WHIMPER!
OKAY, I ADMIT IT.
THAT FREAK LAST NIGHT RATTLED ME.
LATE AGAIN, LATE AGAIN, LATE AGAIN...
IT'S ONE THING TO PUT MY OWN LIFE ON THE LINE, BUT DO I HAVE THE RIGHT TO GAMBLE WITH MY ENTIRE FAMILY TREE?
THIS WORLD WOULD SUCK IF MY PARENTS NEVER EXISTED.
AND JUST WHEN I THOUGHT THINGS WERE DANGEROUS ENOUGH...
SO LATE, SO VERY LATE, SO REALLY COMPLETELY LATE...
UH, PROFESSOR CHOI, DO YOU HAVE JUST A MOMENT?
YIPES!
WELL, UH... DR. ZUEL, I HAVE TO SAY, NO I DON'T, SEE, BECAUSE CLASS, AND...
PLEASE CALL ME DORIS, RYAN.
OH, SURE, HAPPY TO CALL YOU DORIS. OR YOUR SUPERVILLAIN NAME, GIGANTA!
I KNOW WHAT YOU'RE THINKING, AND I CAN'T BLAME YOU.
BUT I WASN'T MYSELF, RYAN. THAT THING...THAT M'NAGALAH...IT WAS CONTROL-LING ME.
BUT I'M FREE OF HIM NOW.
SECOND CHANCE?

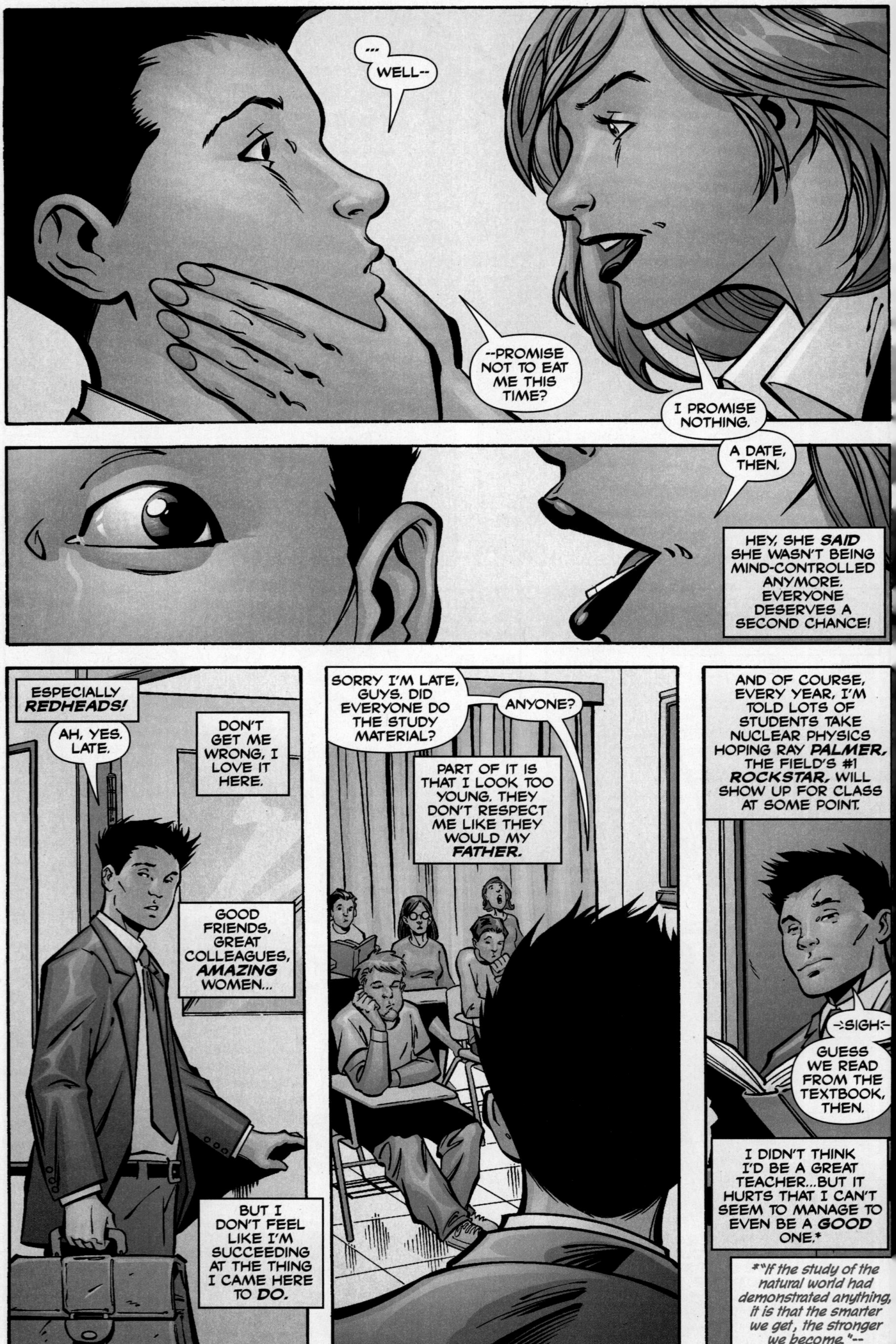
...
WELL--
--PROMISE NOT TO EAT ME THIS TIME?
I PROMISE NOTHING.
A DATE, THEN.
HEY, SHE *SAID* SHE WASN'T BEING MIND-CONTROLLED ANYMORE. EVERYONE DESERVES A SECOND CHANCE!
ESPECIALLY *REDHEADS!*
AH, YES. LATE.
DON'T GET ME WRONG, I LOVE IT HERE.
GOOD FRIENDS, GREAT COLLEAGUES, *AMAZING* WOMEN...
BUT I DON'T FEEL LIKE I'M SUCCEEDING AT THE THING I CAME HERE TO *DO.*
SORRY I'M LATE, GUYS. DID EVERYONE DO THE STUDY MATERIAL?
ANYONE?
PART OF IT IS THAT I LOOK TOO YOUNG. THEY DON'T RESPECT ME LIKE THEY WOULD MY *FATHER.*
AND OF COURSE, EVERY YEAR, I'M TOLD LOTS OF STUDENTS TAKE NUCLEAR PHYSICS HOPING RAY *PALMER,* THE FIELD'S #1 *ROCKSTAR,* WILL SHOW UP FOR CLASS AT SOME POINT.
-SIGH-
GUESS WE READ FROM THE TEXTBOOK, THEN.
I DIDN'T THINK I'D BE A GREAT TEACHER...BUT IT HURTS THAT I CAN'T SEEM TO MANAGE TO EVEN BE A *GOOD* ONE.*
*"If the study of the natural world had demonstrated anything, it is that the smarter we get, the stronger we become."-- DR. JAMES KAKALIOS

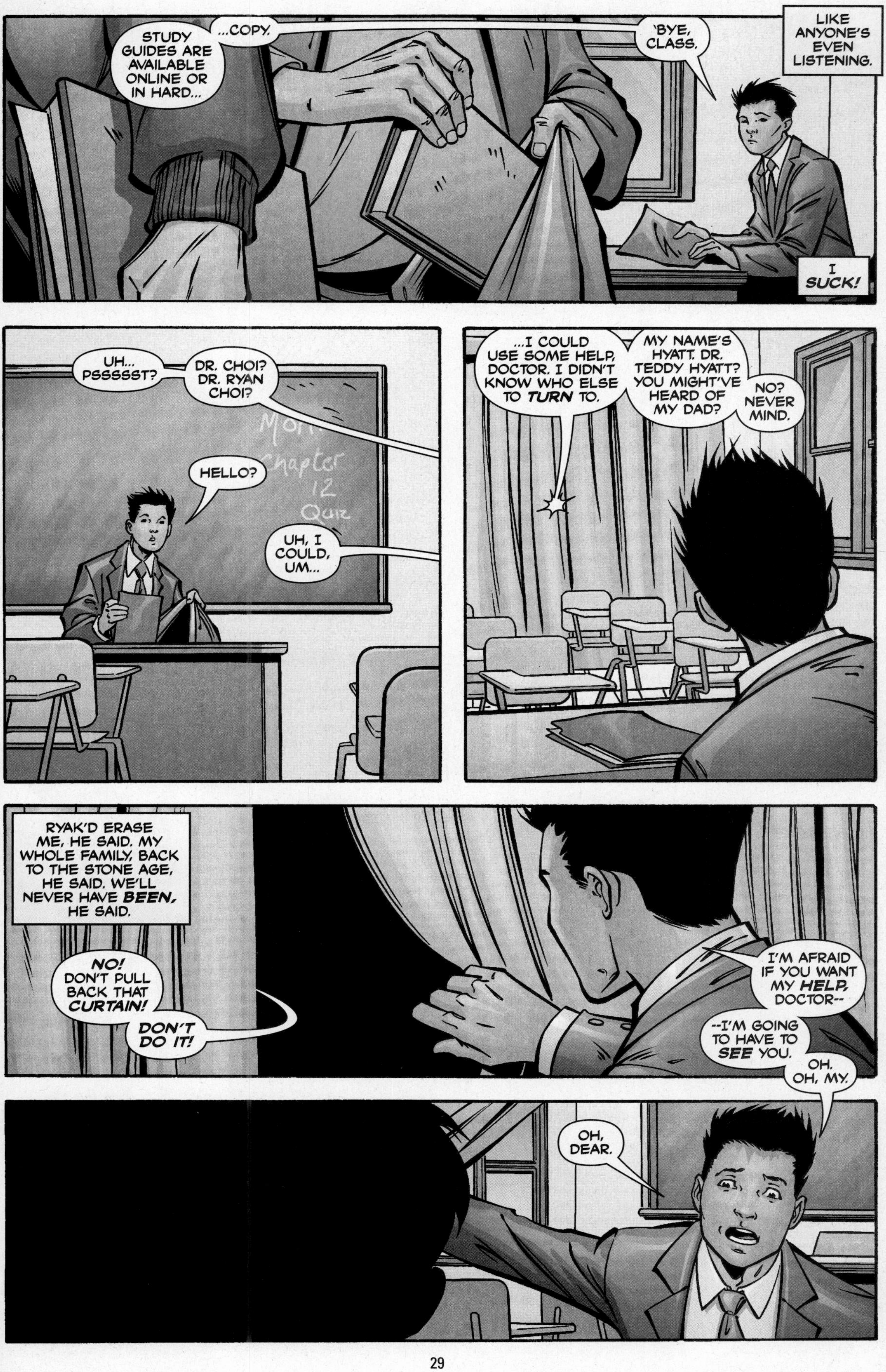
STUDY GUIDES ARE AVAILABLE ONLINE OR IN HARD...
...COPY.
'BYE, CLASS.
LIKE ANYONE'S EVEN LISTENING.
I SUCK!
UH... PSSSSST?
DR. CHOI? DR. RYAN CHOI?
HELLO?
UH, I COULD, UM...
...I COULD USE SOME HELP, DOCTOR. I DIDN'T KNOW WHO ELSE TO TURN TO.
MY NAME'S HYATT. DR. TEDDY HYATT? YOU MIGHT'VE HEARD OF MY DAD?
NO? NEVER MIND.
RYAK'D ERASE ME, HE SAID. MY WHOLE FAMILY, BACK TO THE STONE AGE, HE SAID. WE'LL NEVER HAVE BEEN, HE SAID.
NO! DON'T PULL BACK THAT CURTAIN!
DON'T DO IT!
I'M AFRAID IF YOU WANT MY HELP, DOCTOR--
--I'M GOING TO HAVE TO SEE YOU.
OH. OH, MY.
OH, DEAR.

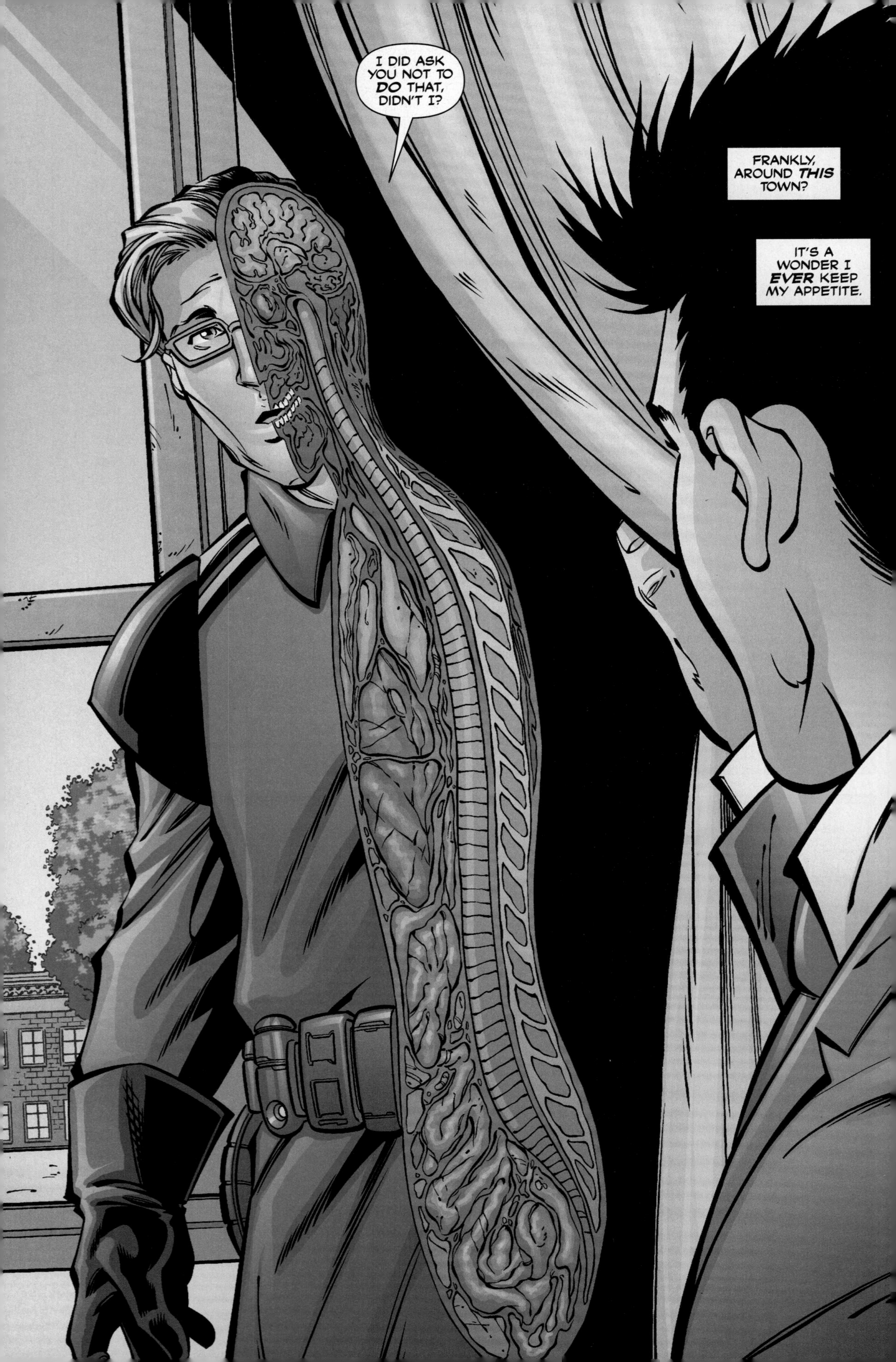
I DID ASK YOU NOT TO DO THAT, DIDN'T I?
FRANKLY, AROUND THIS TOWN?
IT'S A WONDER I EVER KEEP MY APPETITE.

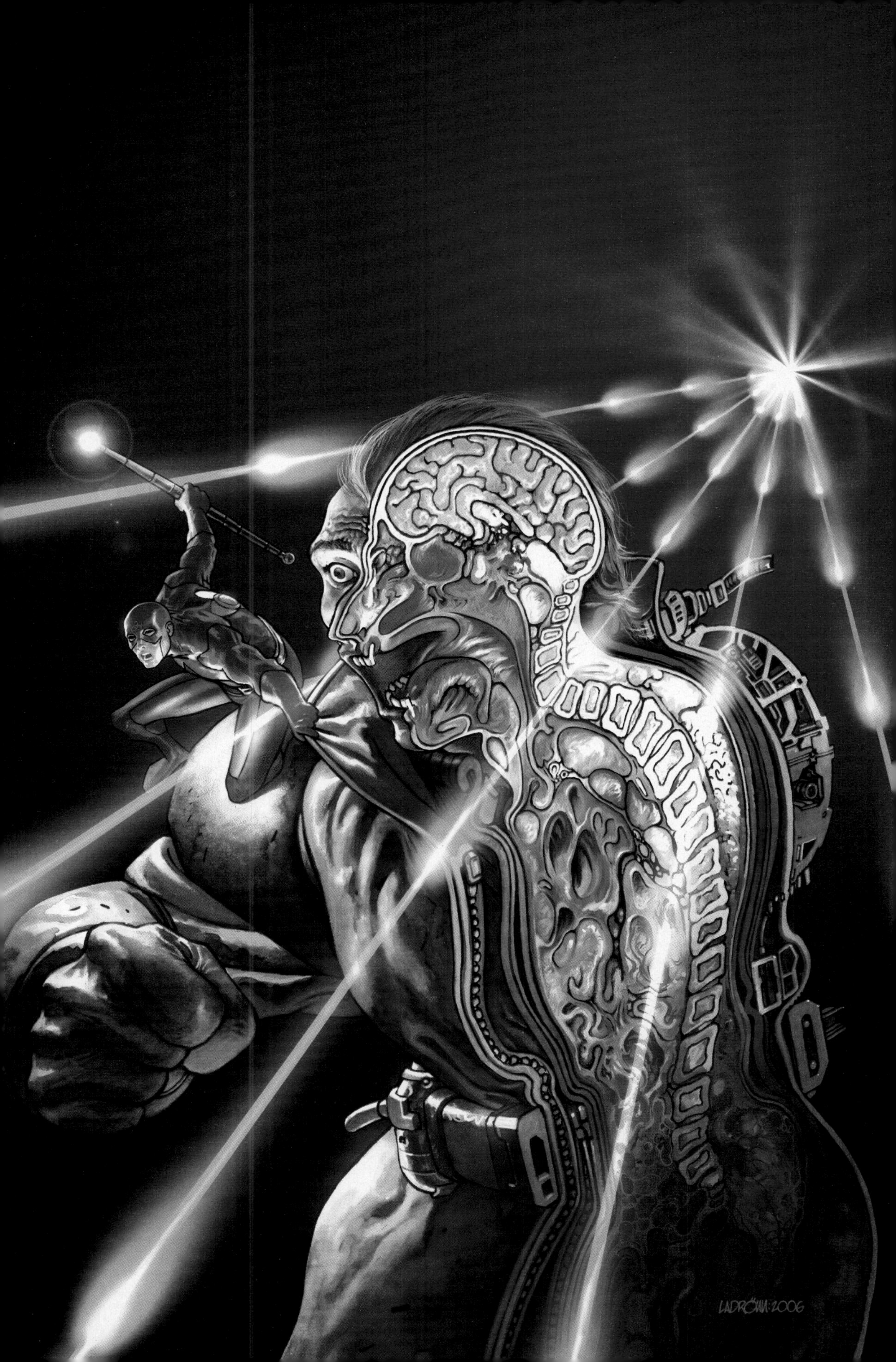
LADRÖNN 2006

THE MAN WHO SWALLOWED ETERNITY: PART TWO
THE ENTROPY OF THE UNIVERSE TENDS TO A MAXIMUM

from **THE ALL NEW ATOM #8**

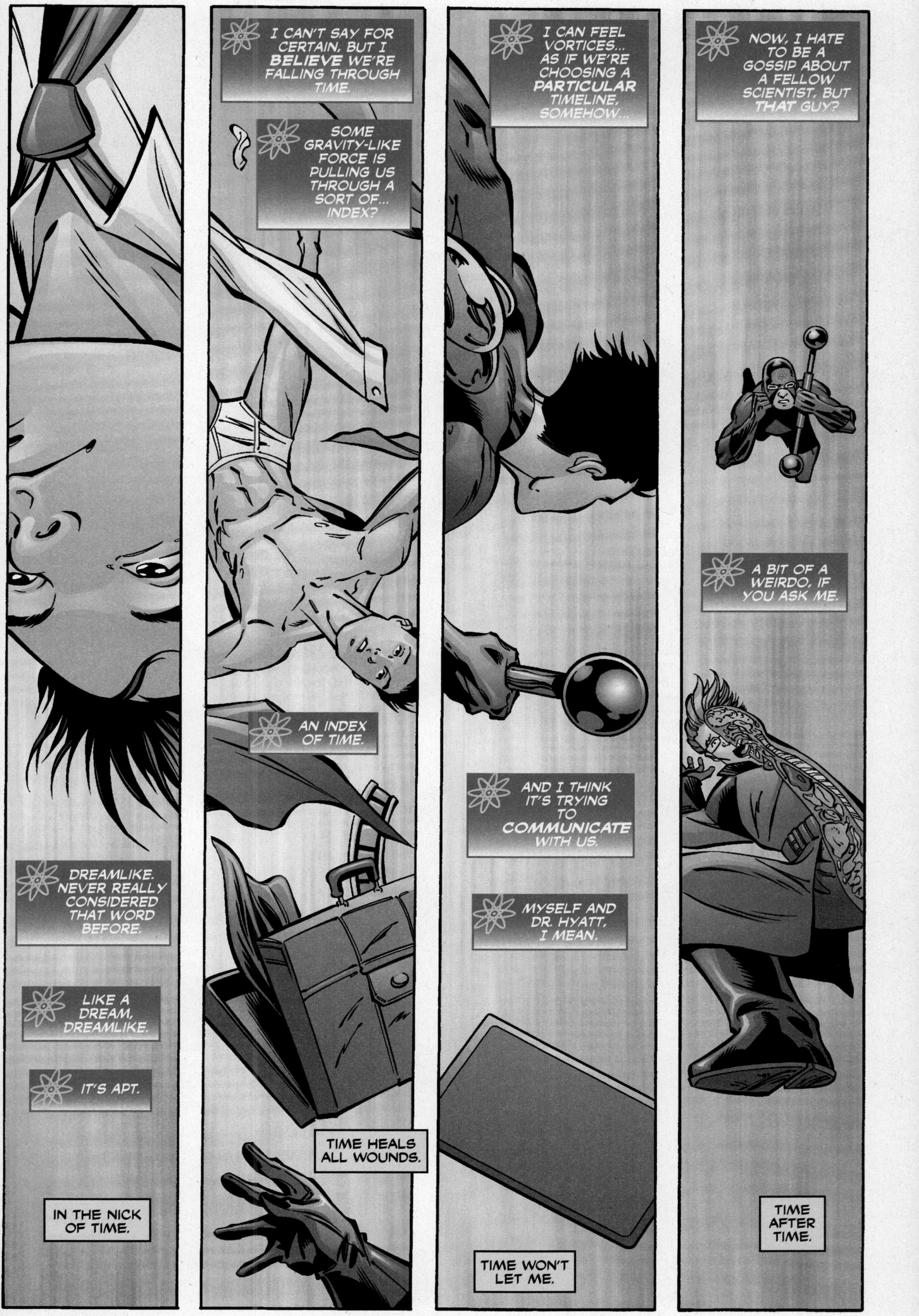
DREAMLIKE. NEVER REALLY CONSIDERED THAT WORD BEFORE.
LIKE A DREAM, DREAMLIKE.
IT'S APT.
IN THE NICK OF TIME.
I CAN'T SAY FOR CERTAIN, BUT I BELIEVE WE'RE FALLING THROUGH TIME.
SOME GRAVITY-LIKE FORCE IS PULLING US THROUGH A SORT OF... INDEX?
AN INDEX OF TIME.
TIME HEALS ALL WOUNDS.
I CAN FEEL VORTICES... AS IF WE'RE CHOOSING A PARTICULAR TIMELINE, SOMEHOW...
AND I THINK IT'S TRYING TO COMMUNICATE WITH US.
MYSELF AND DR. HYATT, I MEAN.
TIME WON'T LET ME.
NOW, I HATE TO BE A GOSSIP ABOUT A FELLOW SCIENTIST, BUT THAT GUY?
A BIT OF A WEIRDO, IF YOU ASK ME.
TIME AFTER TIME.

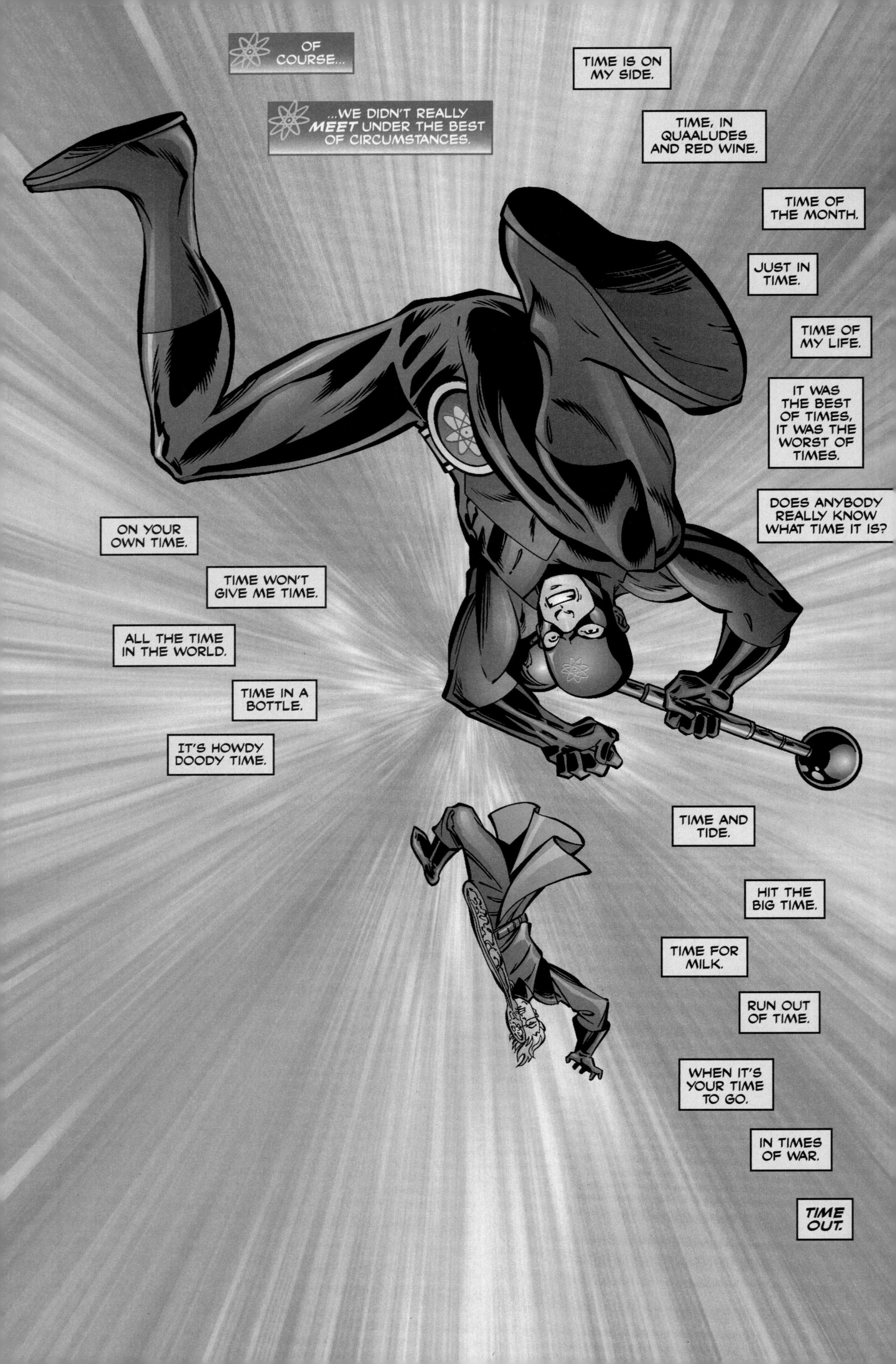
OF COURSE...
...WE DIDN'T REALLY MEET UNDER THE BEST OF CIRCUMSTANCES.
TIME IS ON MY SIDE.
TIME, IN QUAALUDES AND RED WINE.
TIME OF THE MONTH.
JUST IN TIME.
TIME OF MY LIFE.
IT WAS THE BEST OF TIMES, IT WAS THE WORST OF TIMES.
DOES ANYBODY REALLY KNOW WHAT TIME IT IS?
ON YOUR OWN TIME.
TIME WON'T GIVE ME TIME.
ALL THE TIME IN THE WORLD.
TIME IN A BOTTLE.
IT'S HOWDY DOODY TIME.
TIME AND TIDE.
HIT THE BIG TIME.
TIME FOR MILK.
RUN OUT OF TIME.
WHEN IT'S YOUR TIME TO GO.
IN TIMES OF WAR.
TIME OUT.

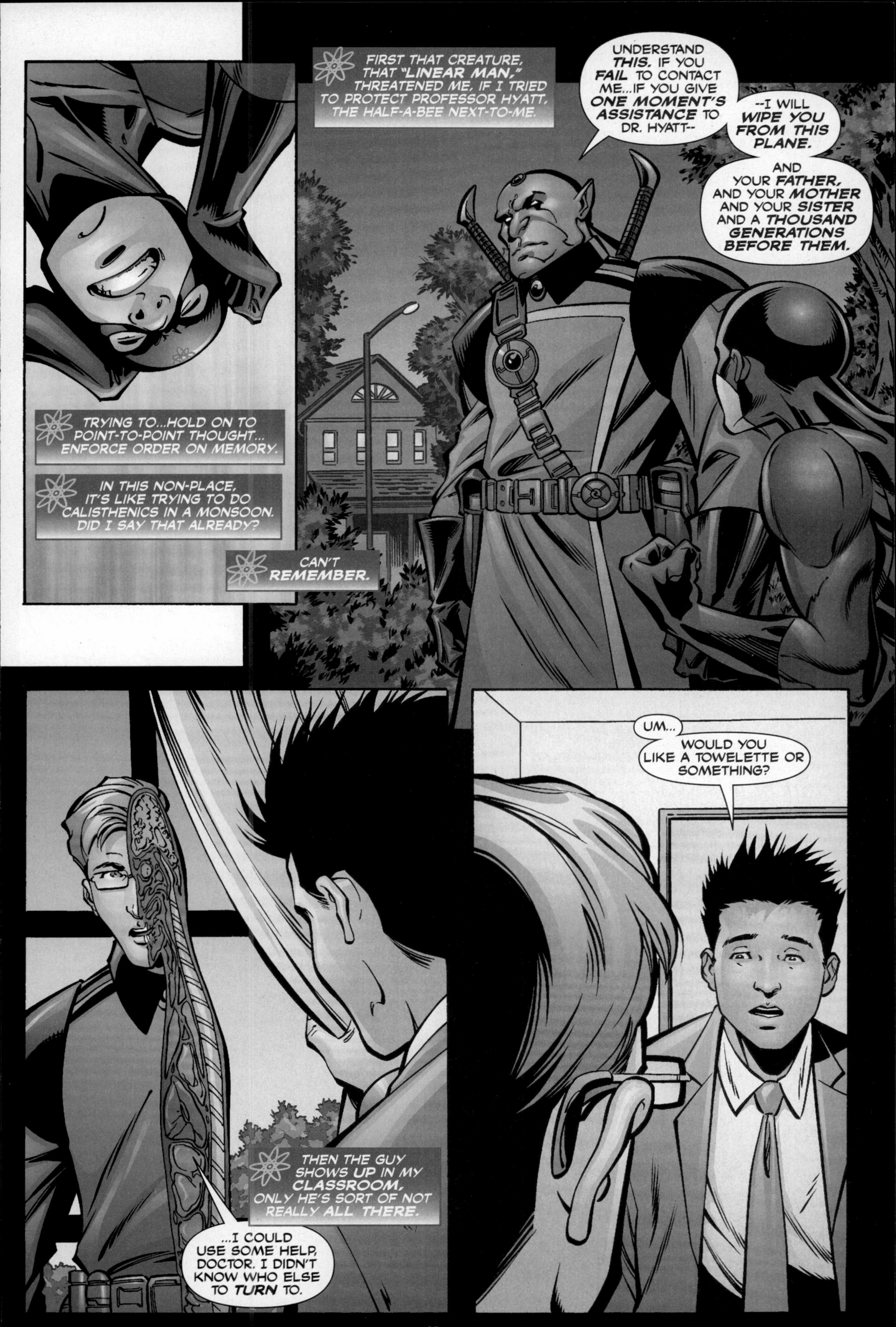
TRYING TO...HOLD ON TO POINT-TO-POINT THOUGHT... ENFORCE ORDER ON MEMORY.
IN THIS NON-PLACE, IT'S LIKE TRYING TO DO CALISTHENICS IN A MONSOON. DID I SAY THAT ALREADY?
CAN'T REMEMBER.
FIRST THAT CREATURE, THAT "LINEAR MAN," THREATENED ME, IF I TRIED TO PROTECT PROFESSOR HYATT, THE HALF-A-BEE NEXT-TO-ME.
UNDERSTAND THIS. IF YOU FAIL TO CONTACT ME...IF YOU GIVE ONE MOMENT'S ASSISTANCE TO DR. HYATT--
--I WILL WIPE YOU FROM THIS PLANE.
AND YOUR FATHER, AND YOUR MOTHER AND YOUR SISTER AND A THOUSAND GENERATIONS BEFORE THEM.
THEN THE GUY SHOWS UP IN MY CLASSROOM, ONLY HE'S SORT OF NOT REALLY ALL THERE.
...I COULD USE SOME HELP, DOCTOR. I DIDN'T KNOW WHO ELSE TO TURN TO.
UM...
WOULD YOU LIKE A TOWELETTE OR SOMETHING?

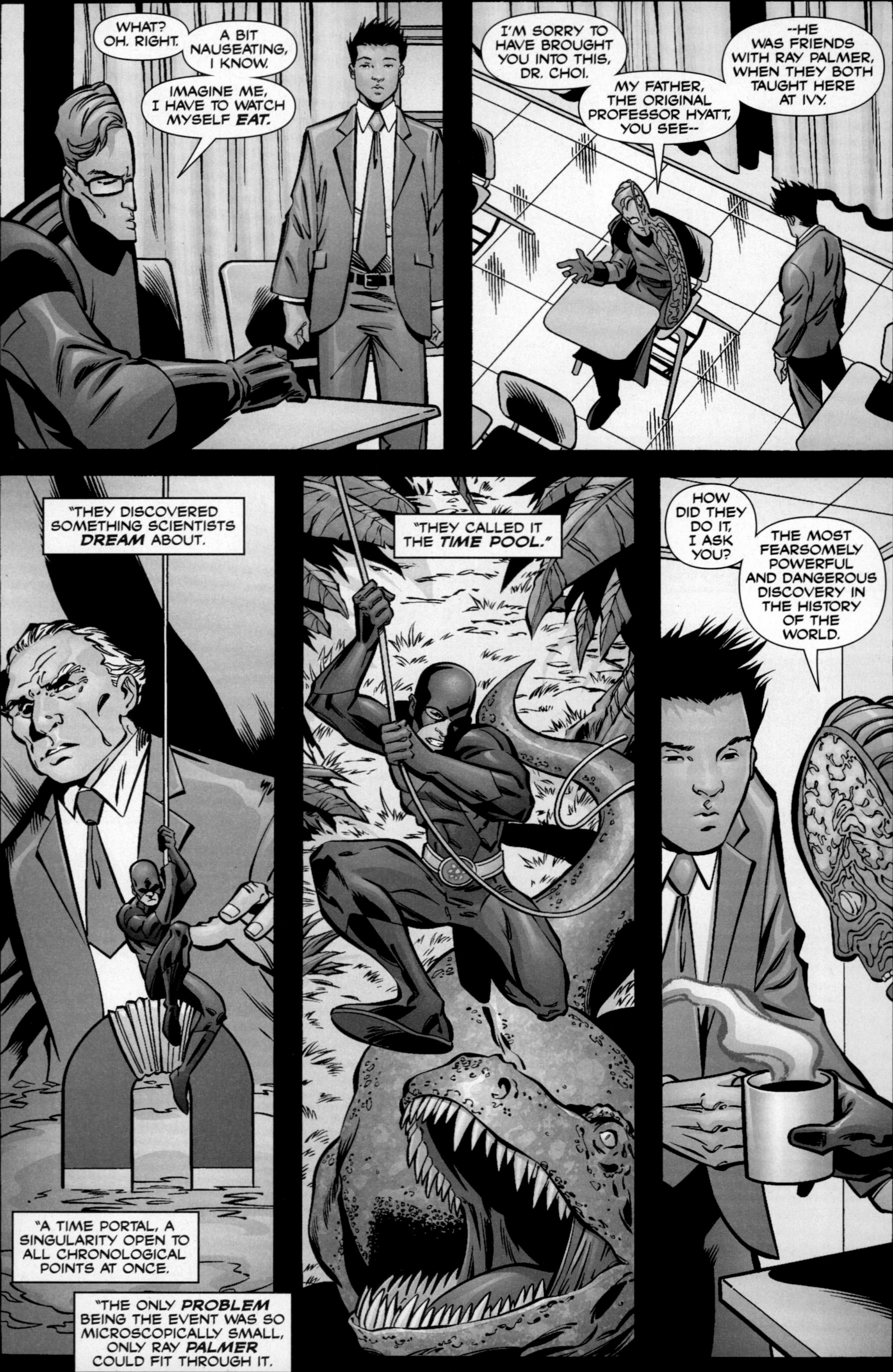
WHAT? OH. RIGHT.
A BIT NAUSEATING, I KNOW.
IMAGINE ME, I HAVE TO WATCH MYSELF *EAT.*
I'M SORRY TO HAVE BROUGHT YOU INTO THIS, DR. CHOI.
MY FATHER, THE ORIGINAL PROFESSOR HYATT, YOU SEE--
--HE WAS FRIENDS WITH RAY PALMER, WHEN THEY BOTH TAUGHT HERE AT IVY.
"THEY DISCOVERED SOMETHING SCIENTISTS *DREAM* ABOUT.
"A TIME PORTAL, A SINGULARITY OPEN TO ALL CHRONOLOGICAL POINTS AT ONCE.
"THE ONLY *PROBLEM* BEING THE EVENT WAS SO MICROSCOPICALLY SMALL, ONLY RAY *PALMER* COULD FIT THROUGH IT.
"THEY CALLED IT THE *TIME POOL.*"
HOW DID THEY DO IT, I ASK YOU?
THE MOST FEARSOMELY POWERFUL AND DANGEROUS DISCOVERY IN THE HISTORY OF THE WORLD.

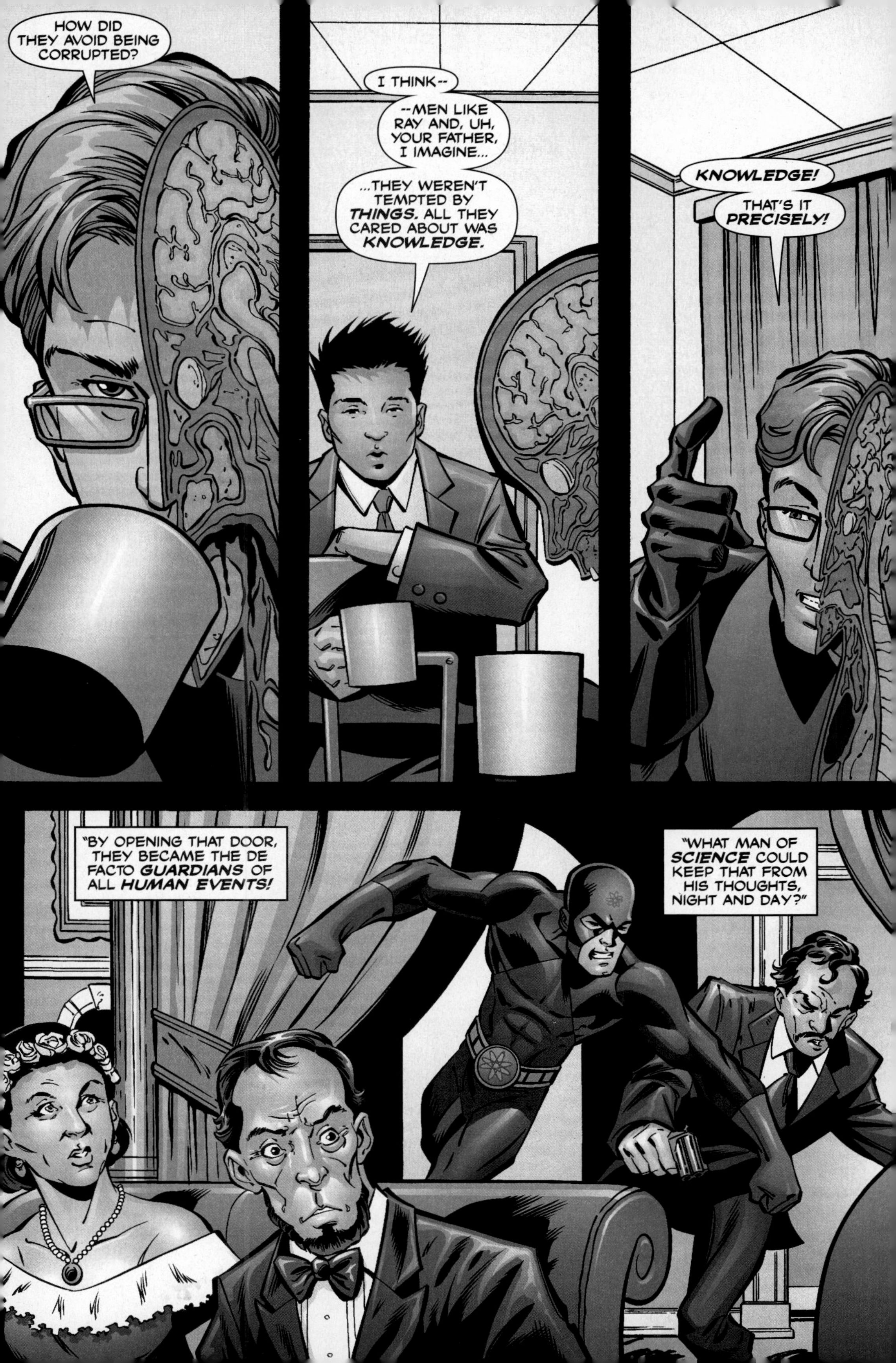
HOW DID THEY AVOID BEING CORRUPTED?
I THINK--
--MEN LIKE RAY AND, UH, YOUR FATHER, I IMAGINE...
...THEY WEREN'T TEMPTED BY THINGS. ALL THEY CARED ABOUT WAS KNOWLEDGE.
KNOWLEDGE!
THAT'S IT PRECISELY!
"BY OPENING THAT DOOR, THEY BECAME THE DE FACTO GUARDIANS OF ALL HUMAN EVENTS!
"WHAT MAN OF SCIENCE COULD KEEP THAT FROM HIS THOUGHTS, NIGHT AND DAY?"

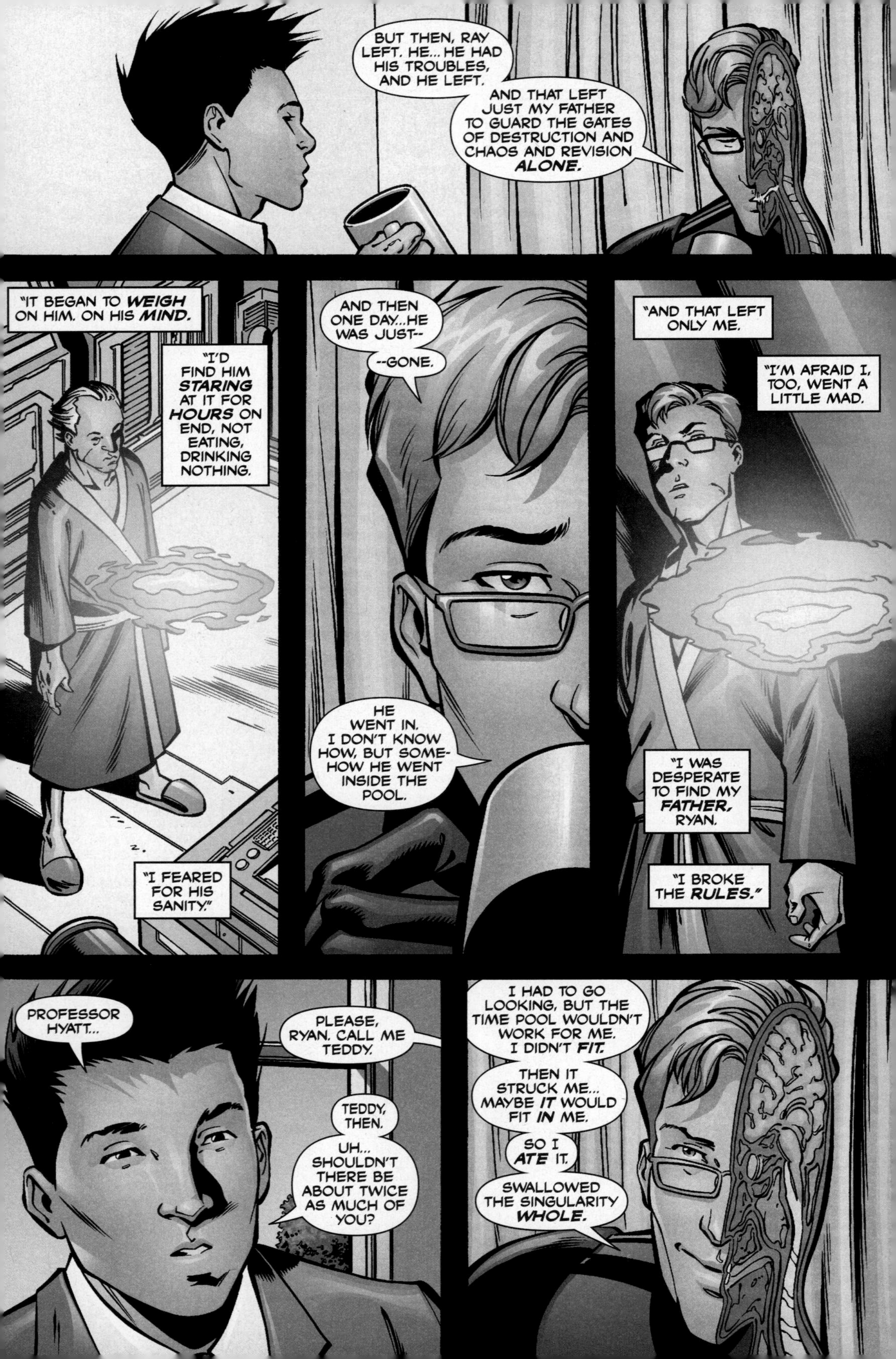
BUT THEN, RAY LEFT. HE... HE HAD HIS TROUBLES, AND HE LEFT.
AND THAT LEFT JUST MY FATHER TO GUARD THE GATES OF DESTRUCTION AND CHAOS AND REVISION ALONE.
"IT BEGAN TO WEIGH ON HIM. ON HIS MIND.
"I'D FIND HIM STARING AT IT FOR HOURS ON END, NOT EATING, DRINKING NOTHING.
"I FEARED FOR HIS SANITY."
AND THEN ONE DAY...HE WAS JUST--
--GONE.
HE WENT IN. I DON'T KNOW HOW, BUT SOMEHOW HE WENT INSIDE THE POOL.
"AND THAT LEFT ONLY ME.
"I'M AFRAID I, TOO, WENT A LITTLE MAD.
"I WAS DESPERATE TO FIND MY FATHER, RYAN.
"I BROKE THE RULES."
PROFESSOR HYATT...
PLEASE, RYAN. CALL ME TEDDY.
TEDDY, THEN.
UH... SHOULDN'T THERE BE ABOUT TWICE AS MUCH OF YOU?
I HAD TO GO LOOKING, BUT THE TIME POOL WOULDN'T WORK FOR ME. I DIDN'T FIT.
THEN IT STRUCK ME... MAYBE IT WOULD FIT IN ME.
SO I ATE IT.
SWALLOWED THE SINGULARITY WHOLE.

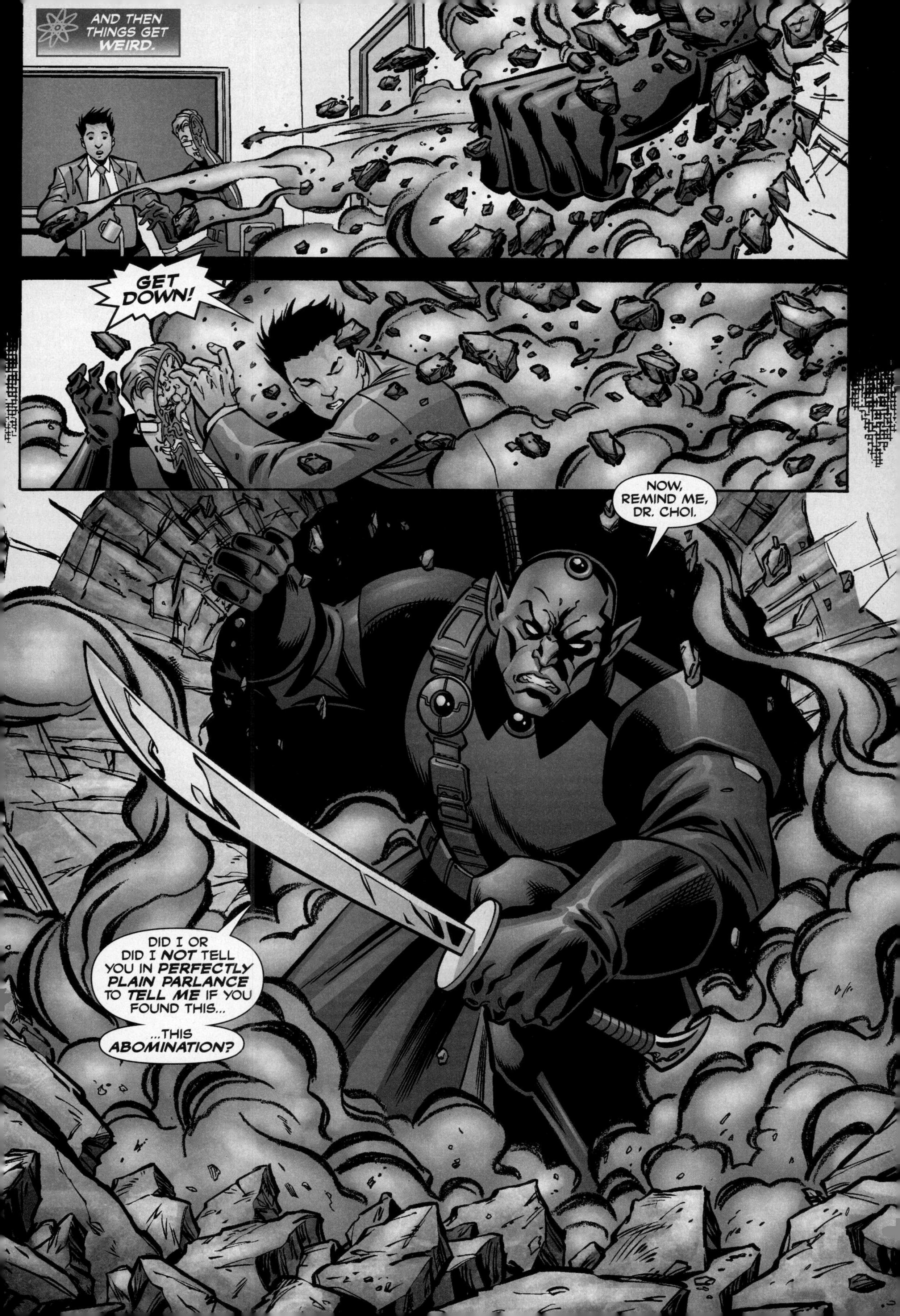
AND THEN THINGS GET *WEIRD*.
GET DOWN!
NOW, REMIND ME, DR. CHOI.
DID I OR DID I ***NOT*** TELL YOU IN ***PERFECTLY PLAIN PARLANCE*** TO ***TELL ME*** IF YOU FOUND THIS...
...THIS ***ABOMINATION?***

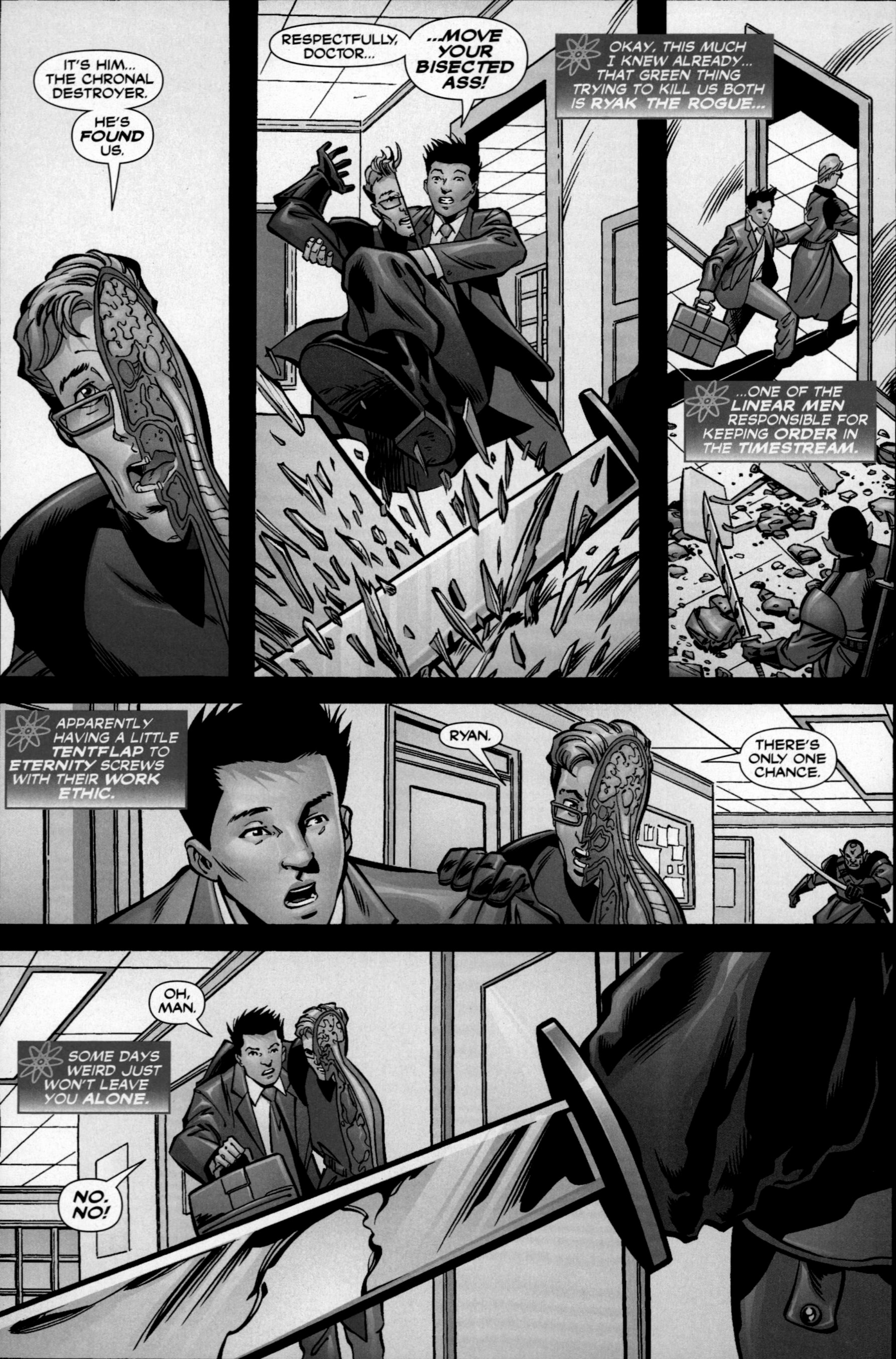
IT'S HIM... THE CHRONAL DESTROYER.
HE'S FOUND US.
RESPECTFULLY, DOCTOR...
...MOVE YOUR BISECTED ASS!
OKAY, THIS MUCH I KNEW ALREADY... THAT GREEN THING TRYING TO KILL US BOTH IS RYAK THE ROGUE...
...ONE OF THE LINEAR MEN RESPONSIBLE FOR KEEPING ORDER IN THE TIMESTREAM.
APPARENTLY HAVING A LITTLE TENTFLAP TO ETERNITY SCREWS WITH THEIR WORK ETHIC.
RYAN.
THERE'S ONLY ONE CHANCE.
OH, MAN.
SOME DAYS WEIRD JUST WON'T LEAVE YOU ALONE.
NO, NO!

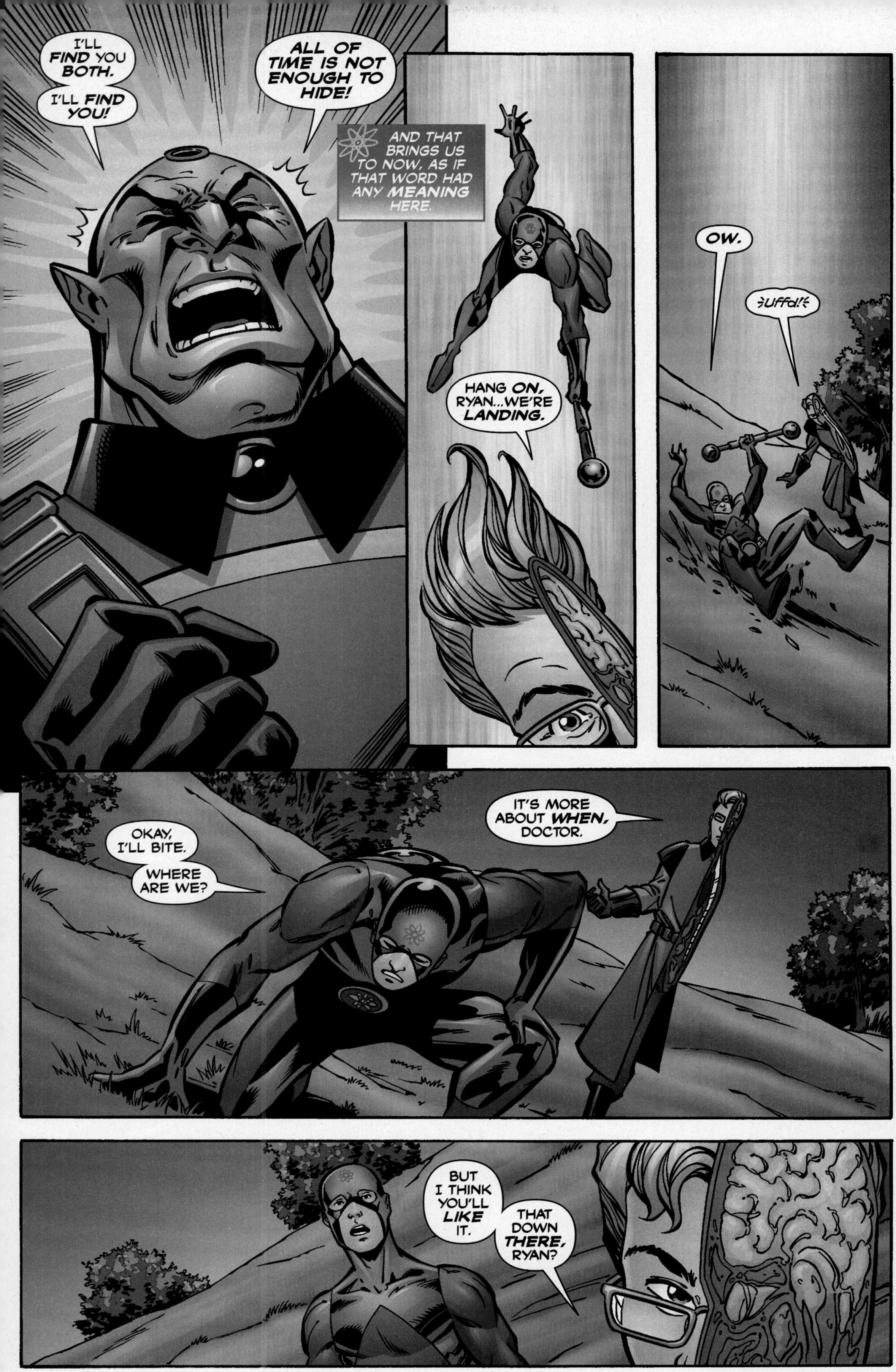
I'LL FIND YOU BOTH.
I'LL FIND YOU!
ALL OF TIME IS NOT ENOUGH TO HIDE!
AND THAT BRINGS US TO NOW, AS IF THAT WORD HAD ANY MEANING HERE.
HANG ON, RYAN...WE'RE LANDING.
OW.
¡Uffa!¡
OKAY, I'LL BITE.
WHERE ARE WE?
IT'S MORE ABOUT WHEN, DOCTOR.
BUT I THINK YOU'LL LIKE IT.
THAT DOWN THERE, RYAN?

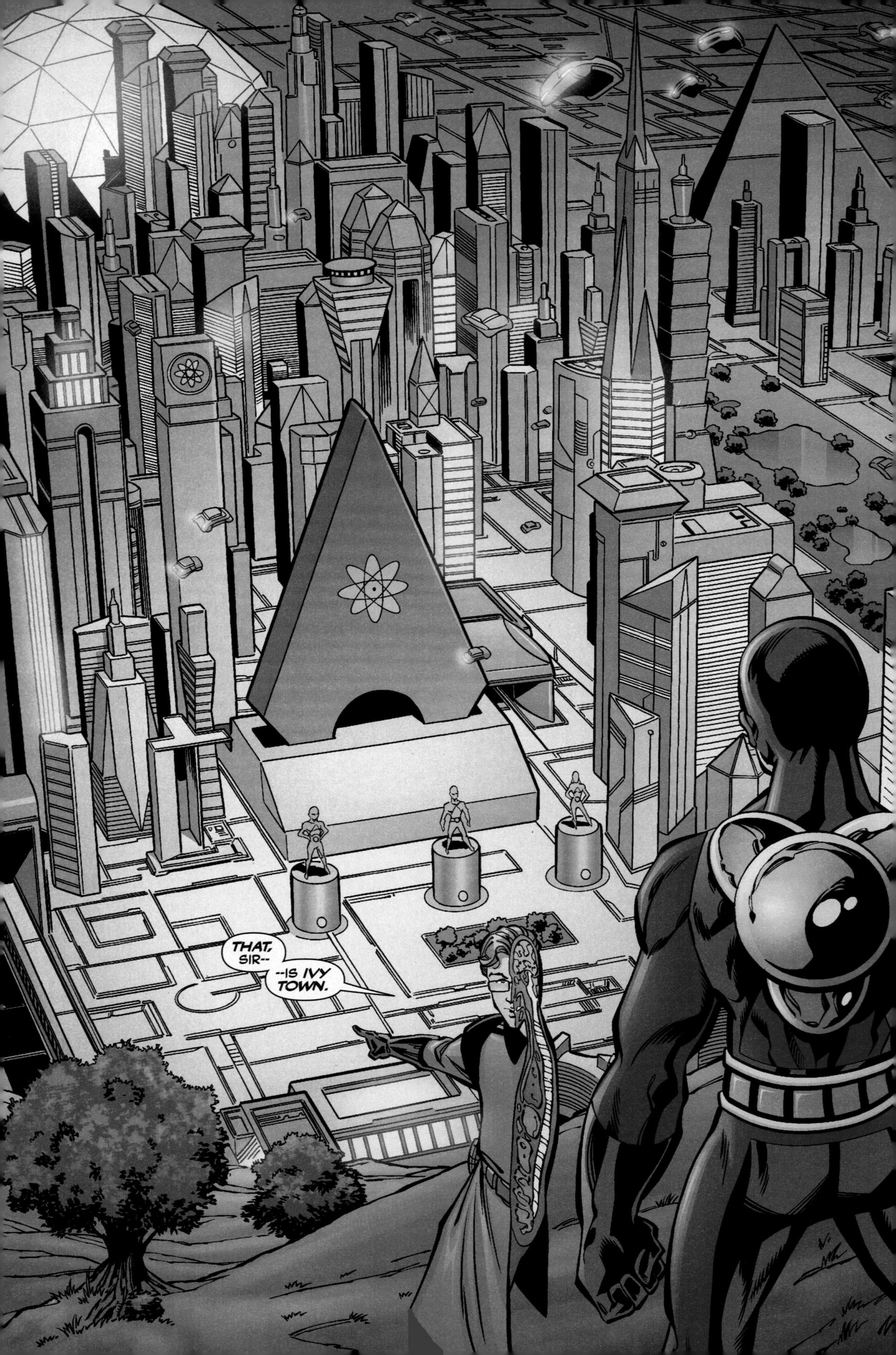
THAT, SIR--
--IS IVY TOWN.

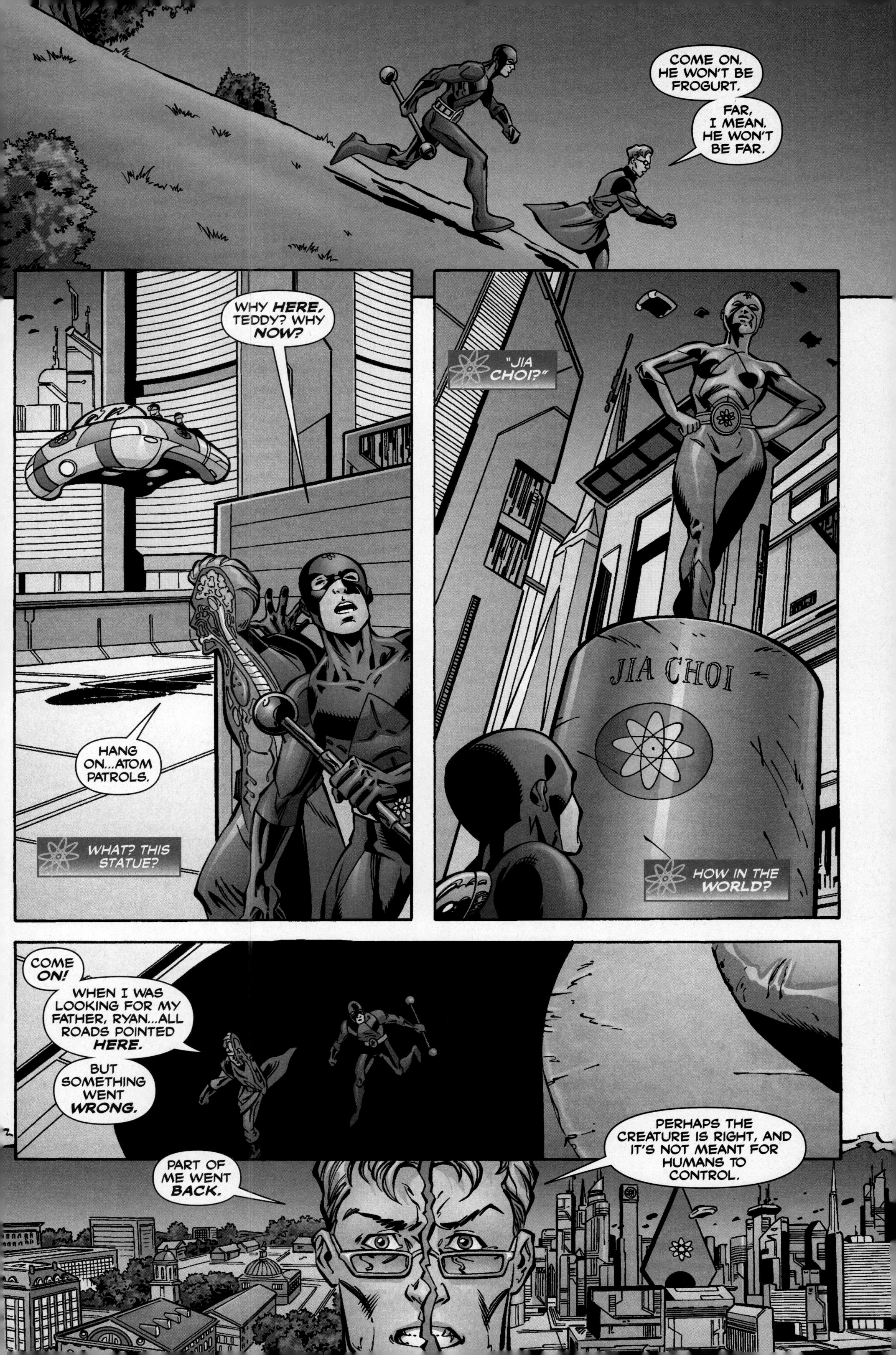
COME ON. HE WON'T BE FROGURT.
FAR, I MEAN. HE WON'T BE FAR.
WHY HERE, TEDDY? WHY NOW?
HANG ON...ATOM PATROLS.
WHAT? THIS STATUE?
"JIA CHOI?"
JIA CHOI
HOW IN THE WORLD?
COME ON!
WHEN I WAS LOOKING FOR MY FATHER, RYAN...ALL ROADS POINTED HERE.
BUT SOMETHING WENT WRONG.
PART OF ME WENT BACK.
PERHAPS THE CREATURE IS RIGHT, AND IT'S NOT MEANT FOR HUMANS TO CONTROL.

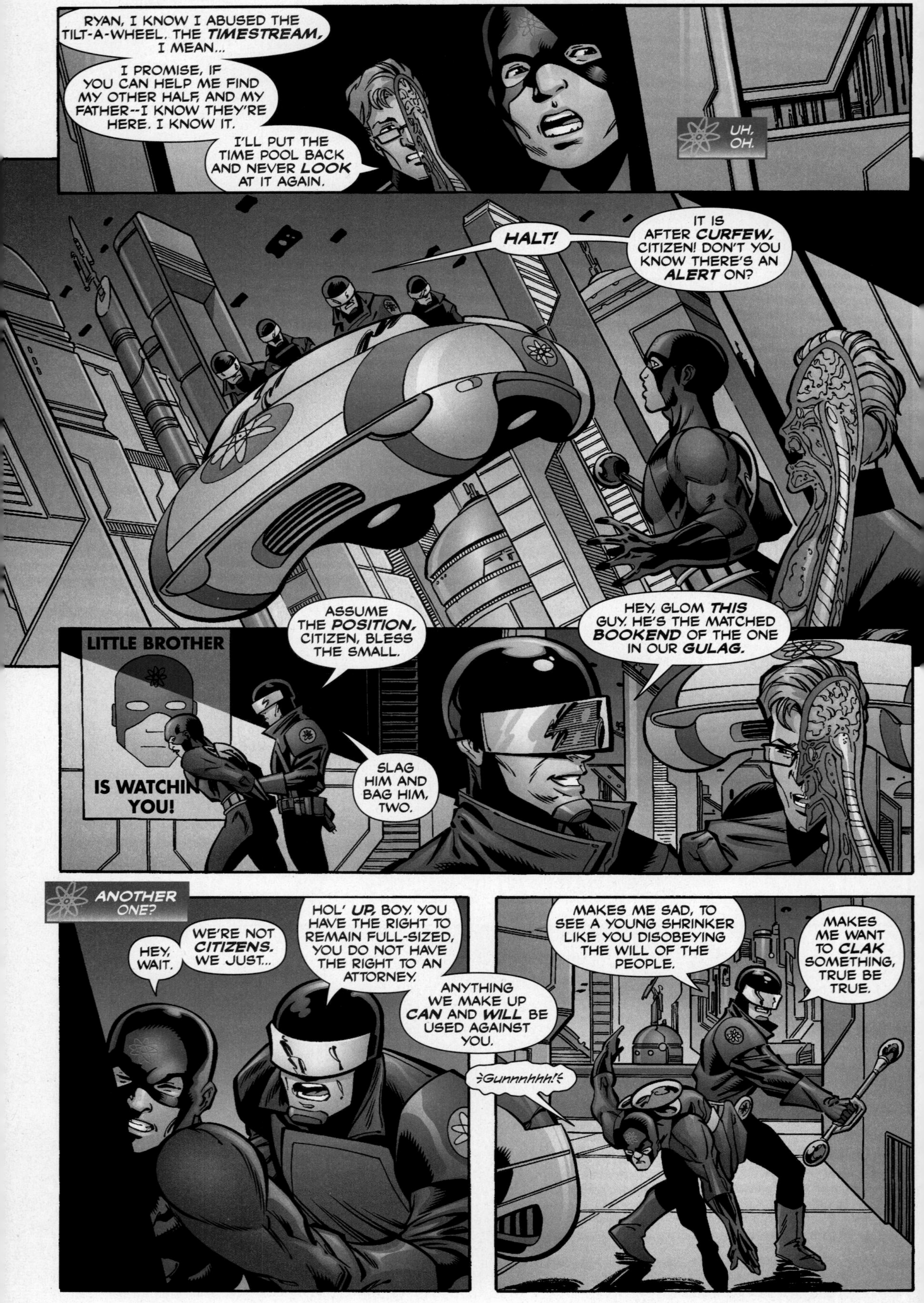
RYAN, I KNOW I ABUSED THE TILT-A-WHEEL. THE TIMESTREAM, I MEAN...
I PROMISE, IF YOU CAN HELP ME FIND MY OTHER HALF, AND MY FATHER--I KNOW THEY'RE HERE. I KNOW IT.
I'LL PUT THE TIME POOL BACK AND NEVER LOOK AT IT AGAIN.
UH, OH.
HALT!
IT IS AFTER CURFEW, CITIZEN! DON'T YOU KNOW THERE'S AN ALERT ON?
LITTLE BROTHER IS WATCHIN YOU!
ASSUME THE POSITION, CITIZEN, BLESS THE SMALL.
SLAG HIM AND BAG HIM, TWO.
HEY, GLOM THIS GUY. HE'S THE MATCHED BOOKEND OF THE ONE IN OUR GULAG.
ANOTHER ONE?
HEY, WAIT.
WE'RE NOT CITIZENS. WE JUST...
HOL' UP, BOY. YOU HAVE THE RIGHT TO REMAIN FULL-SIZED, YOU DO NOT HAVE THE RIGHT TO AN ATTORNEY.
ANYTHING WE MAKE UP CAN AND WILL BE USED AGAINST YOU.
MAKES ME SAD, TO SEE A YOUNG SHRINKER LIKE YOU DISOBEYING THE WILL OF THE PEOPLE.
MAKES ME WANT TO CLAK SOMETHING, TRUE BE TRUE.
Gunnnhhh!

OKAY. MY FIRST MEETING WITH A SENTIENT BEING FROM THE FUTURE AND I GET HIT IN THE FACE.

MAYBE IT'S ME.

NAH, IT'S HIM.

CLAK YOU, CLAKFACE.

CENTRAL MICRO-COMMAND, REQUESTING BACKUP, OFFICER DOWN!

RANDOM SIZE COMBAT MODE, NOW!

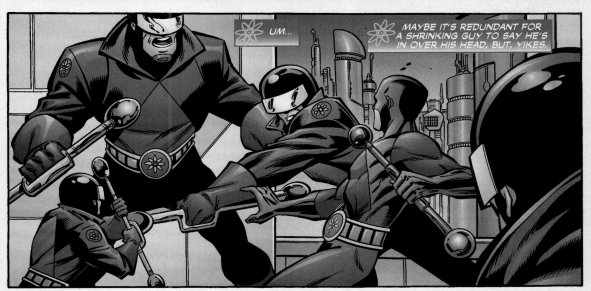

UM...

MAYBE IT'S REDUNDANT FOR A SHRINKING GUY TO SAY HE'S IN OVER HIS HEAD, BUT, YIKES.

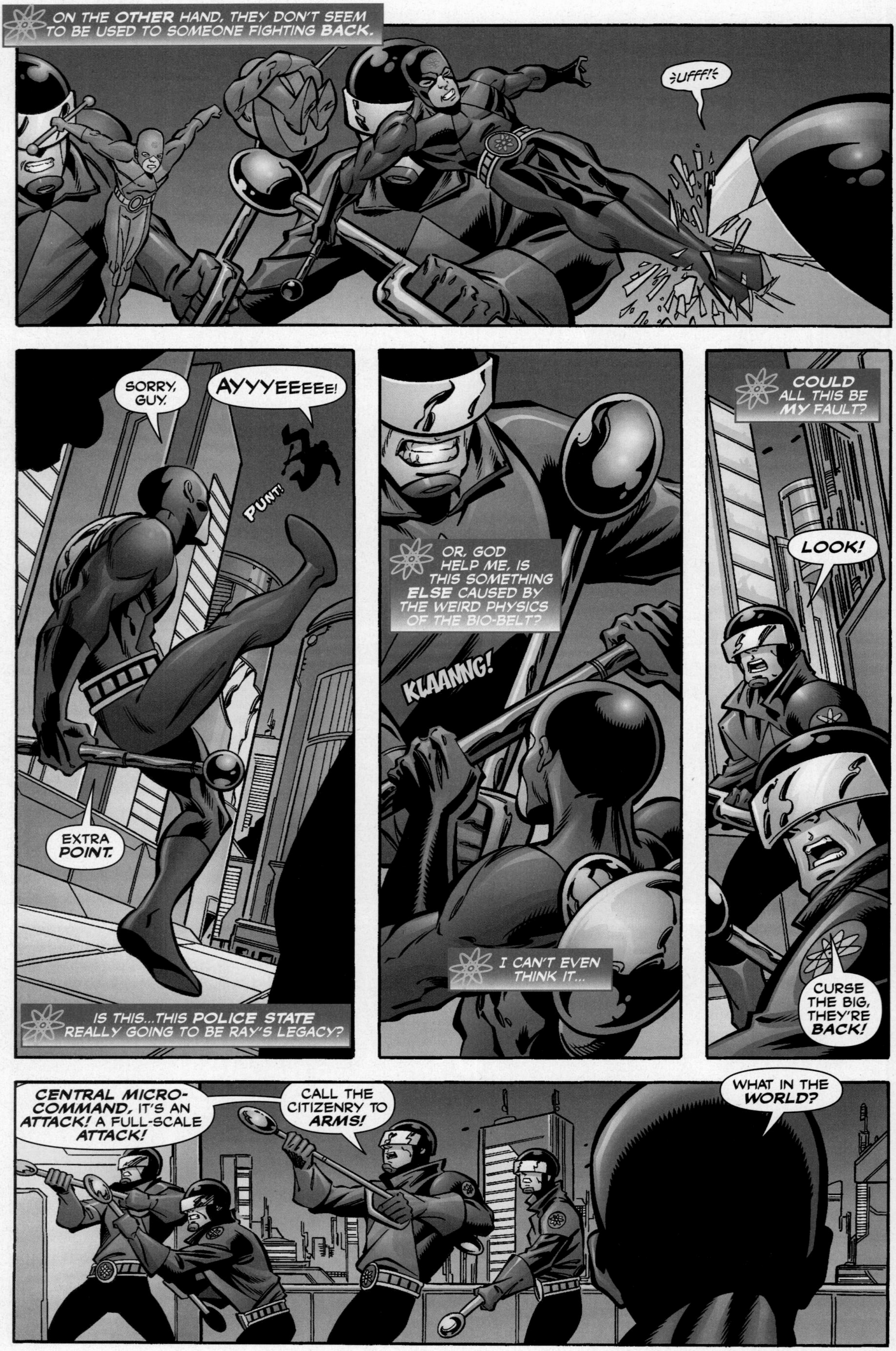
ON THE OTHER HAND, THEY DON'T SEEM TO BE USED TO SOMEONE FIGHTING BACK.
UFFF!
SORRY, GUY.
AYYYEEEEE!
PUNT!
EXTRA POINT.
IS THIS...THIS POLICE STATE REALLY GOING TO BE RAY'S LEGACY?
OR, GOD HELP ME, IS THIS SOMETHING ELSE CAUSED BY THE WEIRD PHYSICS OF THE BIO-BELT?
KLAANNG!
I CAN'T EVEN THINK IT...
COULD ALL THIS BE MY FAULT?
LOOK!
CURSE THE BIG, THEY'RE BACK!
CENTRAL MICRO-COMMAND, IT'S AN ATTACK! A FULL-SCALE ATTACK!
CALL THE CITIZENRY TO ARMS!
WHAT IN THE WORLD?

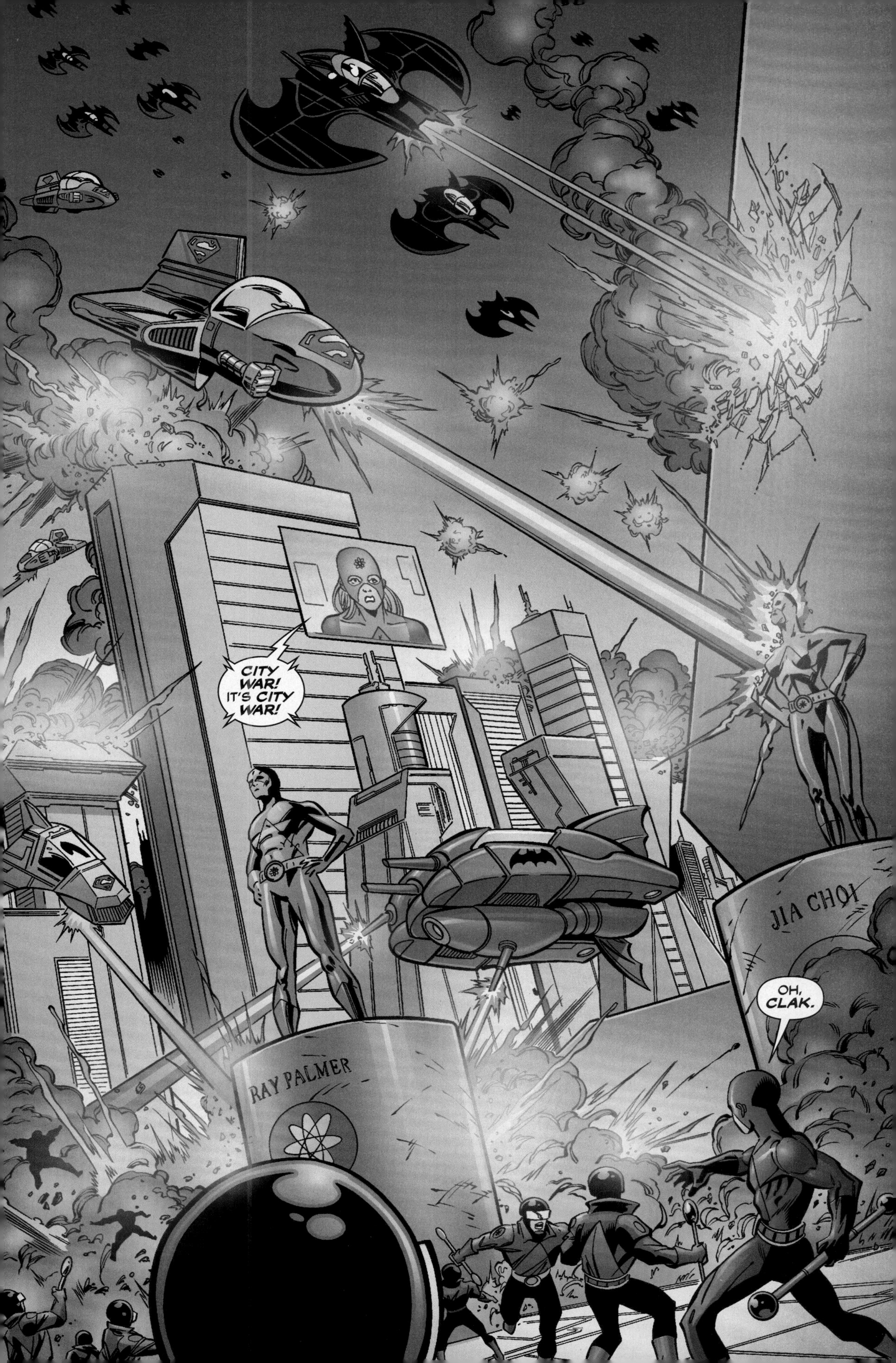
CITY WAR! IT'S CITY WAR!
JIA CHOI
OH, CLAK.
RAY PALMER

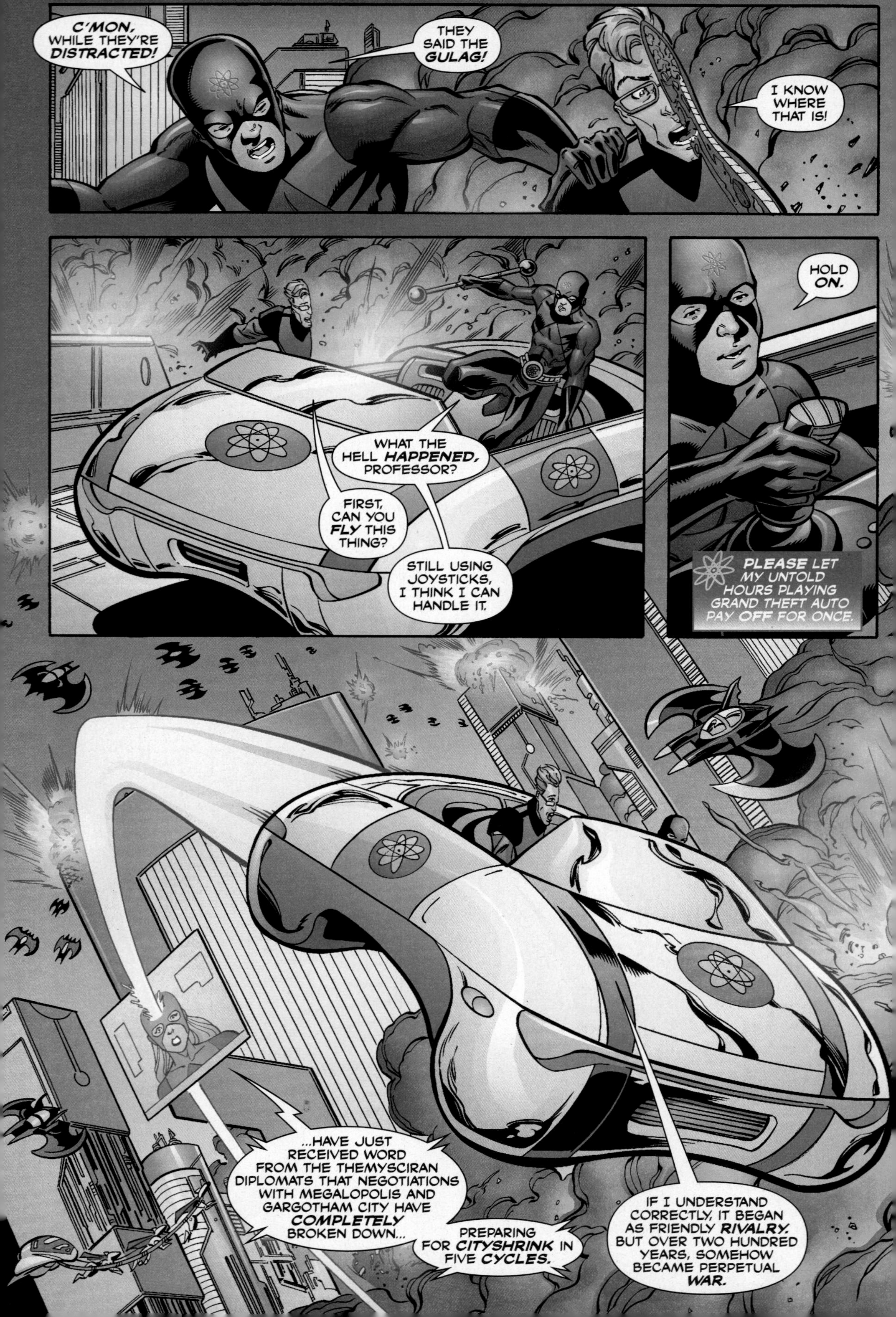
C'MON, WHILE THEY'RE DISTRACTED!
THEY SAID THE GULAG!
I KNOW WHERE THAT IS!
WHAT THE HELL HAPPENED, PROFESSOR?
FIRST, CAN YOU FLY THIS THING?
STILL USING JOYSTICKS, I THINK I CAN HANDLE IT.
HOLD ON.
PLEASE LET MY UNTOLD HOURS PLAYING GRAND THEFT AUTO PAY OFF FOR ONCE.
...HAVE JUST RECEIVED WORD FROM THE THEMYSCIRAN DIPLOMATS THAT NEGOTIATIONS WITH MEGALOPOLIS AND GARGOTHAM CITY HAVE COMPLETELY BROKEN DOWN...
PREPARING FOR CITYSHRINK IN FIVE CYCLES.
IF I UNDERSTAND CORRECTLY, IT BEGAN AS FRIENDLY RIVALRY. BUT OVER TWO HUNDRED YEARS, SOMEHOW BECAME PERPETUAL WAR.

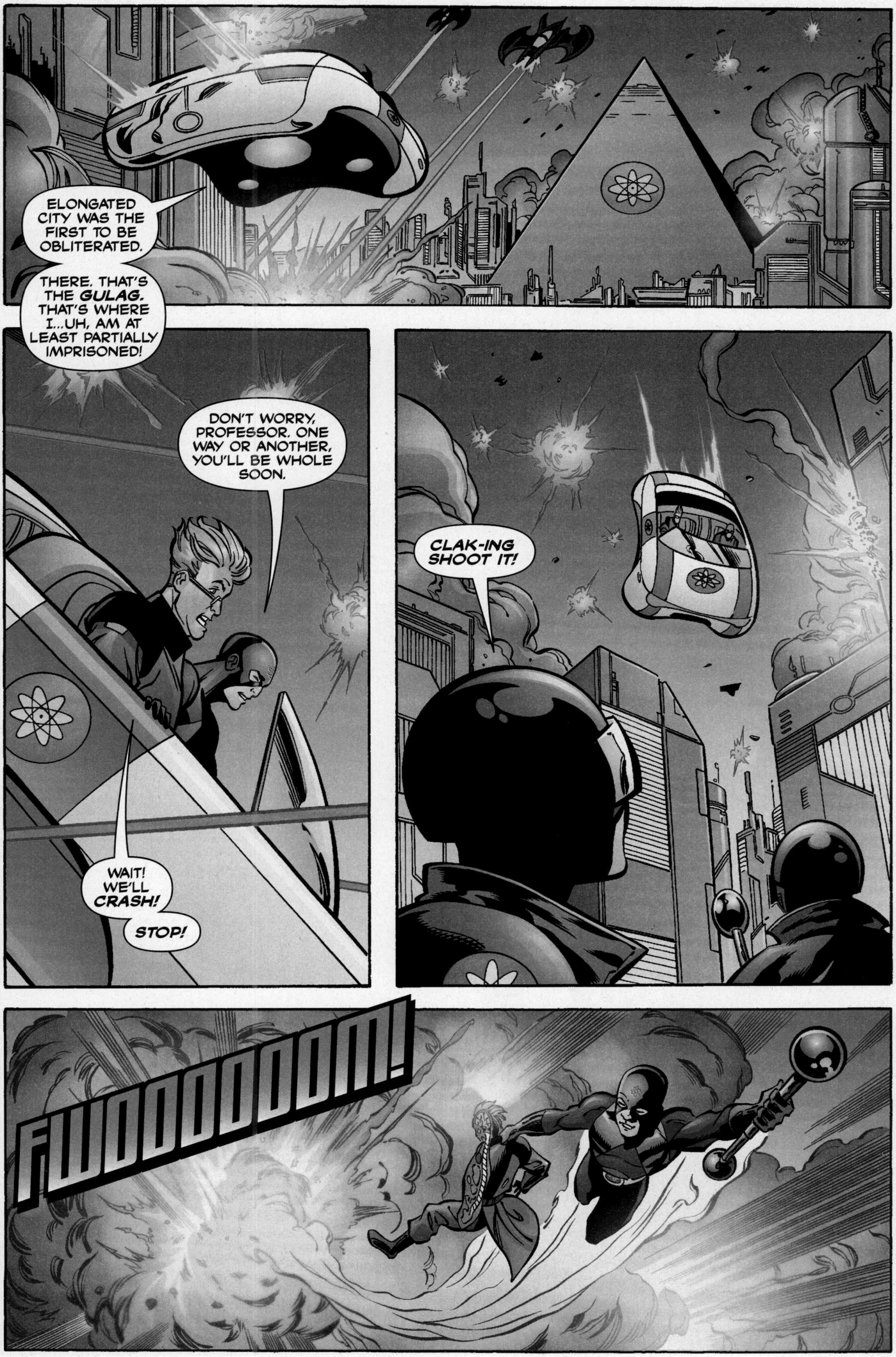

ELONGATED CITY WAS THE FIRST TO BE OBLITERATED.
THERE. THAT'S THE GULAG. THAT'S WHERE I...UH, AM AT LEAST PARTIALLY IMPRISONED!
DON'T WORRY, PROFESSOR. ONE WAY OR ANOTHER, YOU'LL BE WHOLE SOON.
WAIT! WE'LL CRASH!
STOP!
CLAK-ING SHOOT IT!
FWOOOOOOM!

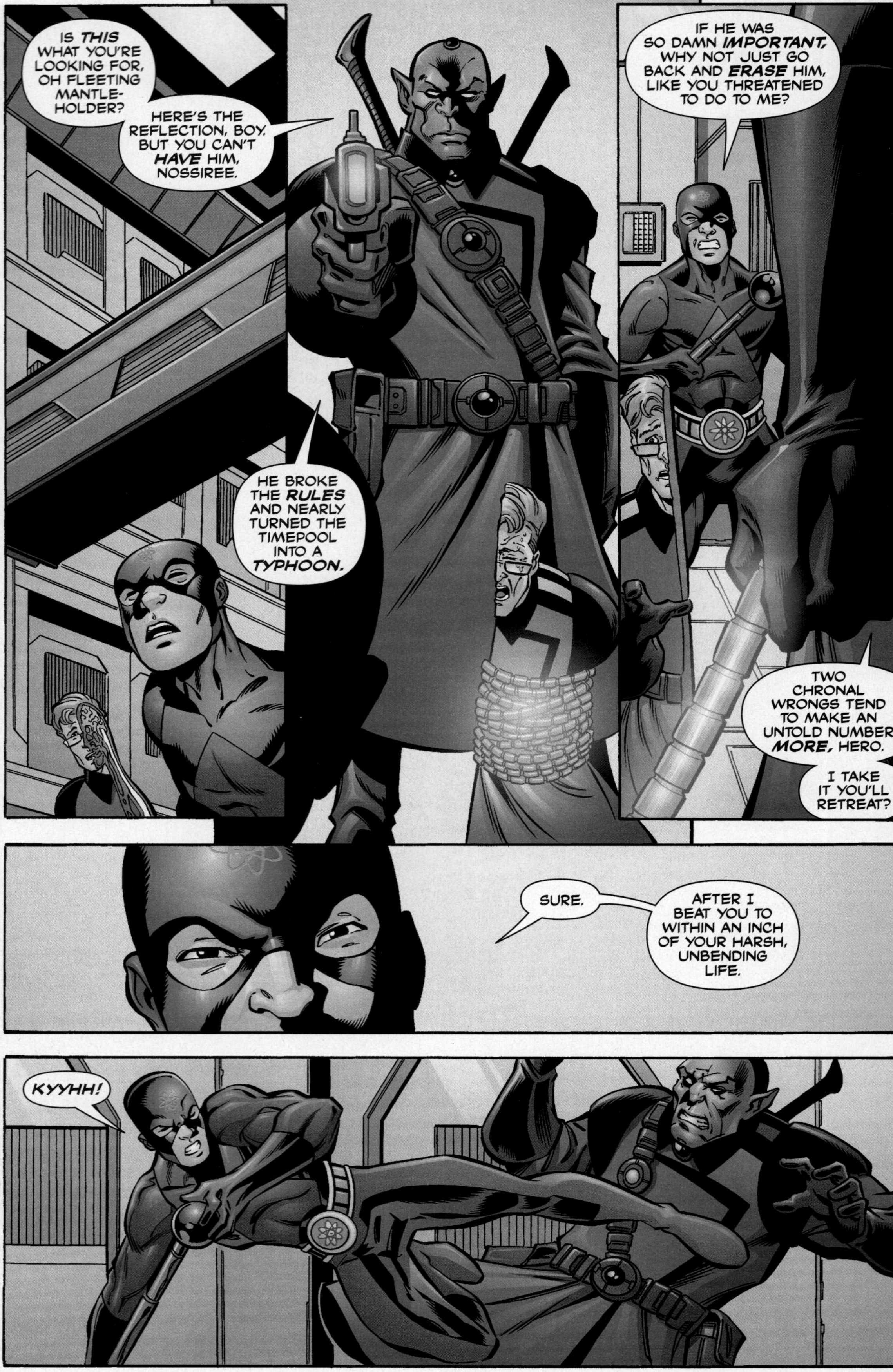
IS THIS WHAT YOU'RE LOOKING FOR, OH FLEETING MANTLE-HOLDER?
HERE'S THE REFLECTION, BOY. BUT YOU CAN'T HAVE HIM, NOSSIREE.
HE BROKE THE RULES AND NEARLY TURNED THE TIMEPOOL INTO A TYPHOON.
IF HE WAS SO DAMN IMPORTANT, WHY NOT JUST GO BACK AND ERASE HIM, LIKE YOU THREATENED TO DO TO ME?
TWO CHRONAL WRONGS TEND TO MAKE AN UNTOLD NUMBER MORE, HERO.
I TAKE IT YOU'LL RETREAT?
SURE.
AFTER I BEAT YOU TO WITHIN AN INCH OF YOUR HARSH, UNBENDING LIFE.
KYYHH!

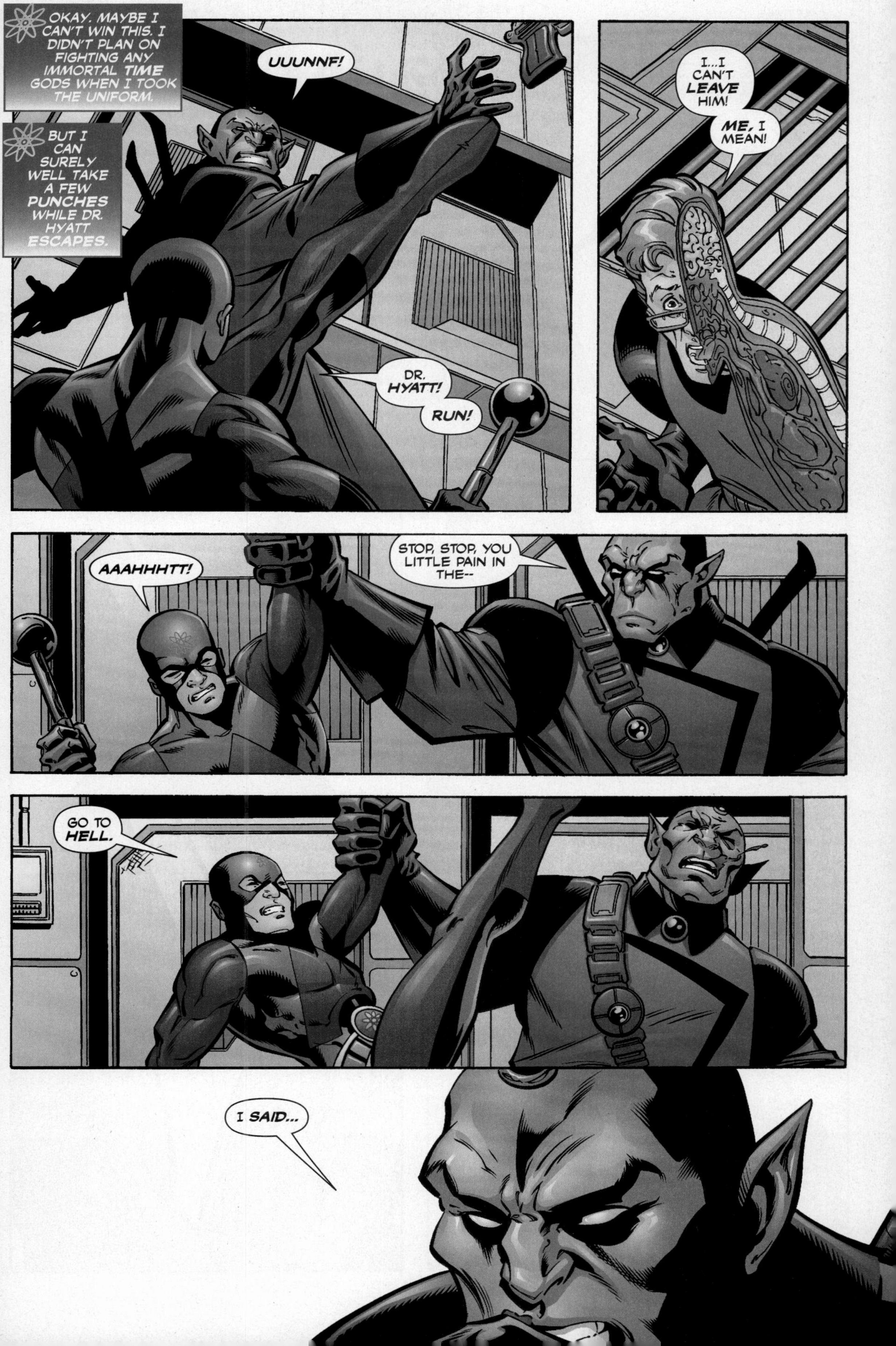
OKAY. MAYBE I CAN'T WIN THIS. I DIDN'T PLAN ON FIGHTING ANY IMMORTAL TIME GODS WHEN I TOOK THE UNIFORM.
BUT I CAN SURELY WELL TAKE A FEW PUNCHES WHILE DR. HYATT ESCAPES.
UUUNNF!
DR. HYATT!
RUN!
I...I CAN'T LEAVE HIM!
ME, I MEAN!
AAAHHHTT!
STOP, STOP, YOU LITTLE PAIN IN THE--
GO TO HELL.
I SAID...

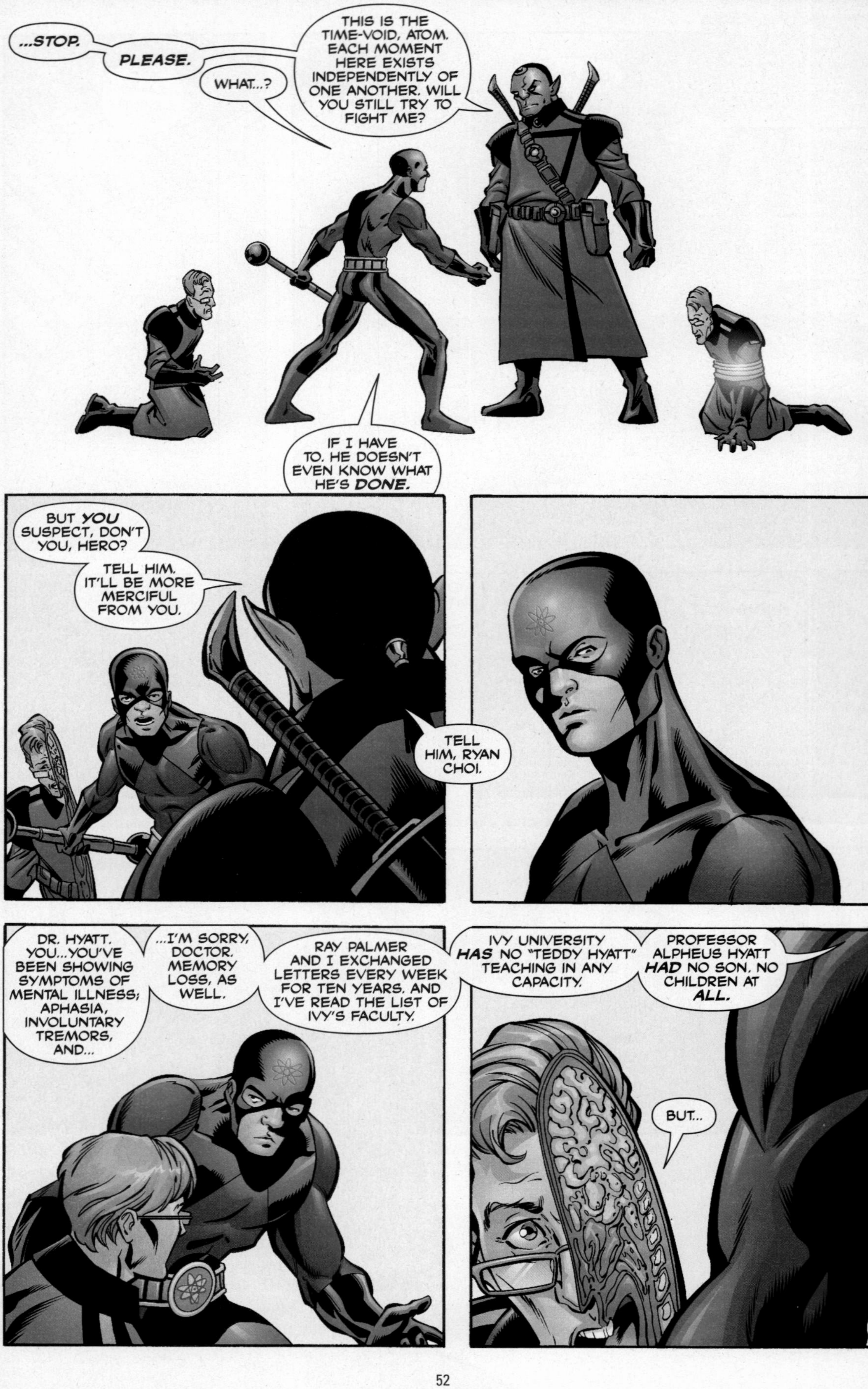
...STOP.
PLEASE.
WHAT...?
THIS IS THE TIME-VOID, ATOM. EACH MOMENT HERE EXISTS INDEPENDENTLY OF ONE ANOTHER. WILL YOU STILL TRY TO FIGHT ME?
IF I HAVE TO. HE DOESN'T EVEN KNOW WHAT HE'S DONE.
BUT YOU SUSPECT, DON'T YOU, HERO?
TELL HIM. IT'LL BE MORE MERCIFUL FROM YOU.
TELL HIM, RYAN CHOI.
DR. HYATT. YOU...YOU'VE BEEN SHOWING SYMPTOMS OF MENTAL ILLNESS; APHASIA, INVOLUNTARY TREMORS, AND...
...I'M SORRY, DOCTOR. MEMORY LOSS, AS WELL.
RAY PALMER AND I EXCHANGED LETTERS EVERY WEEK FOR TEN YEARS, AND I'VE READ THE LIST OF IVY'S FACULTY.
IVY UNIVERSITY HAS NO "TEDDY HYATT" TEACHING IN ANY CAPACITY.
PROFESSOR ALPHEUS HYATT HAD NO SON. NO CHILDREN AT ALL.
BUT...

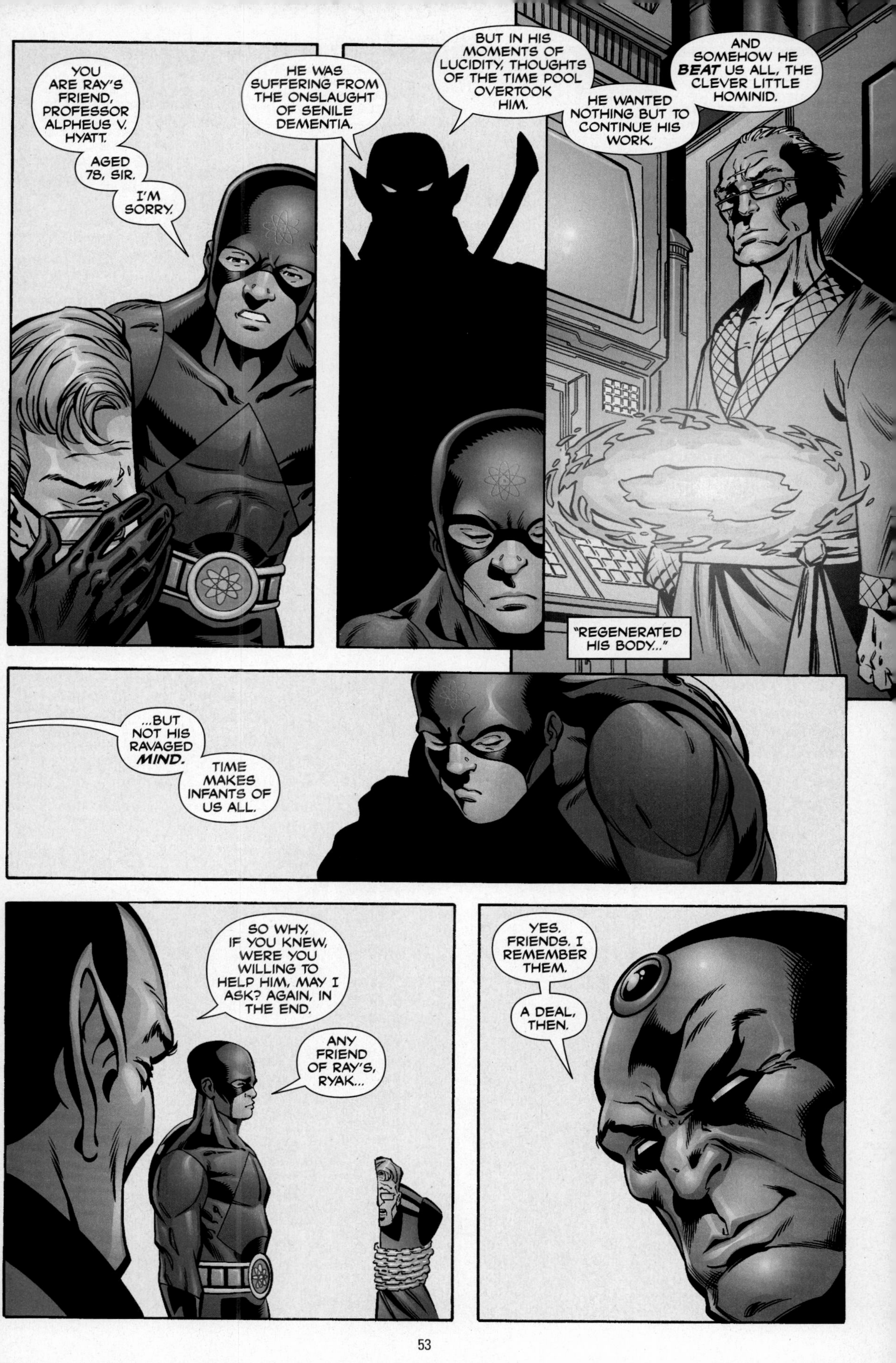

YOU ARE RAY'S FRIEND, PROFESSOR ALPHEUS V. HYATT.
AGED 78, SIR.
I'M SORRY.
HE WAS SUFFERING FROM THE ONSLAUGHT OF SENILE DEMENTIA.
BUT IN HIS MOMENTS OF LUCIDITY, THOUGHTS OF THE TIME POOL OVERTOOK HIM.
HE WANTED NOTHING BUT TO CONTINUE HIS WORK.
AND SOMEHOW HE BEAT US ALL, THE CLEVER LITTLE HOMINID.
"REGENERATED HIS BODY..."
...BUT NOT HIS RAVAGED MIND.
TIME MAKES INFANTS OF US ALL.
SO WHY, IF YOU KNEW, WERE YOU WILLING TO HELP HIM, MAY I ASK? AGAIN, IN THE END.
ANY FRIEND OF RAY'S, RYAK...
YES. FRIENDS. I REMEMBER THEM.
A DEAL, THEN.

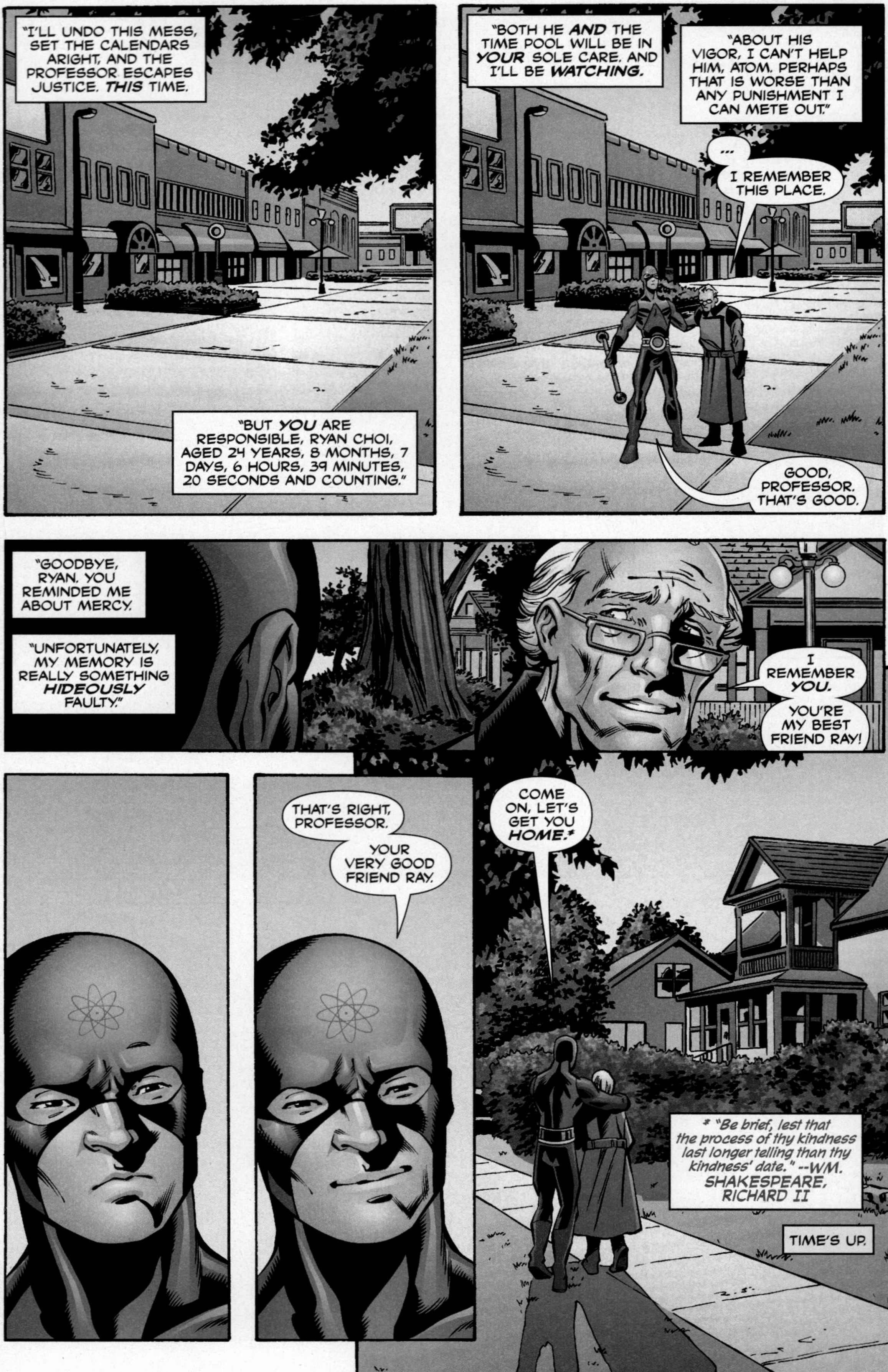
"I'LL UNDO THIS MESS, SET THE CALENDARS ARIGHT, AND THE PROFESSOR ESCAPES JUSTICE. *THIS* TIME.
"BUT *YOU* ARE RESPONSIBLE, RYAN CHOI, AGED 24 YEARS, 8 MONTHS, 7 DAYS, 6 HOURS, 39 MINUTES, 20 SECONDS AND COUNTING."
"BOTH HE *AND* THE TIME POOL WILL BE IN *YOUR* SOLE CARE. AND I'LL BE *WATCHING*.
"ABOUT HIS VIGOR, I CAN'T HELP HIM, ATOM. PERHAPS THAT IS WORSE THAN ANY PUNISHMENT I CAN METE OUT."
...
I REMEMBER THIS PLACE.
GOOD, PROFESSOR. THAT'S GOOD.
"GOODBYE, RYAN. YOU REMINDED ME ABOUT MERCY.
"UNFORTUNATELY, MY MEMORY IS REALLY SOMETHING *HIDEOUSLY* FAULTY."
I REMEMBER *YOU*.
YOU'RE MY BEST FRIEND RAY!
THAT'S RIGHT, PROFESSOR.
YOUR VERY GOOD FRIEND RAY.
COME ON, LET'S GET YOU *HOME*.*
* "Be brief, lest that the process of thy kindness last longer telling than thy kindness' date." --WM. SHAKESPEARE, RICHARD II
TIME'S UP.

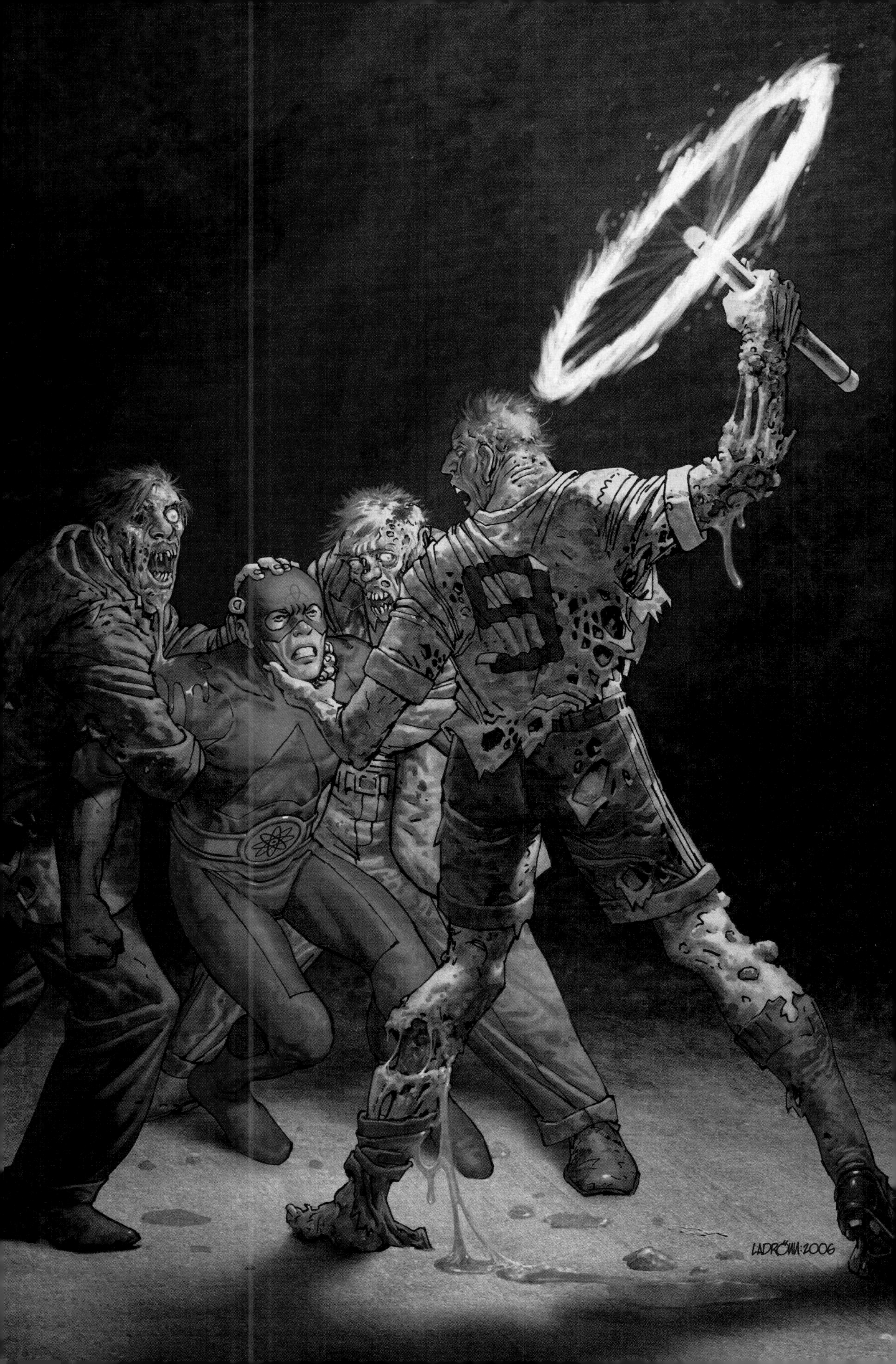
LADRÖNN:2006

JIA: PART ONE
HER NAME MEANT BEAUTY

from **THE ALL NEW ATOM #9**

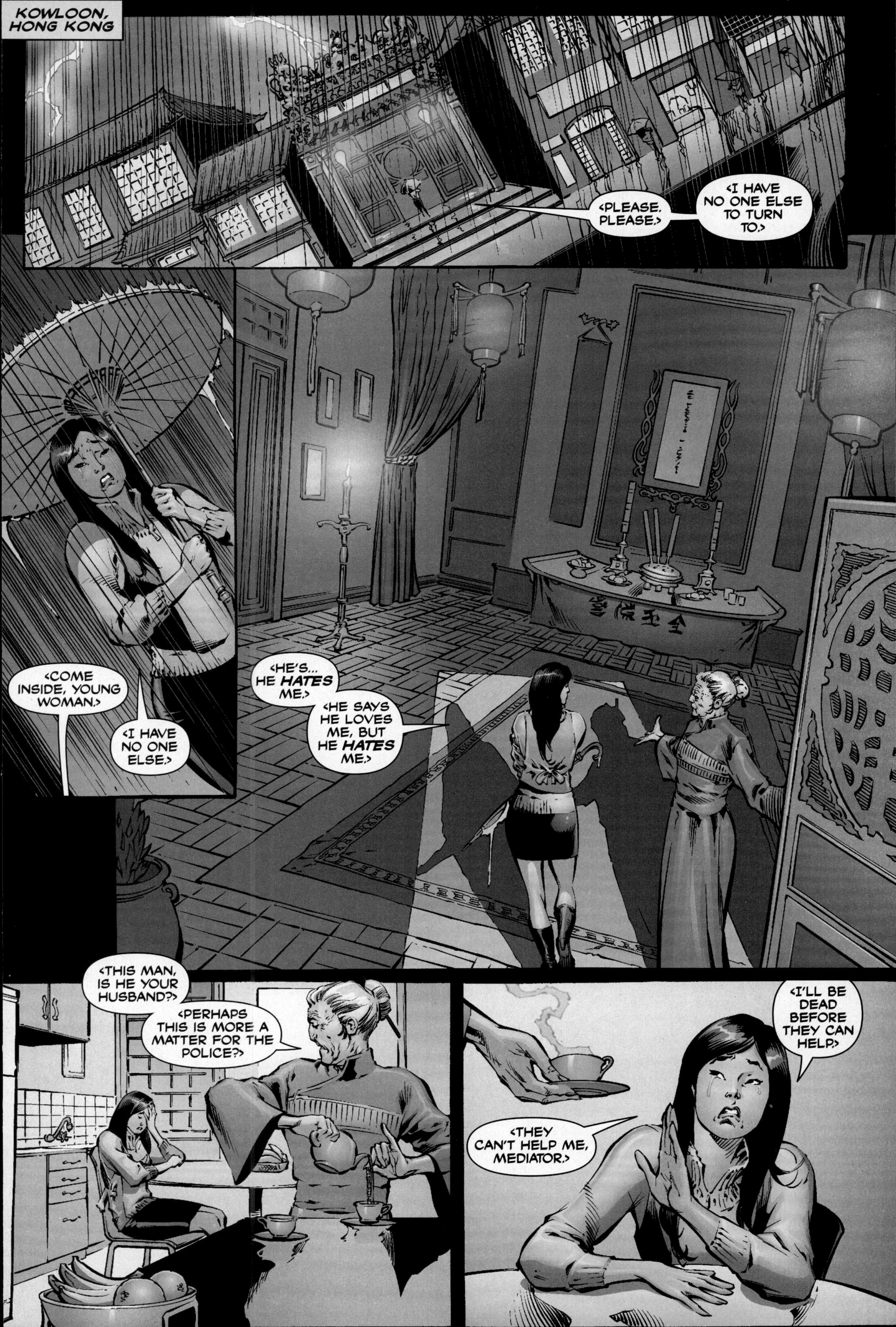
KOWLOON, HONG KONG
<PLEASE. PLEASE.>
<I HAVE NO ONE ELSE TO TURN TO.>
<COME INSIDE, YOUNG WOMAN.>
<I HAVE NO ONE ELSE.>
<HE'S... HE HATES ME.>
<HE SAYS HE LOVES ME, BUT HE HATES ME.>
<THIS MAN, IS HE YOUR HUSBAND?>
<PERHAPS THIS IS MORE A MATTER FOR THE POLICE?>
<I'LL BE DEAD BEFORE THEY CAN HELP.>
<THEY CAN'T HELP ME, MEDIATOR.>

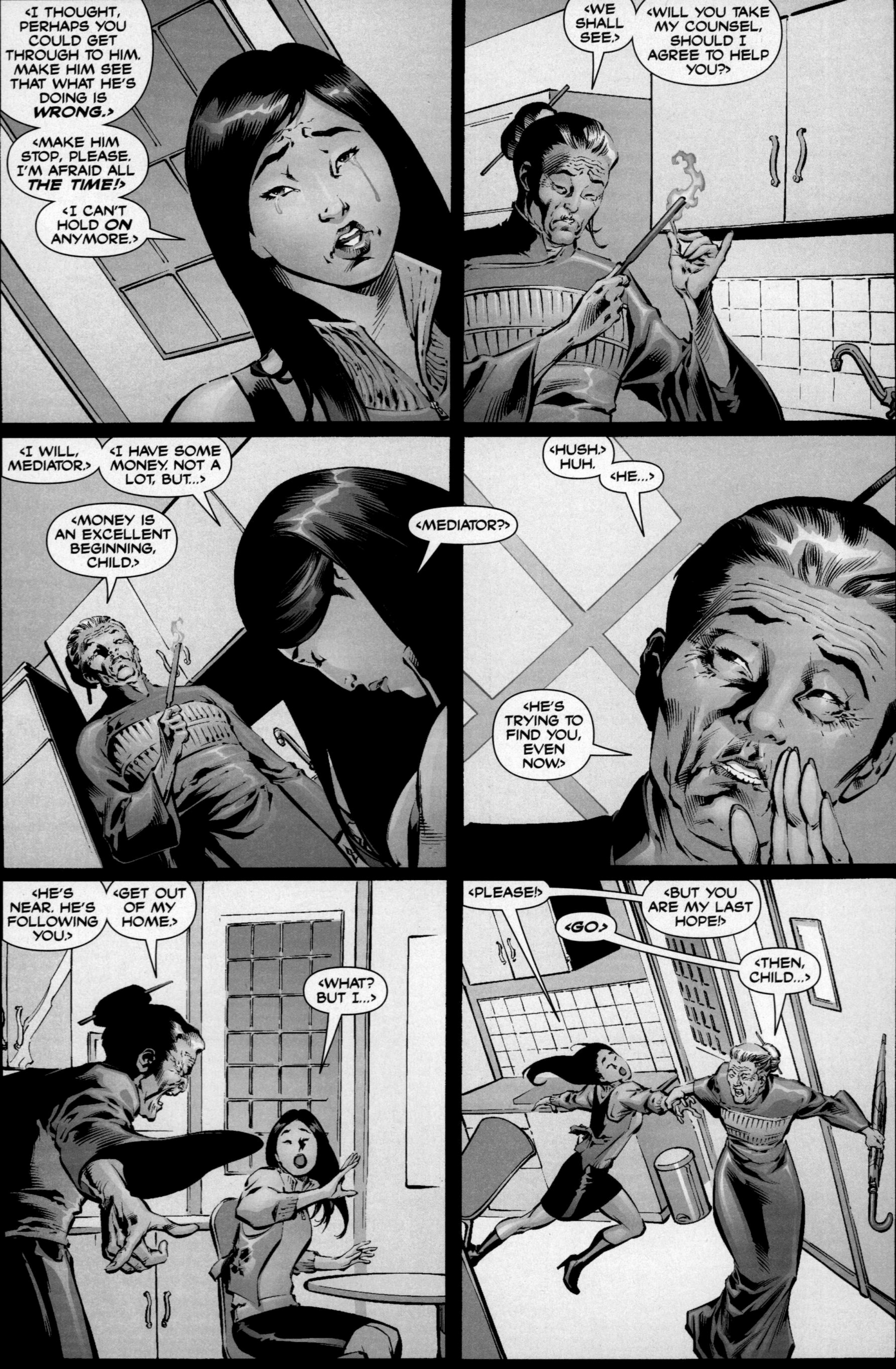
‹I THOUGHT, PERHAPS YOU COULD GET THROUGH TO HIM. MAKE HIM SEE THAT WHAT HE'S DOING IS *WRONG*.›
‹MAKE HIM STOP, PLEASE. I'M AFRAID ALL *THE TIME!*›
‹I CAN'T HOLD *ON* ANYMORE.›
‹WE SHALL SEE.›
‹WILL YOU TAKE MY COUNSEL, SHOULD I AGREE TO HELP YOU?›
‹I WILL, MEDIATOR.›
‹I HAVE SOME MONEY. NOT A LOT, BUT...›
‹MONEY IS AN EXCELLENT BEGINNING, CHILD.›
‹MEDIATOR?›
‹HUSH.› HUH.
‹HE...›
‹HE'S TRYING TO FIND YOU, EVEN NOW.›
‹HE'S NEAR. HE'S FOLLOWING YOU.›
‹GET OUT OF MY HOME.›
‹WHAT? BUT I...›
‹PLEASE!›
‹BUT YOU ARE MY LAST HOPE!›
‹*GO*.›
‹THEN, CHILD...›

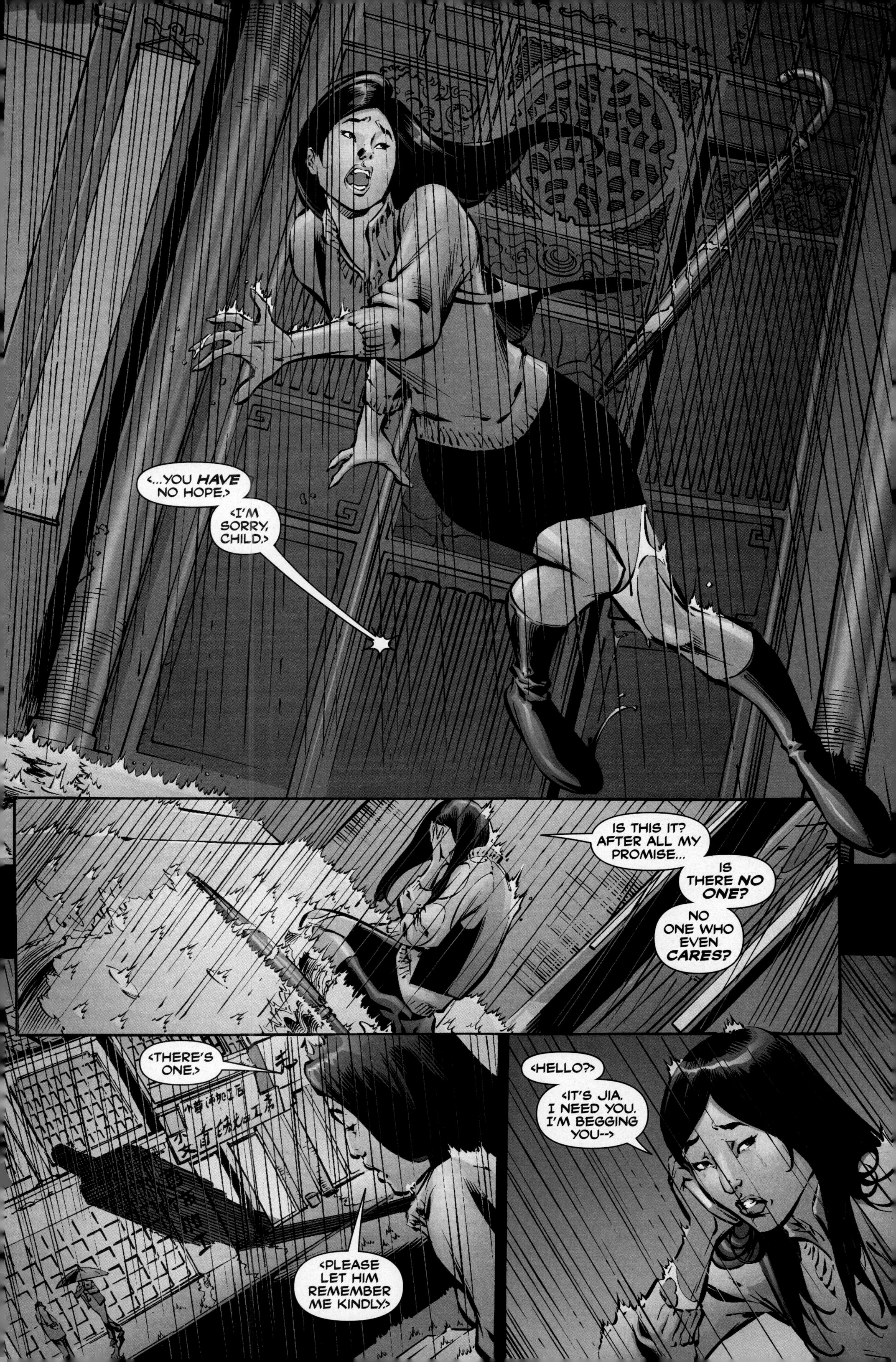
<...YOU HAVE NO HOPE.>
<I'M SORRY, CHILD.>
IS THIS IT? AFTER ALL MY PROMISE...
IS THERE NO ONE?
NO ONE WHO EVEN CARES?
<THERE'S ONE.>
<PLEASE LET HIM REMEMBER ME KINDLY.>
<HELLO?>
<IT'S JIA. I NEED YOU. I'M BEGGING YOU-->

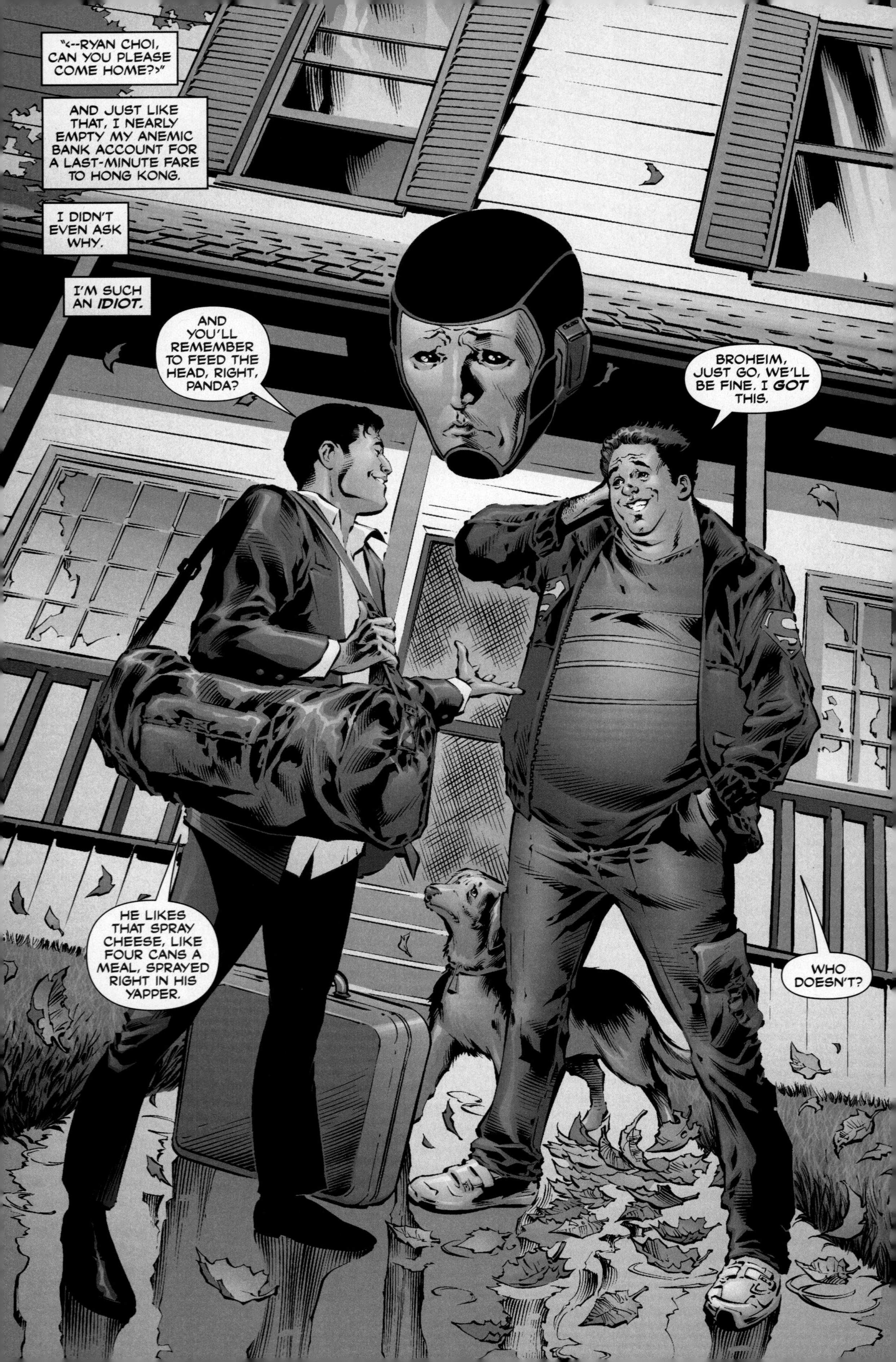
"<--RYAN CHOI, CAN YOU PLEASE COME HOME?>"
AND JUST LIKE THAT, I NEARLY EMPTY MY ANEMIC BANK ACCOUNT FOR A LAST-MINUTE FARE TO HONG KONG.
I DIDN'T EVEN ASK WHY.
I'M SUCH AN *IDIOT.*
AND YOU'LL REMEMBER TO FEED THE HEAD, RIGHT, PANDA?
BROHEIM, JUST GO, WE'LL BE FINE. I *GOT* THIS.
HE LIKES THAT SPRAY CHEESE, LIKE FOUR CANS A MEAL, SPRAYED RIGHT IN HIS YAPPER.
WHO DOESN'T?

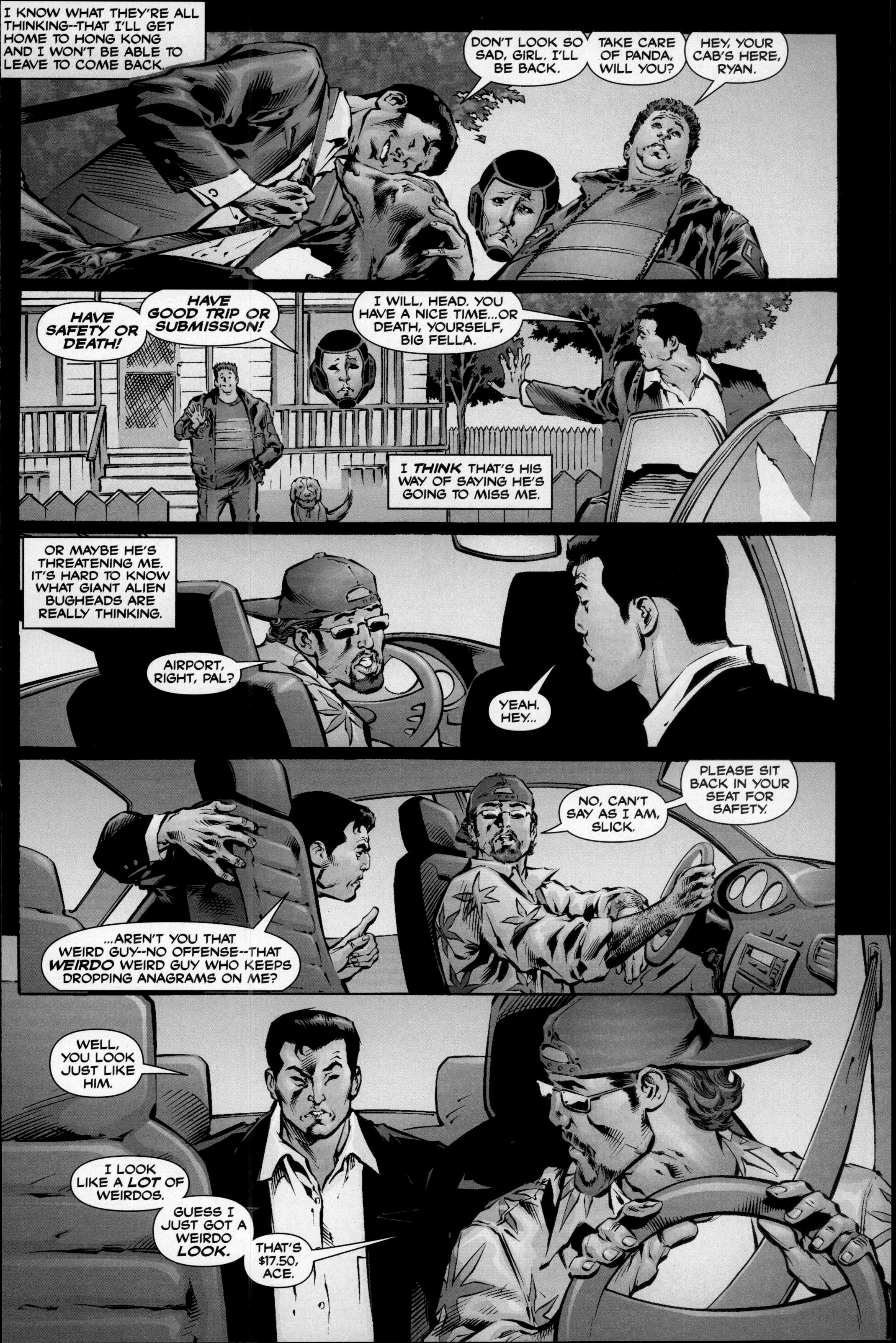
I KNOW WHAT THEY'RE ALL THINKING--THAT I'LL GET HOME TO HONG KONG AND I WON'T BE ABLE TO LEAVE TO COME BACK.
DON'T LOOK SO SAD, GIRL. I'LL BE BACK.
TAKE CARE OF PANDA, WILL YOU?
HEY, YOUR CAB'S HERE, RYAN.
HAVE SAFETY OR DEATH!
HAVE GOOD TRIP OR SUBMISSION!
I WILL, HEAD. YOU HAVE A NICE TIME...OR DEATH, YOURSELF, BIG FELLA.
I THINK THAT'S HIS WAY OF SAYING HE'S GOING TO MISS ME.
OR MAYBE HE'S THREATENING ME. IT'S HARD TO KNOW WHAT GIANT ALIEN BUGHEADS ARE REALLY THINKING.
AIRPORT, RIGHT, PAL?
YEAH. HEY...
...AREN'T YOU THAT WEIRD GUY--NO OFFENSE--THAT WEIRDO WEIRD GUY WHO KEEPS DROPPING ANAGRAMS ON ME?
NO, CAN'T SAY AS I AM, SLICK.
PLEASE SIT BACK IN YOUR SEAT FOR SAFETY.
WELL, YOU LOOK JUST LIKE HIM.
I LOOK LIKE A LOT OF WEIRDOS.
GUESS I JUST GOT A WEIRDO LOOK.
THAT'S $17.50, ACE.

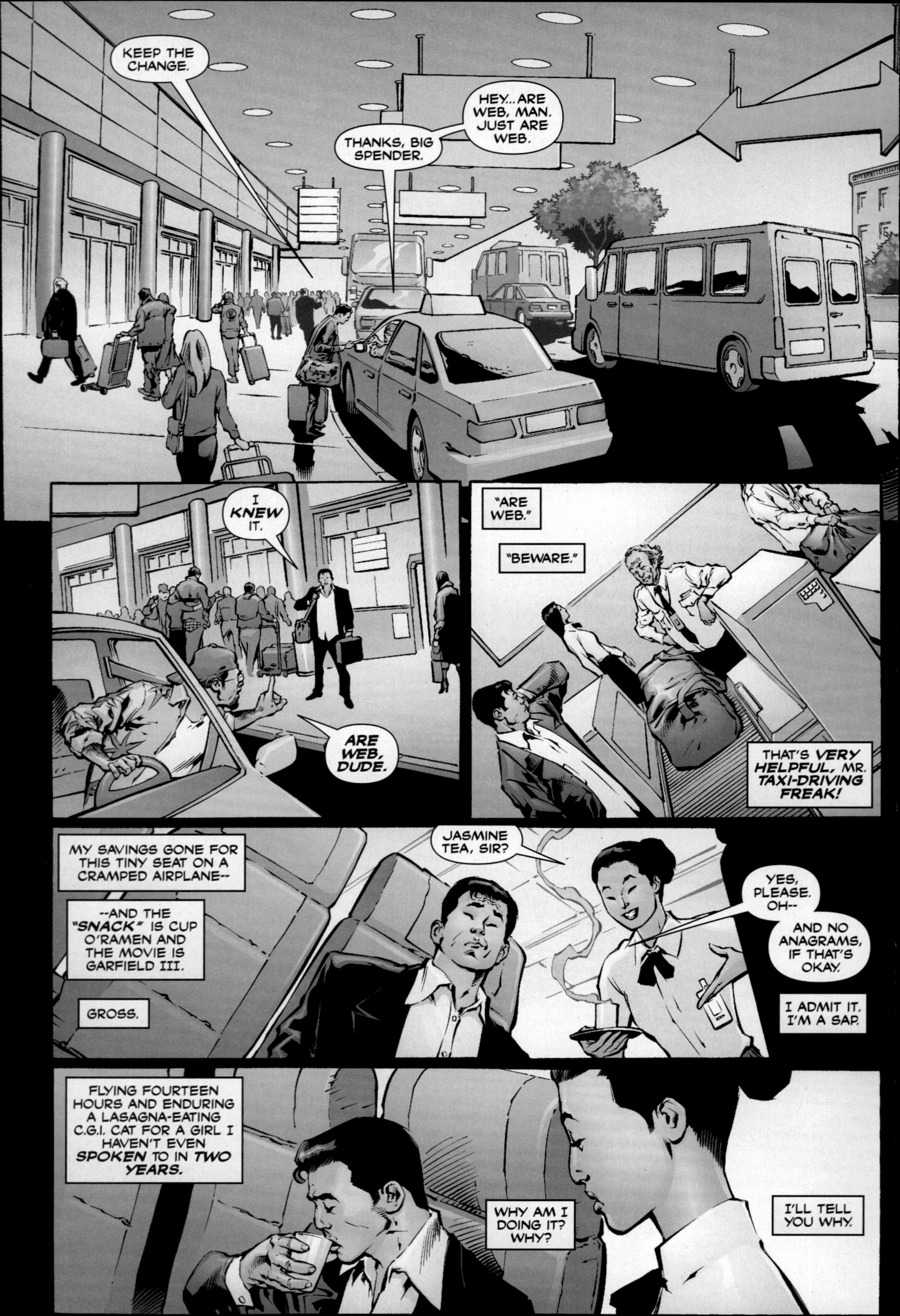
KEEP THE CHANGE.
THANKS, BIG SPENDER.
HEY... ARE WEB, MAN. JUST ARE WEB.
I KNEW IT.
ARE WEB, DUDE.
"ARE WEB."
"BEWARE."
THAT'S VERY HELPFUL, MR. TAXI-DRIVING FREAK!
MY SAVINGS GONE FOR THIS TINY SEAT ON A CRAMPED AIRPLANE--
--AND THE "SNACK" IS CUP O'RAMEN AND THE MOVIE IS GARFIELD III.
GROSS.
JASMINE TEA, SIR?
YES, PLEASE. OH--
AND NO ANAGRAMS, IF THAT'S OKAY.
I ADMIT IT. I'M A SAP.
FLYING FOURTEEN HOURS AND ENDURING A LASAGNA-EATING C.G.I. CAT FOR A GIRL I HAVEN'T EVEN SPOKEN TO IN TWO YEARS.
WHY AM I DOING IT? WHY?
I'LL TELL YOU WHY.

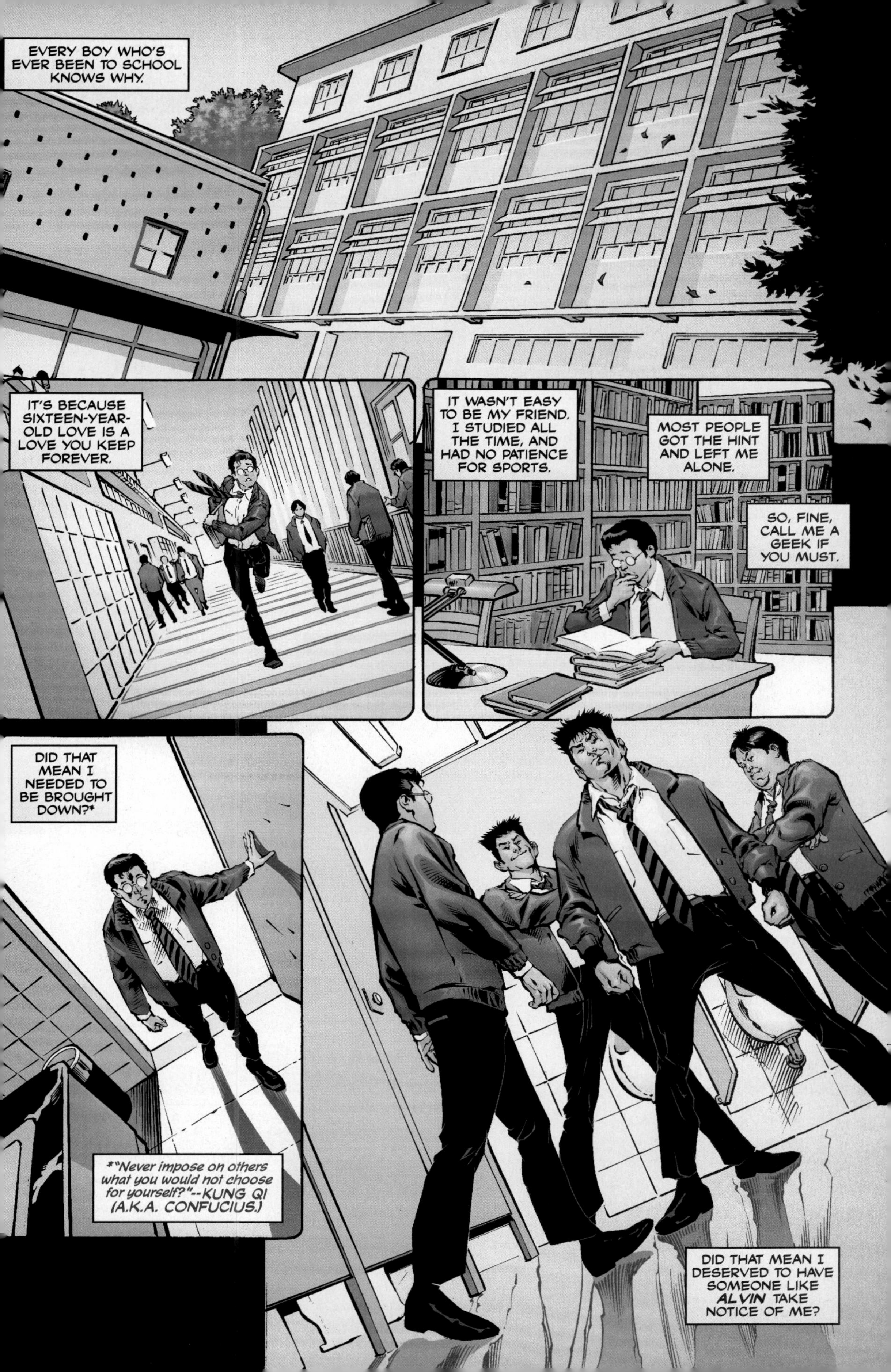
EVERY BOY WHO'S EVER BEEN TO SCHOOL KNOWS WHY.
IT'S BECAUSE SIXTEEN-YEAR-OLD LOVE IS A LOVE YOU KEEP FOREVER.
IT WASN'T EASY TO BE MY FRIEND. I STUDIED ALL THE TIME, AND HAD NO PATIENCE FOR SPORTS.
MOST PEOPLE GOT THE HINT AND LEFT ME ALONE.
SO, FINE, CALL ME A GEEK IF YOU MUST.
DID THAT MEAN I NEEDED TO BE BROUGHT DOWN?*
*"Never impose on others what you would not choose for yourself?"--KUNG QI (A.K.A. CONFUCIUS.)
DID THAT MEAN I DESERVED TO HAVE SOMEONE LIKE ALVIN TAKE NOTICE OF ME?

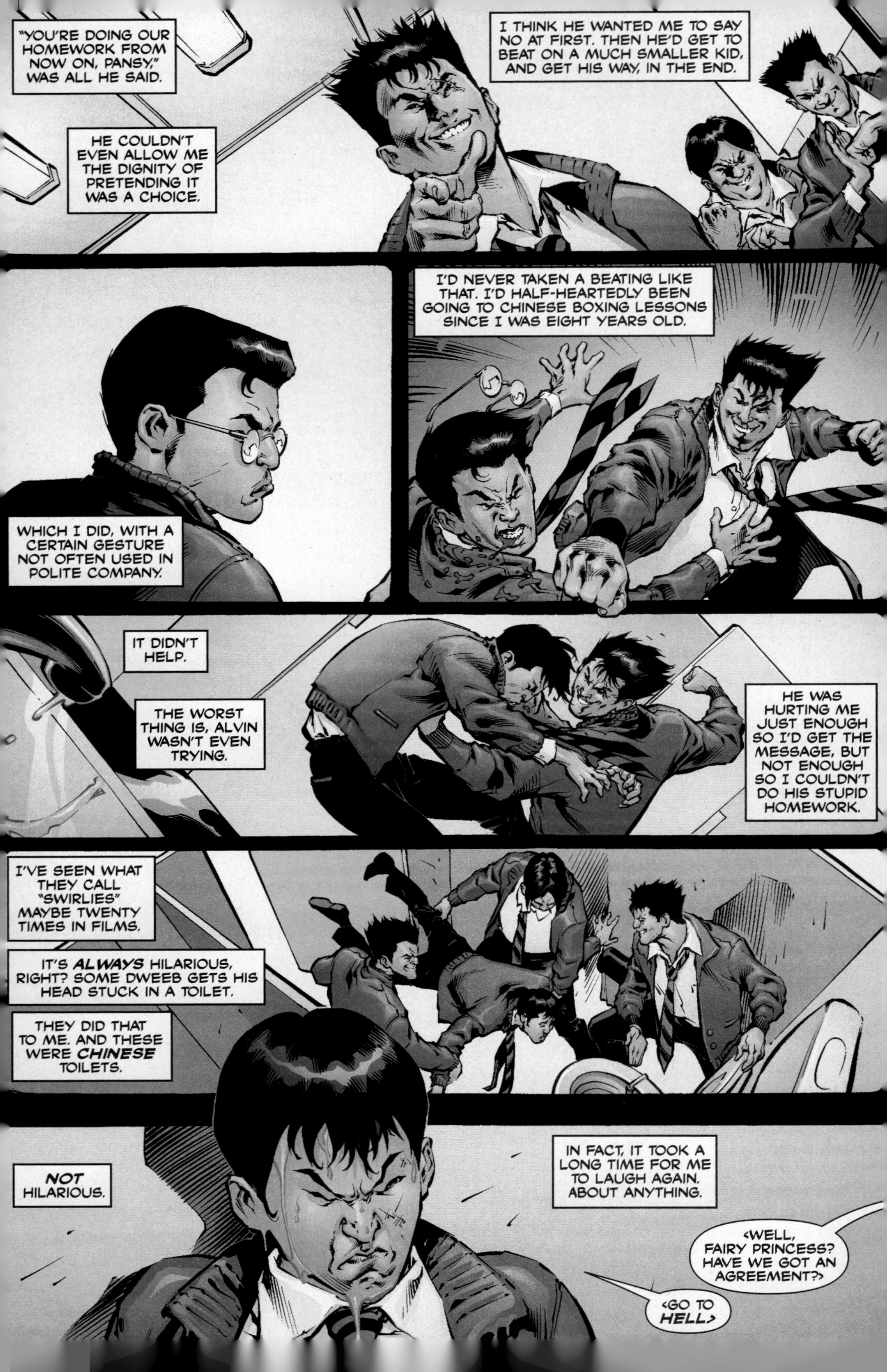
"YOU'RE DOING OUR HOMEWORK FROM NOW ON, PANSY," WAS ALL HE SAID.
I THINK HE WANTED ME TO SAY NO AT FIRST. THEN HE'D GET TO BEAT ON A MUCH SMALLER KID, AND GET HIS WAY, IN THE END.
HE COULDN'T EVEN ALLOW ME THE DIGNITY OF PRETENDING IT WAS A CHOICE.
WHICH I DID, WITH A CERTAIN GESTURE NOT OFTEN USED IN POLITE COMPANY.
I'D NEVER TAKEN A BEATING LIKE THAT. I'D HALF-HEARTEDLY BEEN GOING TO CHINESE BOXING LESSONS SINCE I WAS EIGHT YEARS OLD.
IT DIDN'T HELP.
THE WORST THING IS, ALVIN WASN'T EVEN TRYING.
HE WAS HURTING ME JUST ENOUGH SO I'D GET THE MESSAGE, BUT NOT ENOUGH SO I COULDN'T DO HIS STUPID HOMEWORK.
I'VE SEEN WHAT THEY CALL "SWIRLIES" MAYBE TWENTY TIMES IN FILMS.
IT'S ***ALWAYS*** HILARIOUS, RIGHT? SOME DWEEB GETS HIS HEAD STUCK IN A TOILET.
THEY DID THAT TO ME. AND THESE WERE ***CHINESE*** TOILETS.
NOT HILARIOUS.
IN FACT, IT TOOK A LONG TIME FOR ME TO LAUGH AGAIN. ABOUT ANYTHING.
‹WELL, FAIRY PRINCESS? HAVE WE GOT AN AGREEMENT?›
‹GO TO ***HELL.***›

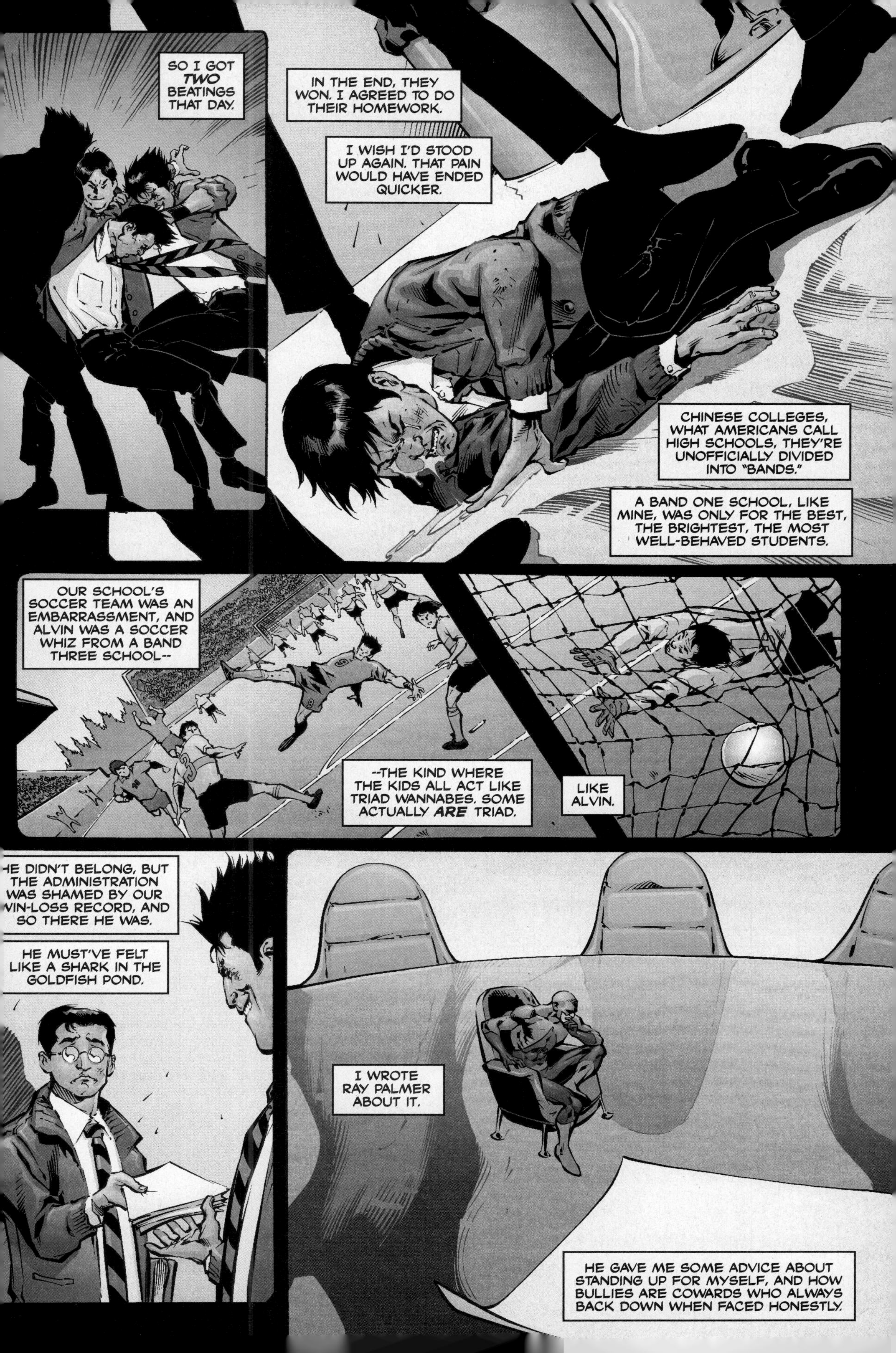
SO I GOT *TWO* BEATINGS THAT DAY.
IN THE END, THEY WON. I AGREED TO DO THEIR HOMEWORK.
I WISH I'D STOOD UP AGAIN. THAT PAIN WOULD HAVE ENDED QUICKER.
CHINESE COLLEGES, WHAT AMERICANS CALL HIGH SCHOOLS, THEY'RE UNOFFICIALLY DIVIDED INTO "BANDS."
A BAND ONE SCHOOL, LIKE MINE, WAS ONLY FOR THE BEST, THE BRIGHTEST, THE MOST WELL-BEHAVED STUDENTS.
OUR SCHOOL'S SOCCER TEAM WAS AN EMBARRASSMENT, AND ALVIN WAS A SOCCER WHIZ FROM A BAND THREE SCHOOL--
--THE KIND WHERE THE KIDS ALL ACT LIKE TRIAD WANNABES. SOME ACTUALLY *ARE* TRIAD.
LIKE ALVIN.
HE DIDN'T BELONG, BUT THE ADMINISTRATION WAS SHAMED BY OUR WIN-LOSS RECORD, AND SO THERE HE WAS.
HE MUST'VE FELT LIKE A SHARK IN THE GOLDFISH POND.
I WROTE RAY PALMER ABOUT IT.
HE GAVE ME SOME ADVICE ABOUT STANDING UP FOR MYSELF, AND HOW BULLIES ARE COWARDS WHO ALWAYS BACK DOWN WHEN FACED HONESTLY.

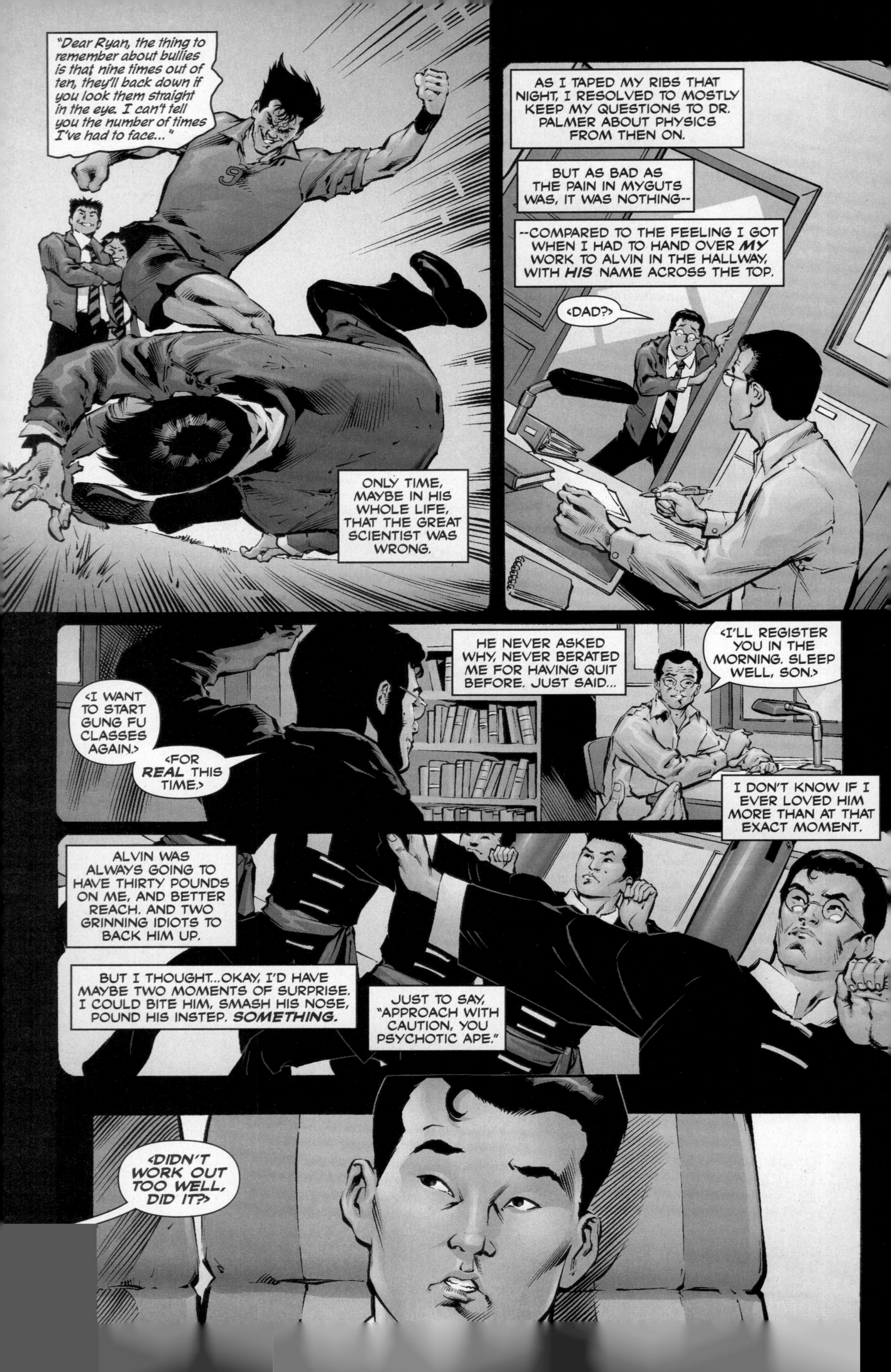
"Dear Ryan, the thing to remember about bullies is that nine times out of ten, they'll back down if you look them straight in the eye. I can't tell you the number of times I've had to face..."
ONLY TIME, MAYBE IN HIS WHOLE LIFE, THAT THE GREAT SCIENTIST WAS WRONG.
AS I TAPED MY RIBS THAT NIGHT, I RESOLVED TO MOSTLY KEEP MY QUESTIONS TO DR. PALMER ABOUT PHYSICS FROM THEN ON.
BUT AS BAD AS THE PAIN IN MYGUTS WAS, IT WAS NOTHING--
--COMPARED TO THE FEELING I GOT WHEN I HAD TO HAND OVER MY WORK TO ALVIN IN THE HALLWAY, WITH HIS NAME ACROSS THE TOP.
<DAD?>
<I WANT TO START GUNG FU CLASSES AGAIN.>
<FOR REAL THIS TIME.>
HE NEVER ASKED WHY, NEVER BERATED ME FOR HAVING QUIT BEFORE. JUST SAID...
<I'LL REGISTER YOU IN THE MORNING. SLEEP WELL, SON.>
I DON'T KNOW IF I EVER LOVED HIM MORE THAN AT THAT EXACT MOMENT.
ALVIN WAS ALWAYS GOING TO HAVE THIRTY POUNDS ON ME, AND BETTER REACH, AND TWO GRINNING IDIOTS TO BACK HIM UP.
BUT I THOUGHT...OKAY, I'D HAVE MAYBE TWO MOMENTS OF SURPRISE. I COULD BITE HIM, SMASH HIS NOSE, POUND HIS INSTEP. SOMETHING.
JUST TO SAY, "APPROACH WITH CAUTION, YOU PSYCHOTIC APE."
<DIDN'T WORK OUT TOO WELL, DID IT?>

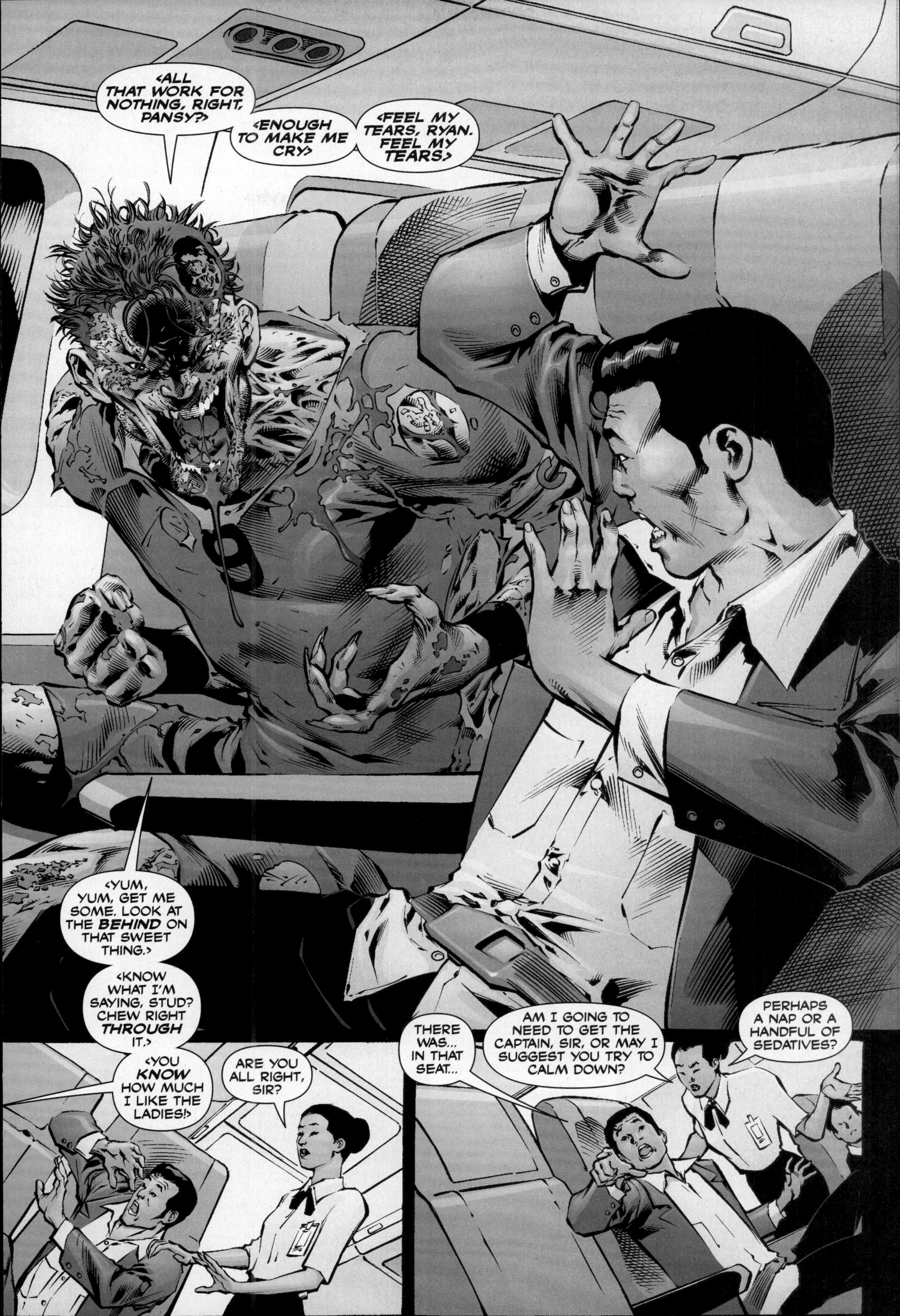
<ALL THAT WORK FOR NOTHING, RIGHT, PANSY?>
<ENOUGH TO MAKE ME CRY>
<FEEL MY TEARS, RYAN. FEEL MY TEARS.>
<YUM, YUM, GET ME SOME. LOOK AT THE **BEHIND** ON THAT SWEET THING.>
<KNOW WHAT I'M SAYING, STUD? CHEW RIGHT **THROUGH** IT.>
<YOU **KNOW** HOW MUCH I LIKE THE LADIES!>
ARE YOU ALL RIGHT, SIR?
THERE WAS... IN THAT SEAT...
AM I GOING TO NEED TO GET THE CAPTAIN, SIR, OR MAY I SUGGEST YOU TRY TO CALM DOWN?
PERHAPS A NAP OR A HANDFUL OF SEDATIVES?

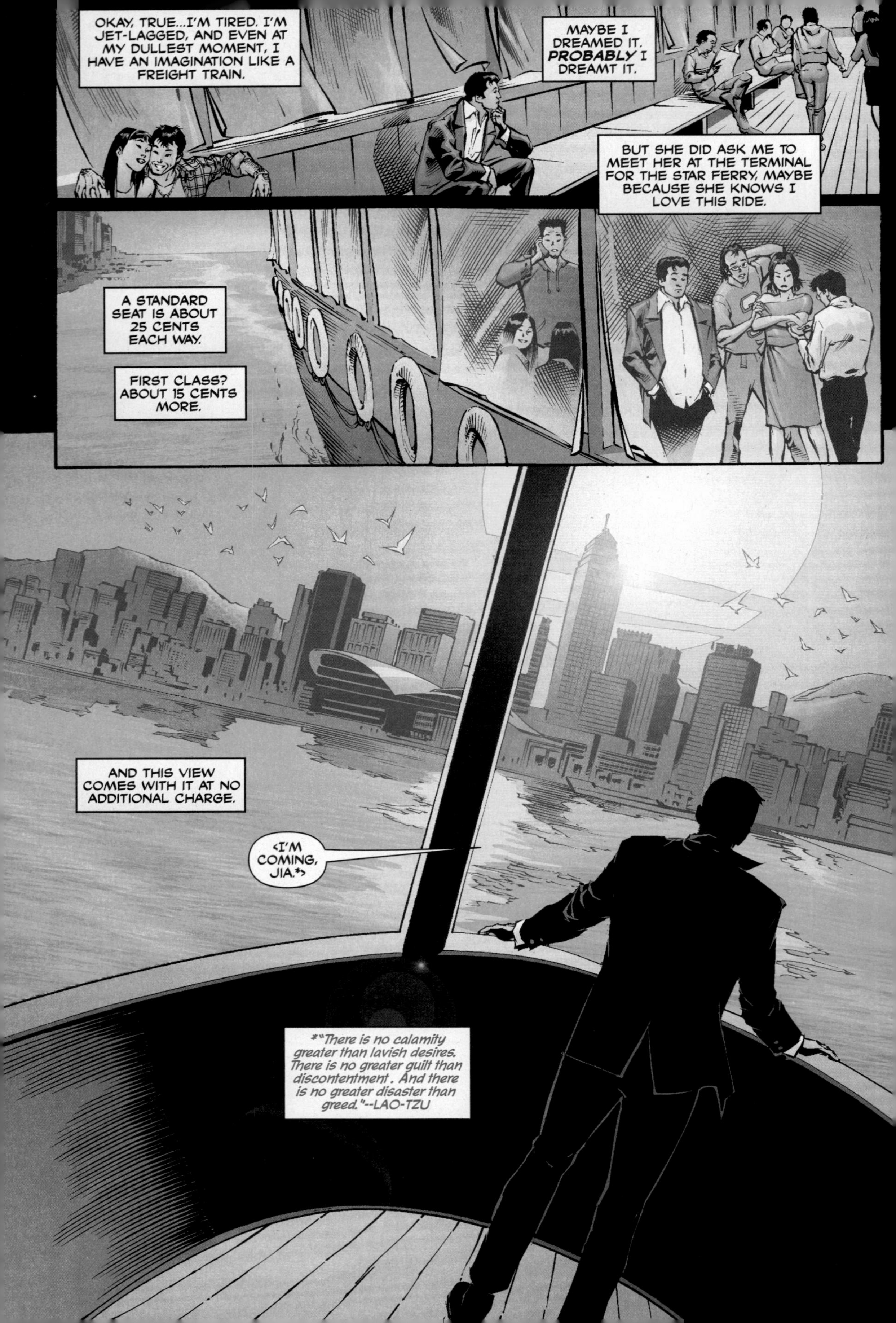

OKAY, TRUE...I'M TIRED. I'M JET-LAGGED, AND EVEN AT MY DULLEST MOMENT, I HAVE AN IMAGINATION LIKE A FREIGHT TRAIN.
MAYBE I DREAMED IT. *PROBABLY* I DREAMT IT.
BUT SHE DID ASK ME TO MEET HER AT THE TERMINAL FOR THE STAR FERRY, MAYBE BECAUSE SHE KNOWS I LOVE THIS RIDE.
A STANDARD SEAT IS ABOUT 25 CENTS EACH WAY.
FIRST CLASS? ABOUT 15 CENTS MORE.
AND THIS VIEW COMES WITH IT AT NO ADDITIONAL CHARGE.
<I'M COMING, JIA.*>
*"There is no calamity greater than lavish desires. There is no greater guilt than discontentment . And there is no greater disaster than greed."--LAO-TZU

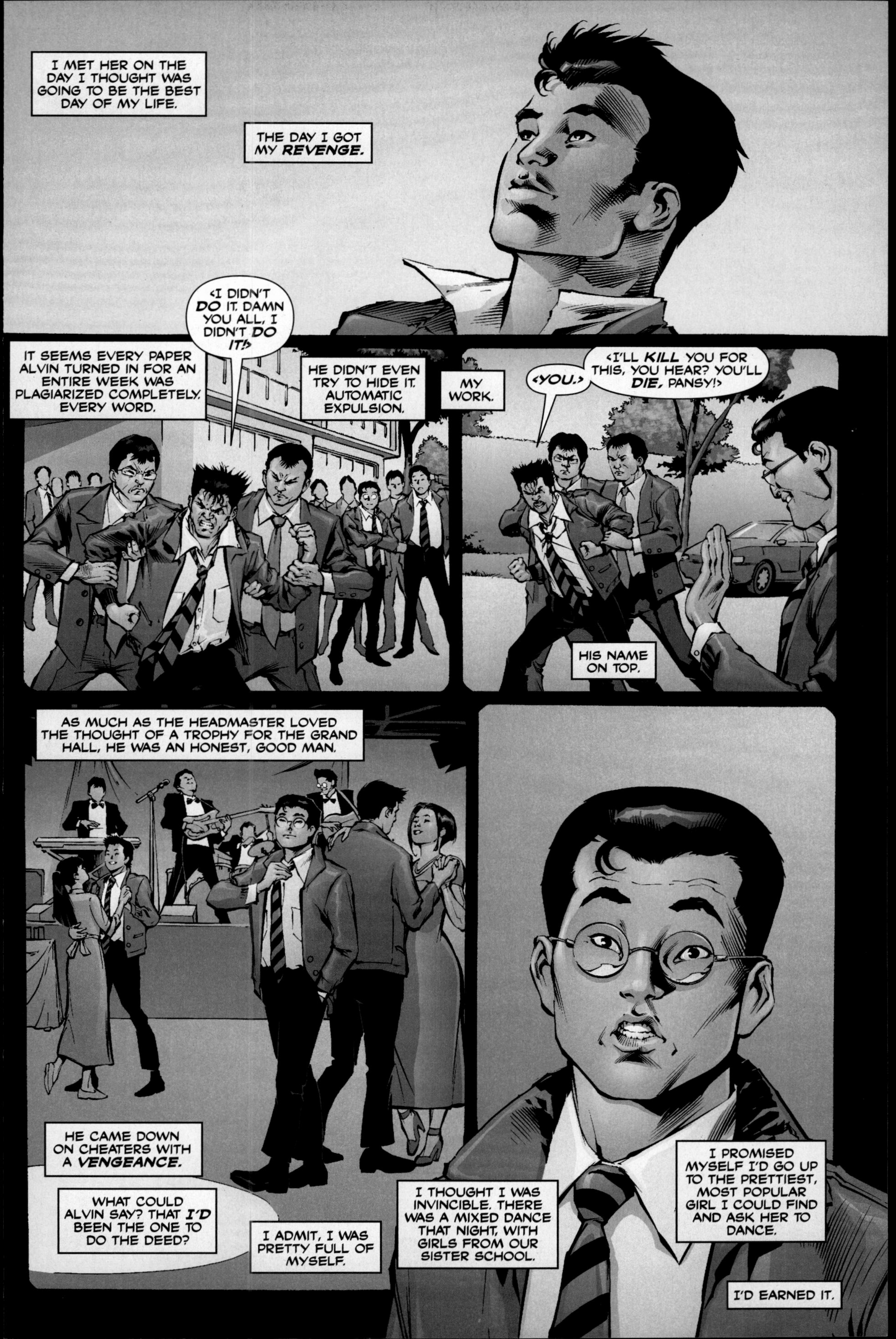
I MET HER ON THE DAY I THOUGHT WAS GOING TO BE THE BEST DAY OF MY LIFE.
THE DAY I GOT MY *REVENGE.*
IT SEEMS EVERY PAPER ALVIN TURNED IN FOR AN ENTIRE WEEK WAS PLAGIARIZED COMPLETELY. EVERY WORD.
<I DIDN'T *DO* IT. DAMN YOU ALL, I DIDN'T *DO* IT!>
HE DIDN'T EVEN TRY TO HIDE IT. AUTOMATIC EXPULSION.
MY WORK.
<*YOU.*>
<I'LL *KILL* YOU FOR THIS, YOU HEAR? YOU'LL *DIE,* PANSY!>
HIS NAME ON TOP.
AS MUCH AS THE HEADMASTER LOVED THE THOUGHT OF A TROPHY FOR THE GRAND HALL, HE WAS AN HONEST, GOOD MAN.
HE CAME DOWN ON CHEATERS WITH A *VENGEANCE.*
WHAT COULD ALVIN SAY? THAT *I'D* BEEN THE ONE TO DO THE DEED?
I ADMIT, I WAS PRETTY FULL OF MYSELF.
I THOUGHT I WAS INVINCIBLE. THERE WAS A MIXED DANCE THAT NIGHT, WITH GIRLS FROM OUR SISTER SCHOOL.
I PROMISED MYSELF I'D GO UP TO THE PRETTIEST, MOST POPULAR GIRL I COULD FIND AND ASK HER TO DANCE.
I'D EARNED IT.

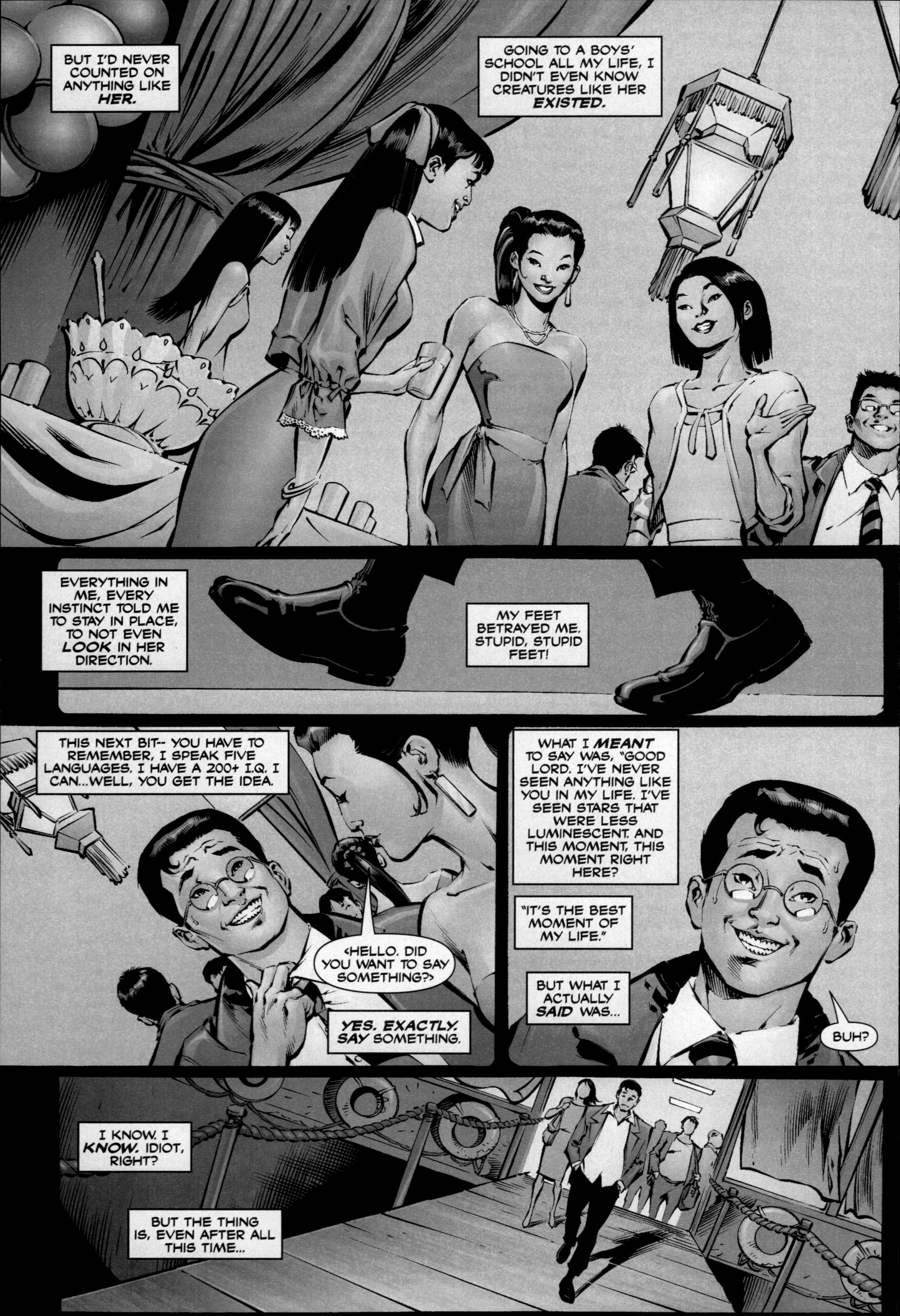
BUT I'D NEVER COUNTED ON ANYTHING LIKE HER.
GOING TO A BOYS' SCHOOL ALL MY LIFE, I DIDN'T EVEN KNOW CREATURES LIKE HER EXISTED.
EVERYTHING IN ME, EVERY INSTINCT TOLD ME TO STAY IN PLACE, TO NOT EVEN LOOK IN HER DIRECTION.
MY FEET BETRAYED ME. STUPID, STUPID FEET!
THIS NEXT BIT-- YOU HAVE TO REMEMBER, I SPEAK FIVE LANGUAGES. I HAVE A 200+ I.Q. I CAN...WELL, YOU GET THE IDEA.
<HELLO. DID YOU WANT TO SAY SOMETHING?>
YES. EXACTLY. SAY SOMETHING.
WHAT I MEANT TO SAY WAS, "GOOD LORD. I'VE NEVER SEEN ANYTHING LIKE YOU IN MY LIFE. I'VE SEEN STARS THAT WERE LESS LUMINESCENT. AND THIS MOMENT, THIS MOMENT RIGHT HERE?
"IT'S THE BEST MOMENT OF MY LIFE."
BUT WHAT I ACTUALLY SAID WAS...
BUH?
I KNOW. I KNOW. IDIOT, RIGHT?
BUT THE THING IS, EVEN AFTER ALL THIS TIME...

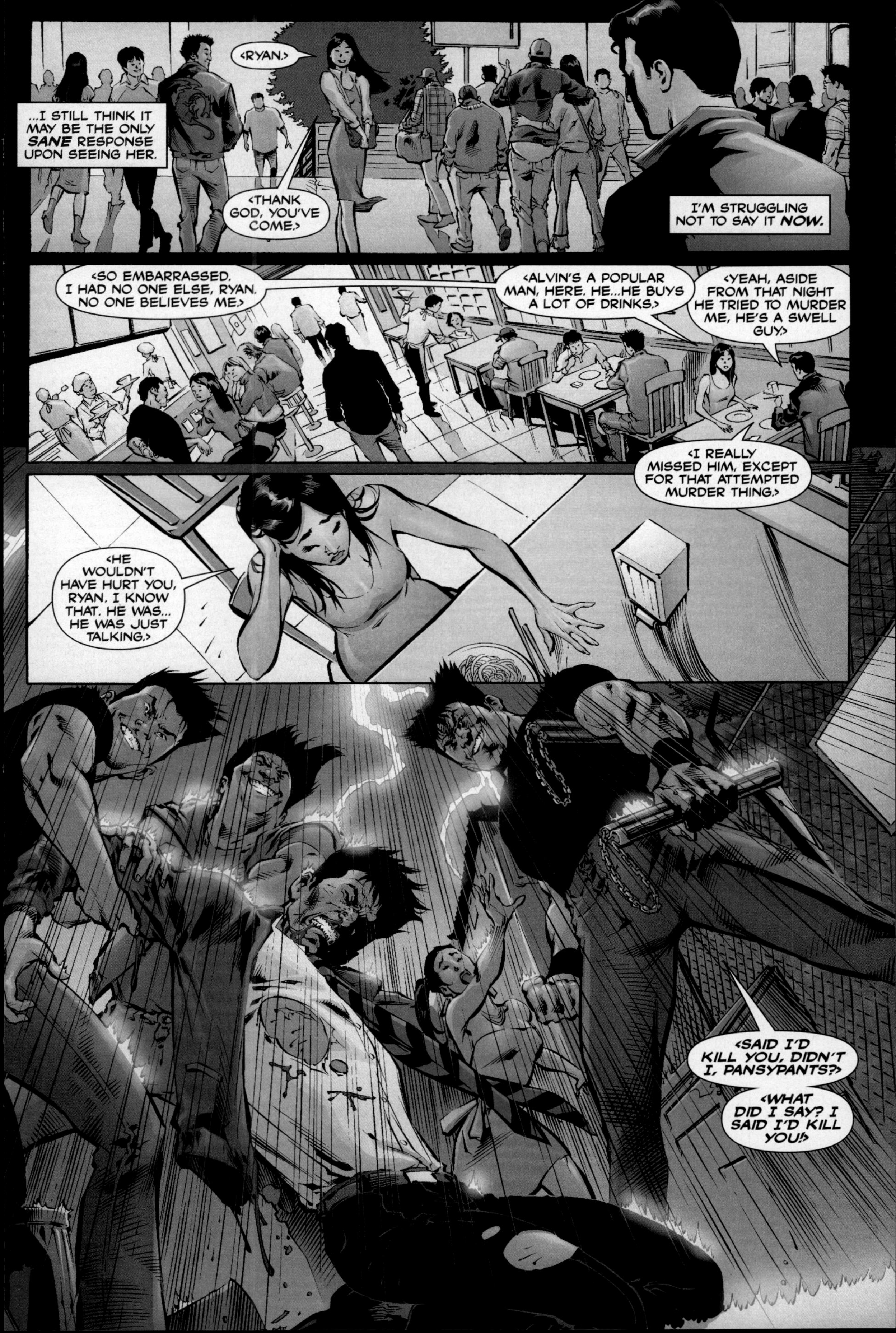
...I STILL THINK IT MAY BE THE ONLY SANE RESPONSE UPON SEEING HER.
<RYAN.>
<THANK GOD, YOU'VE COME.>
I'M STRUGGLING NOT TO SAY IT NOW.
<SO EMBARRASSED. I HAD NO ONE ELSE, RYAN. NO ONE BELIEVES ME.>
<ALVIN'S A POPULAR MAN, HERE. HE...HE BUYS A LOT OF DRINKS.>
<YEAH, ASIDE FROM THAT NIGHT HE TRIED TO MURDER ME, HE'S A SWELL GUY.>
<I REALLY MISSED HIM, EXCEPT FOR THAT ATTEMPTED MURDER THING.>
<HE WOULDN'T HAVE HURT YOU, RYAN. I KNOW THAT. HE WAS... HE WAS JUST TALKING.>
<SAID I'D KILL YOU, DIDN'T I, PANSYPANTS?>
<WHAT DID I SAY? I SAID I'D KILL YOU!>

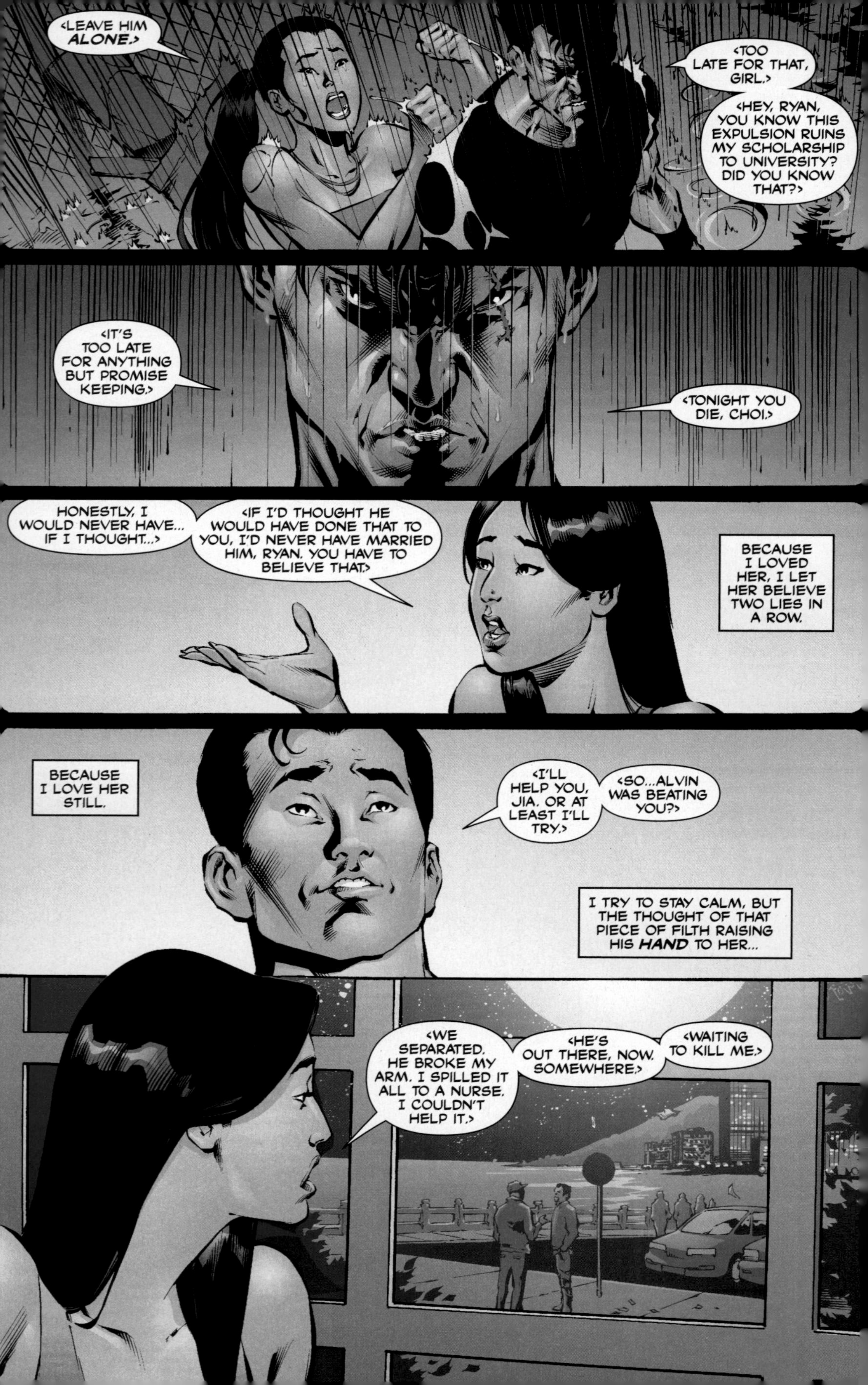
‹LEAVE HIM ALONE.›
‹TOO LATE FOR THAT, GIRL.›
‹HEY, RYAN, YOU KNOW THIS EXPULSION RUINS MY SCHOLARSHIP TO UNIVERSITY? DID YOU KNOW THAT?›
‹IT'S TOO LATE FOR ANYTHING BUT PROMISE KEEPING.›
‹TONIGHT YOU DIE, CHOI.›
HONESTLY, I WOULD NEVER HAVE... IF I THOUGHT...›
‹IF I'D THOUGHT HE WOULD HAVE DONE THAT TO YOU, I'D NEVER HAVE MARRIED HIM, RYAN. YOU HAVE TO BELIEVE THAT.›
BECAUSE I LOVED HER, I LET HER BELIEVE TWO LIES IN A ROW.
BECAUSE I LOVE HER STILL.
‹I'LL HELP YOU, JIA. OR AT LEAST I'LL TRY.›
‹SO...ALVIN WAS BEATING YOU?›
I TRY TO STAY CALM, BUT THE THOUGHT OF THAT PIECE OF FILTH RAISING HIS HAND TO HER...
‹WE SEPARATED. HE BROKE MY ARM. I SPILLED IT ALL TO A NURSE. I COULDN'T HELP IT.›
‹HE'S OUT THERE, NOW. SOMEWHERE.›
‹WAITING TO KILL ME.›

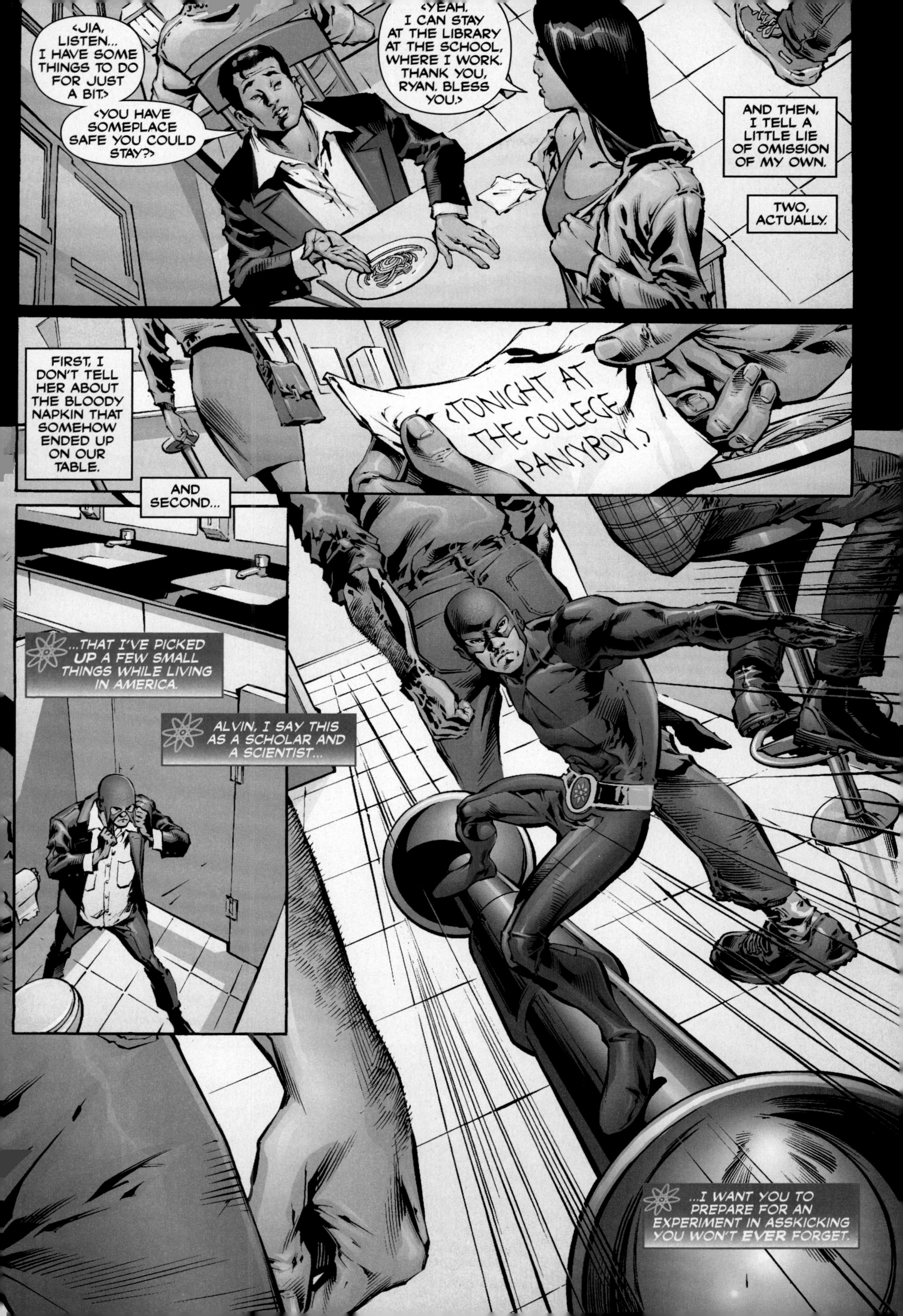

<JIA, LISTEN... I HAVE SOME THINGS TO DO FOR JUST A BIT>
<YOU HAVE SOMEPLACE SAFE YOU COULD STAY?>
<YEAH. I CAN STAY AT THE LIBRARY AT THE SCHOOL, WHERE I WORK. THANK YOU, RYAN. BLESS YOU.>
AND THEN, I TELL A LITTLE LIE OF OMISSION OF MY OWN.
TWO, ACTUALLY.
FIRST, I DON'T TELL HER ABOUT THE BLOODY NAPKIN THAT SOMEHOW ENDED UP ON OUR TABLE.
<TONIGHT AT THE COLLEGE PANSYBOY.>
AND SECOND...
...THAT I'VE PICKED UP A FEW SMALL THINGS WHILE LIVING IN AMERICA.
ALVIN, I SAY THIS AS A SCHOLAR AND A SCIENTIST...
...I WANT YOU TO PREPARE FOR AN EXPERIMENT IN ASSKICKING YOU WON'T EVER FORGET.

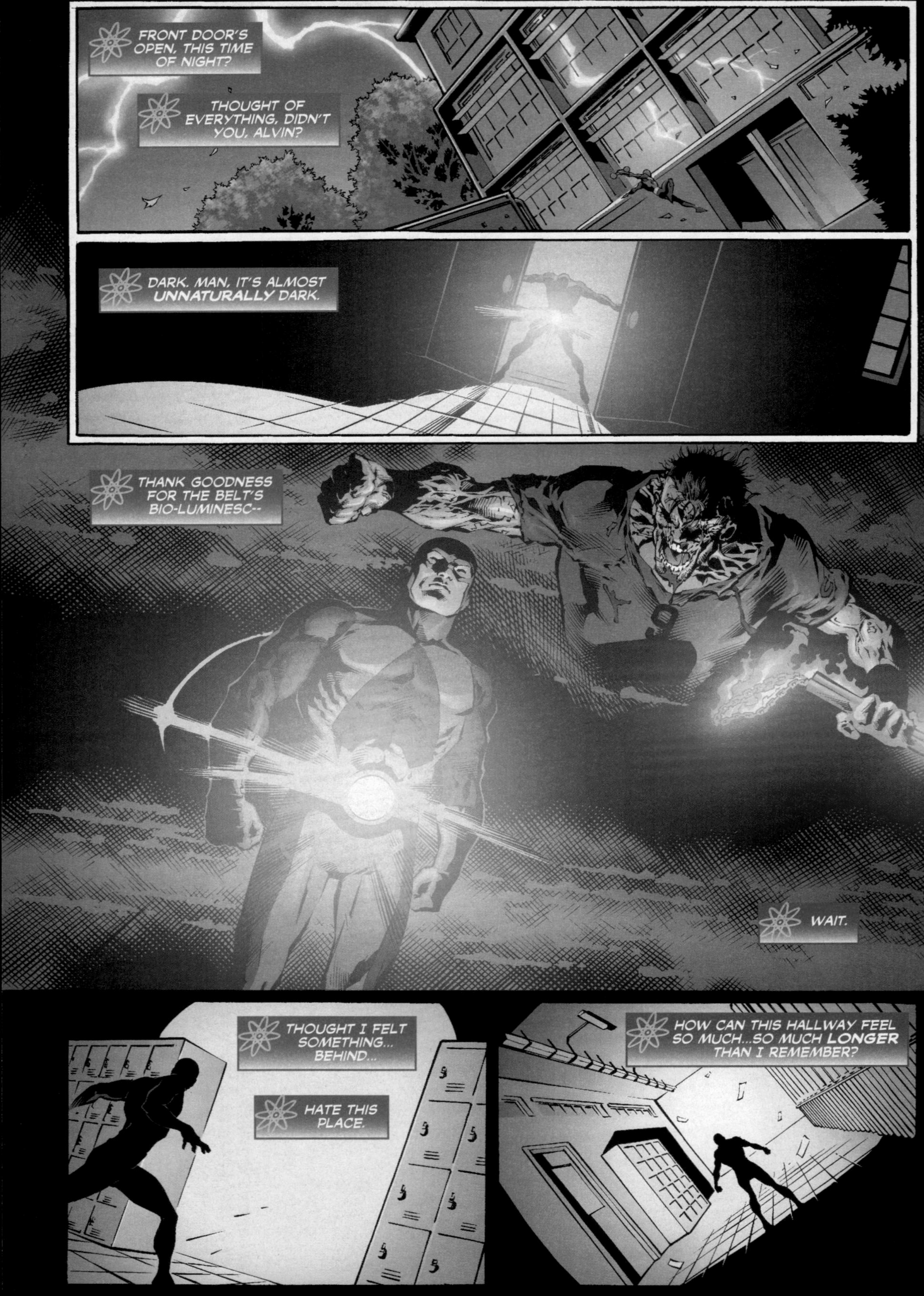
FRONT DOOR'S OPEN, THIS TIME OF NIGHT?
THOUGHT OF EVERYTHING, DIDN'T YOU, ALVIN?
DARK. MAN, IT'S ALMOST UNNATURALLY DARK.
THANK GOODNESS FOR THE BELT'S BIO-LUMINESC--
WAIT.
THOUGHT I FELT SOMETHING... BEHIND...
HATE THIS PLACE.
HOW CAN THIS HALLWAY FEEL SO MUCH...SO MUCH LONGER THAN I REMEMBER?

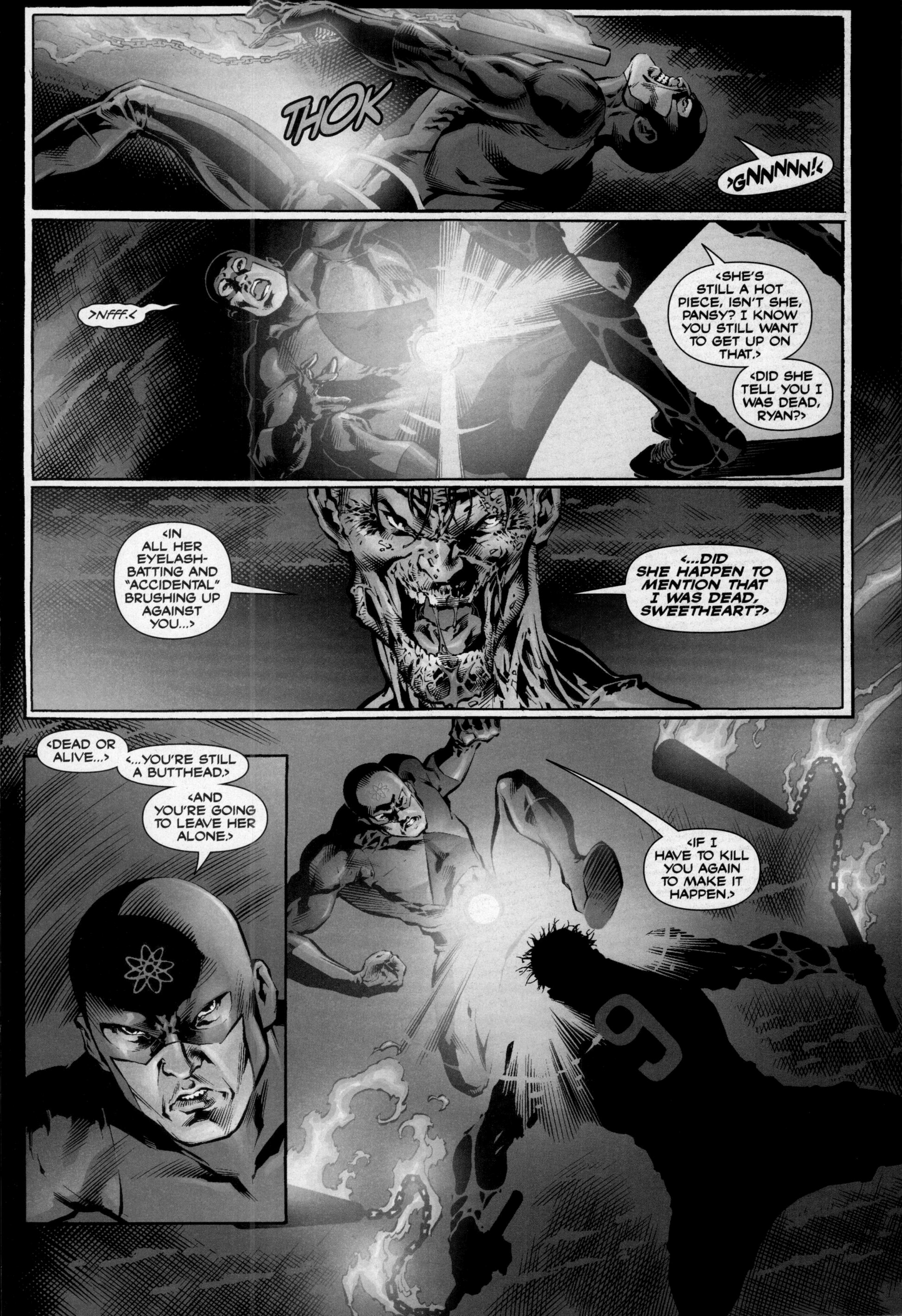
THOK
>GNNNNN!<
>NFFF.<
<SHE'S STILL A HOT PIECE, ISN'T SHE, PANSY? I KNOW YOU STILL WANT TO GET UP ON THAT.>
<DID SHE TELL YOU I WAS DEAD, RYAN?>
<IN ALL HER EYELASH-BATTING AND "ACCIDENTAL" BRUSHING UP AGAINST YOU...>
<...DID SHE HAPPEN TO MENTION THAT I WAS DEAD, SWEETHEART?>
<DEAD OR ALIVE...>
<...YOU'RE STILL A BUTTHEAD.>
<AND YOU'RE GOING TO LEAVE HER ALONE.>
<IF I HAVE TO KILL YOU AGAIN TO MAKE IT HAPPEN.>

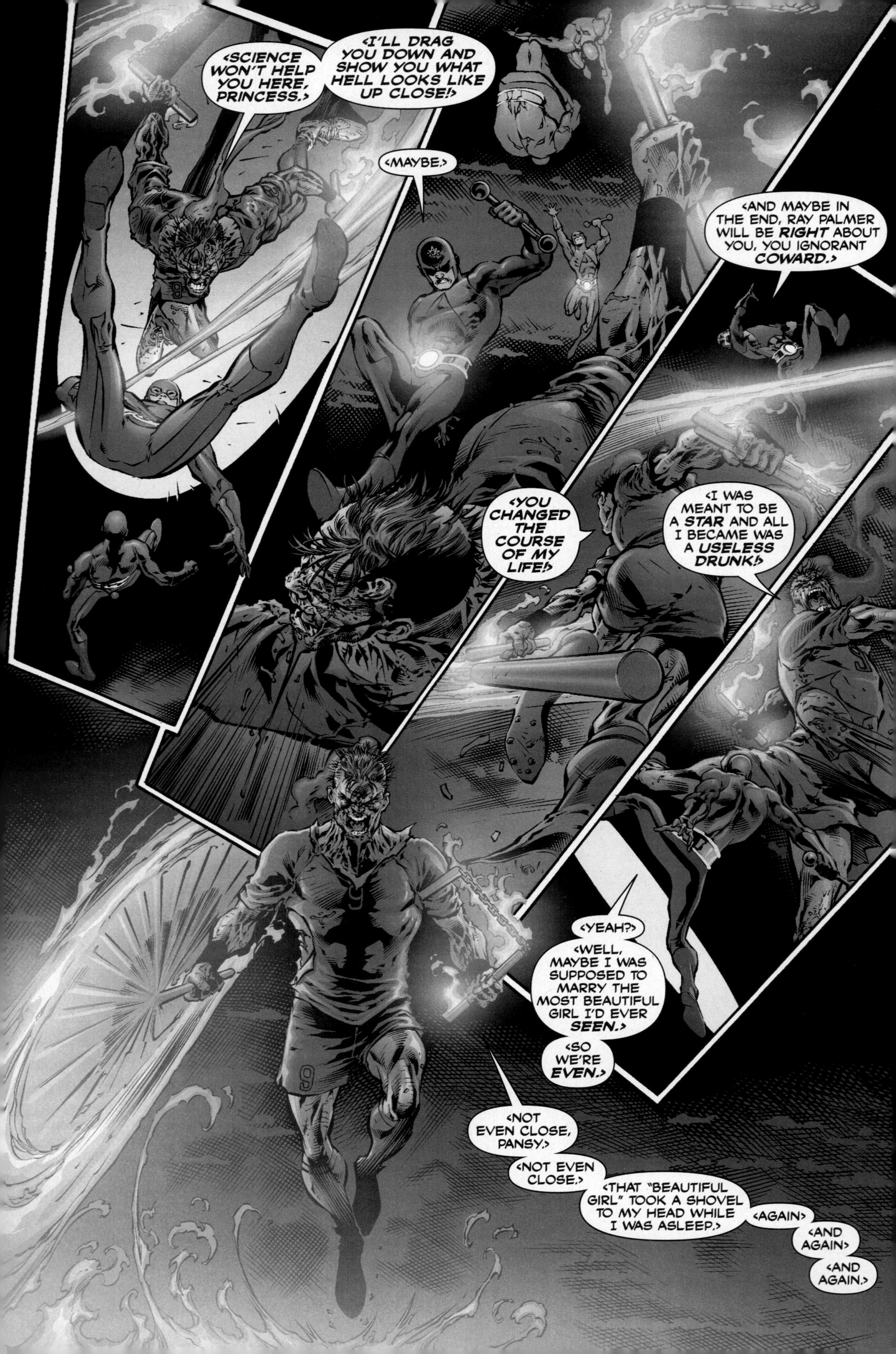
‹SCIENCE WON'T HELP YOU HERE, PRINCESS.›
‹I'LL DRAG YOU DOWN AND SHOW YOU WHAT HELL LOOKS LIKE UP CLOSE!›
‹MAYBE.›
‹AND MAYBE IN THE END, RAY PALMER WILL BE RIGHT ABOUT YOU, YOU IGNORANT COWARD.›
‹YOU CHANGED THE COURSE OF MY LIFE!›
‹I WAS MEANT TO BE A STAR AND ALL I BECAME WAS A USELESS DRUNK!›
‹YEAH?›
‹WELL, MAYBE I WAS SUPPOSED TO MARRY THE MOST BEAUTIFUL GIRL I'D EVER SEEN.›
‹SO WE'RE EVEN.›
‹NOT EVEN CLOSE, PANSY.›
‹NOT EVEN CLOSE.›
‹THAT "BEAUTIFUL GIRL" TOOK A SHOVEL TO MY HEAD WHILE I WAS ASLEEP.›
‹AGAIN›
‹AND AGAIN›
‹AND AGAIN.›

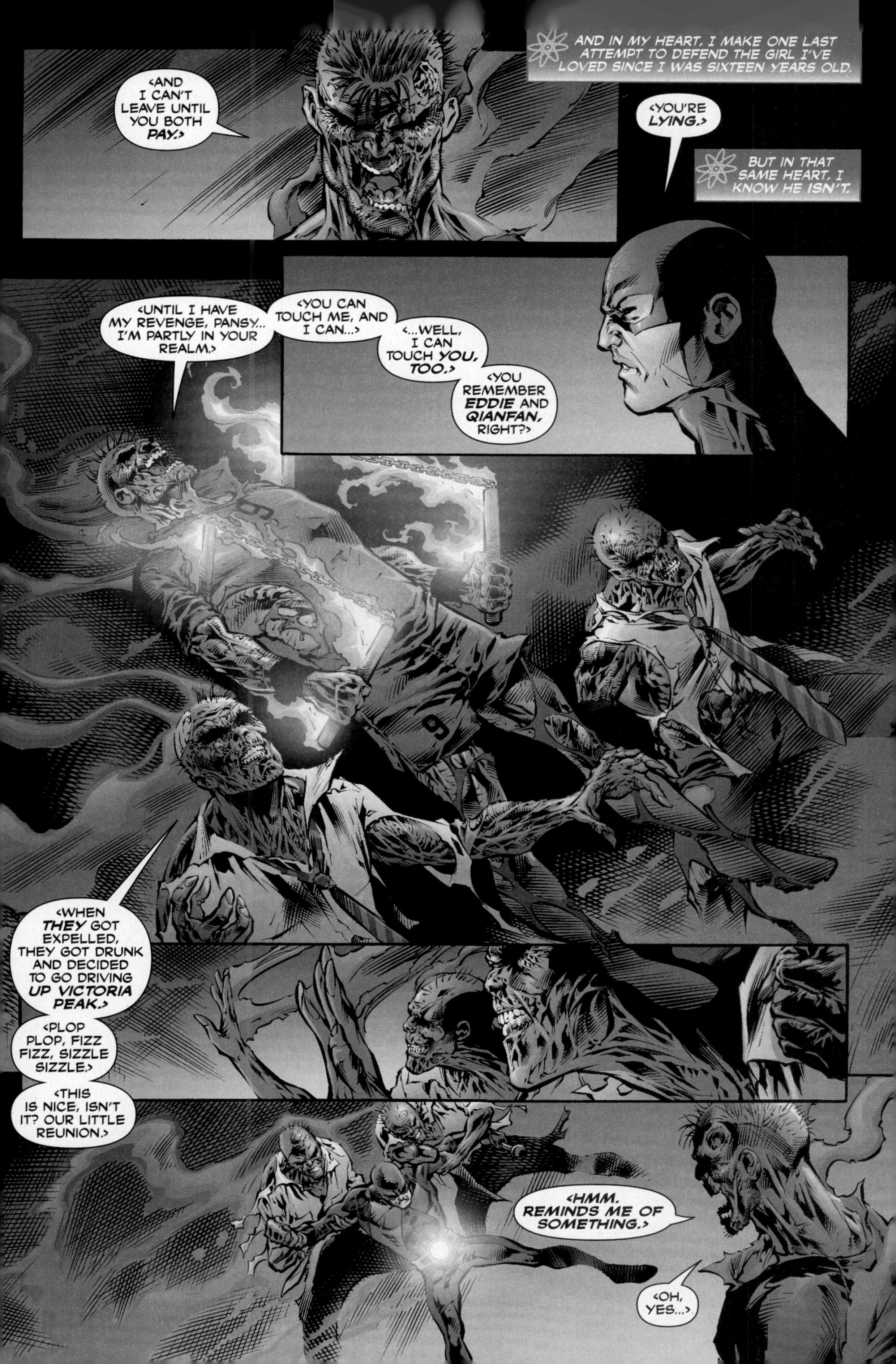
AND IN MY HEART, I MAKE ONE LAST ATTEMPT TO DEFEND THE GIRL I'VE LOVED SINCE I WAS SIXTEEN YEARS OLD.
<AND I CAN'T LEAVE UNTIL YOU BOTH PAY.>
<YOU'RE LYING.>
BUT IN THAT SAME HEART, I KNOW HE ISN'T.
<UNTIL I HAVE MY REVENGE, PANSY... I'M PARTLY IN YOUR REALM.>
<YOU CAN TOUCH ME, AND I CAN...>
<...WELL, I CAN TOUCH YOU, TOO.>
<YOU REMEMBER EDDIE AND QIANFAN, RIGHT?>
<WHEN THEY GOT EXPELLED, THEY GOT DRUNK AND DECIDED TO GO DRIVING UP VICTORIA PEAK.>
<PLOP PLOP, FIZZ FIZZ, SIZZLE SIZZLE.>
<THIS IS NICE, ISN'T IT? OUR LITTLE REUNION.>
<HMM. REMINDS ME OF SOMETHING.>
<OH, YES...>

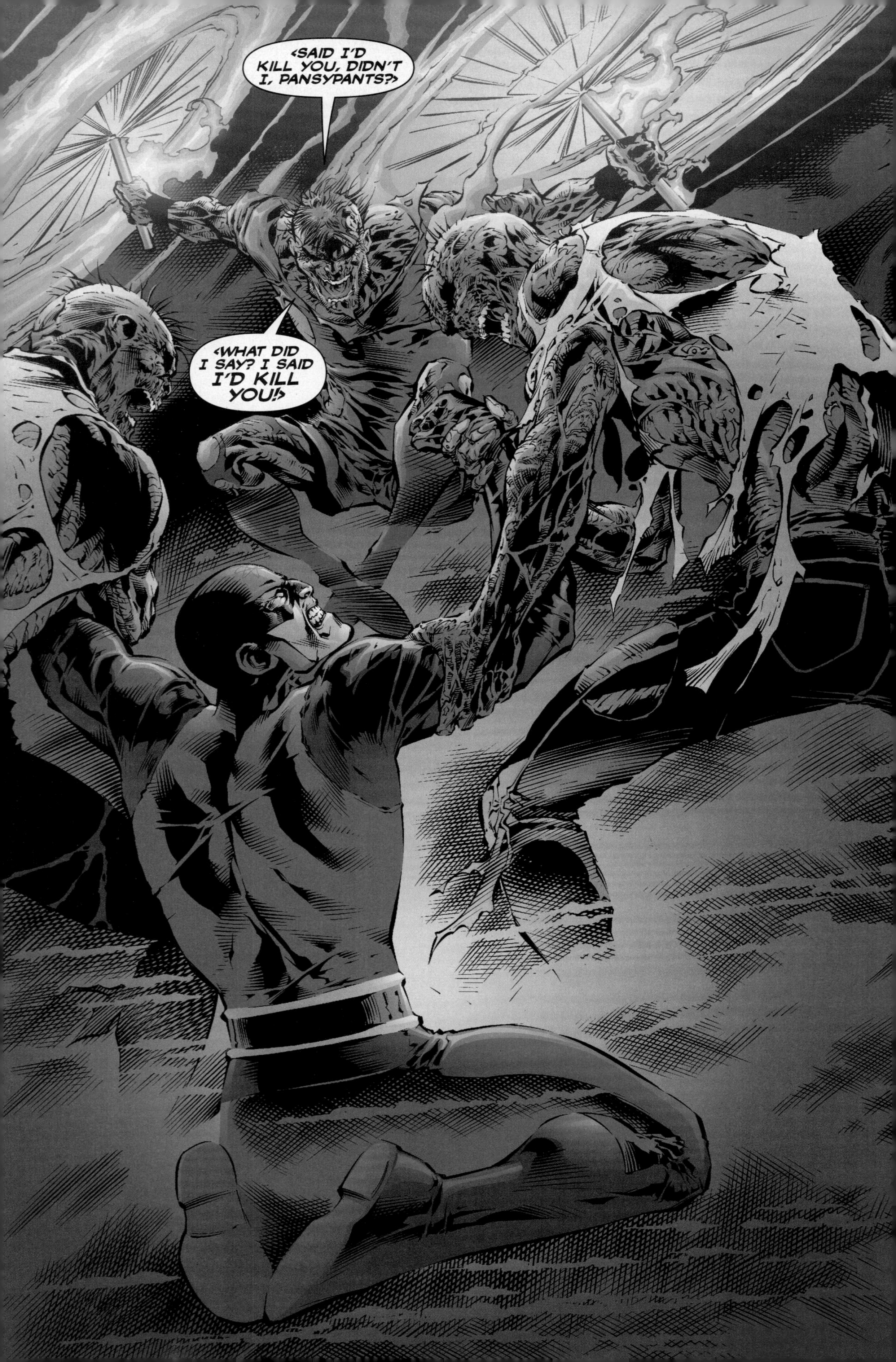
‹SAID I'D KILL YOU, DIDN'T I, PANSYPANTS?›
‹WHAT DID I SAY? I SAID I'D KILL YOU!›

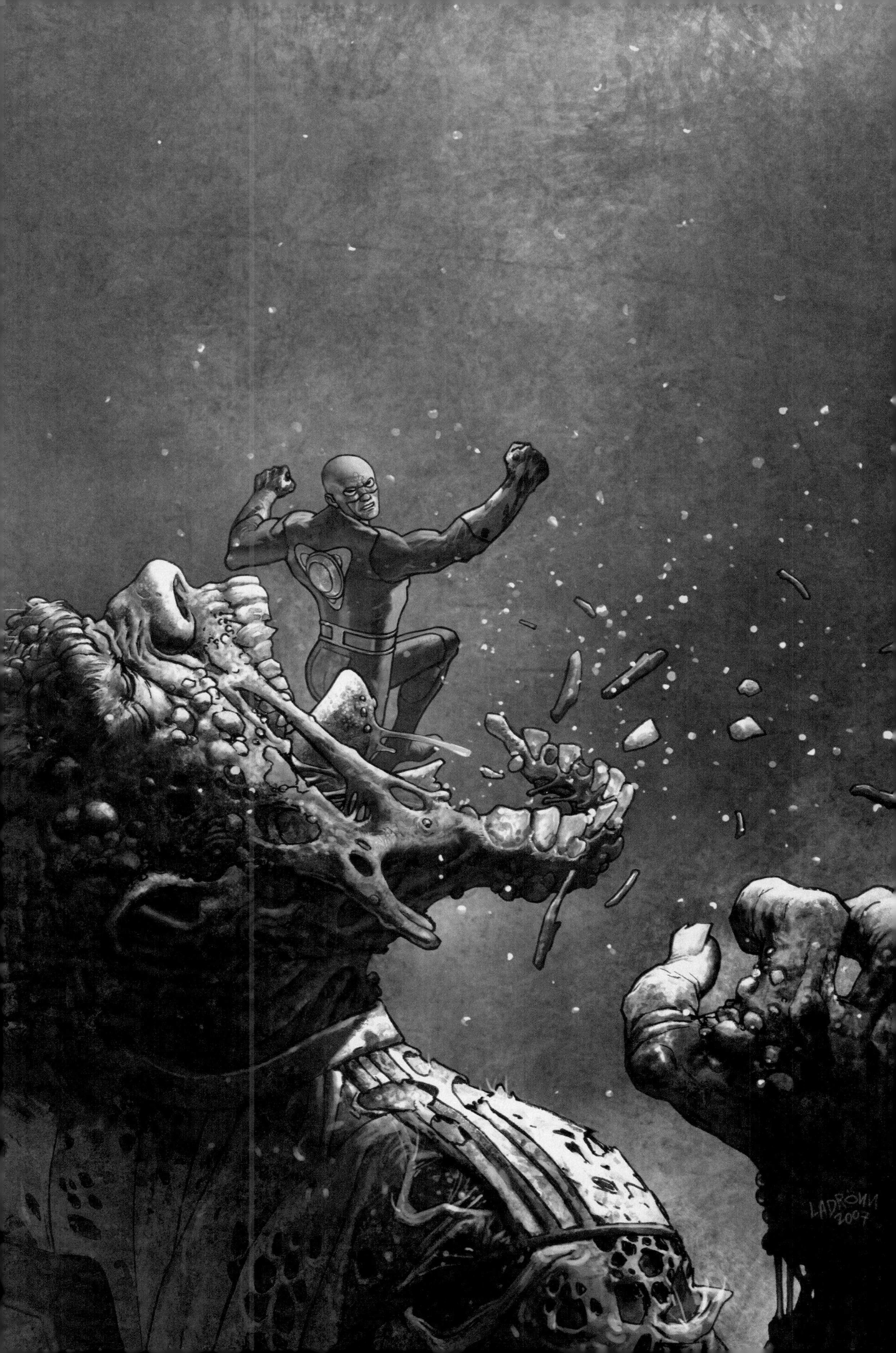
LADRONN
2007

JIA: PART TWO
UNWANTED ADVANCES

from **THE ALL NEW ATOM #10**

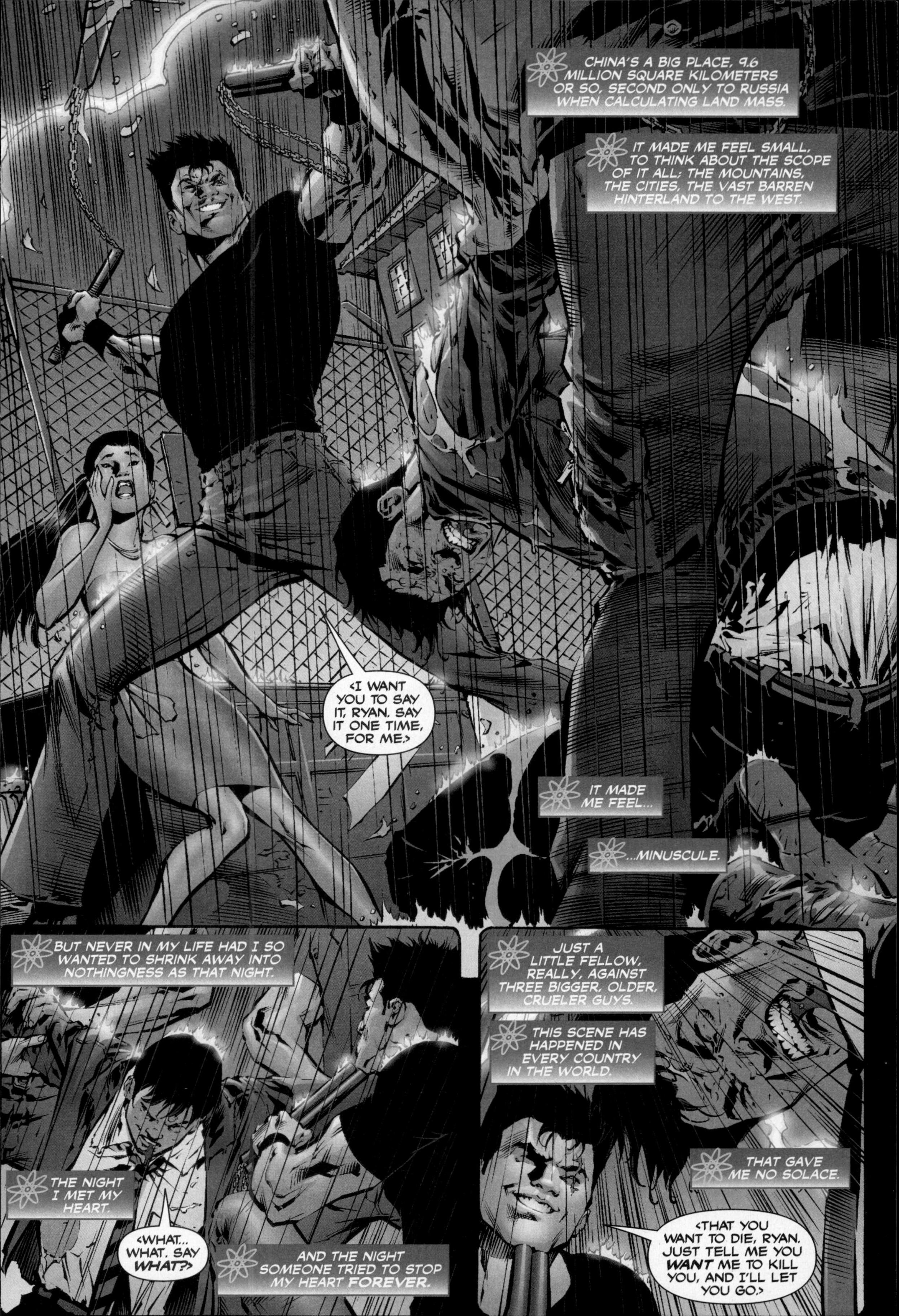
CHINA'S A BIG PLACE, 9.6 MILLION SQUARE KILOMETERS OR SO, SECOND ONLY TO RUSSIA WHEN CALCULATING LAND MASS.
IT MADE ME FEEL SMALL, TO THINK ABOUT THE SCOPE OF IT ALL; THE MOUNTAINS, THE CITIES, THE VAST BARREN HINTERLAND TO THE WEST.
<I WANT YOU TO SAY IT, RYAN. SAY IT ONE TIME, FOR ME.>
IT MADE ME FEEL...
...MINUSCULE.
BUT NEVER IN MY LIFE HAD I SO WANTED TO SHRINK AWAY INTO NOTHINGNESS AS THAT NIGHT.
THE NIGHT I MET MY HEART.
<WHAT... WHAT. SAY WHAT?>
AND THE NIGHT SOMEONE TRIED TO STOP MY HEART FOREVER.
JUST A LITTLE FELLOW, REALLY, AGAINST THREE BIGGER, OLDER, CRUELER GUYS.
THIS SCENE HAS HAPPENED IN EVERY COUNTRY IN THE WORLD.
THAT GAVE ME NO SOLACE.
<THAT YOU WANT TO DIE, RYAN. JUST TELL ME YOU WANT ME TO KILL YOU, AND I'LL LET YOU GO.>

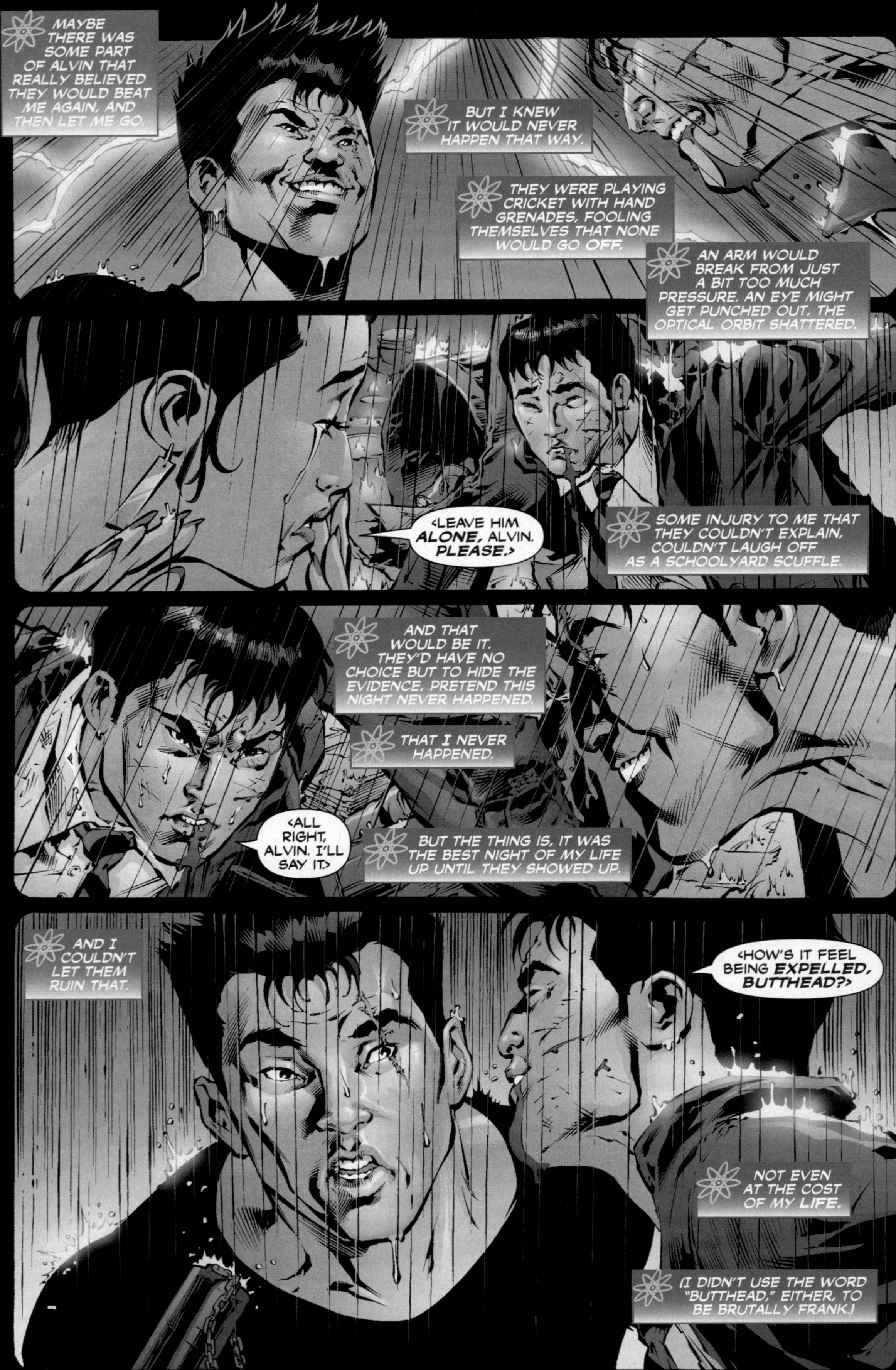
MAYBE THERE WAS SOME PART OF ALVIN THAT REALLY BELIEVED THEY WOULD BEAT ME AGAIN, AND THEN LET ME GO.
BUT I KNEW IT WOULD NEVER HAPPEN THAT WAY.
THEY WERE PLAYING CRICKET WITH HAND GRENADES, FOOLING THEMSELVES THAT NONE WOULD GO OFF.
AN ARM WOULD BREAK FROM JUST A BIT TOO MUCH PRESSURE. AN EYE MIGHT GET PUNCHED OUT, THE OPTICAL ORBIT SHATTERED.
<LEAVE HIM ALONE, ALVIN. PLEASE.>
SOME INJURY TO ME THAT THEY COULDN'T EXPLAIN, COULDN'T LAUGH OFF AS A SCHOOLYARD SCUFFLE.
AND THAT WOULD BE IT. THEY'D HAVE NO CHOICE BUT TO HIDE THE EVIDENCE, PRETEND THIS NIGHT NEVER HAPPENED.
THAT I NEVER HAPPENED.
<ALL RIGHT, ALVIN. I'LL SAY IT.>
BUT THE THING IS, IT WAS THE BEST NIGHT OF MY LIFE UP UNTIL THEY SHOWED UP.
AND I COULDN'T LET THEM RUIN THAT.
<HOW'S IT FEEL BEING EXPELLED, BUTTHEAD?>
NOT EVEN AT THE COST OF MY LIFE.
(I DIDN'T USE THE WORD "BUTTHEAD," EITHER, TO BE BRUTALLY FRANK.)

AND THEN I DON'T REMEMBER MUCH FOR A BIT.

BUT WHATEVER BRAVADO I HAD DIED WHEN I REALIZED I WAS TIED UP IN THE TRUNK OF ALVIN'S CAR.

THAT MOMENT OF NO-RETURN WAS WHISPERING, THAT MOMENT WHEN THEY COULDN'T TURN BACK WAS LAUGHING AT ME, IN THE DARK.

<LAST CHANCE, PANSY.>

<SAY YOU *WANT* IT. SAY YOU *WANT* ME TO KILL YOU.>

<THEN WE LET YOU GO.>

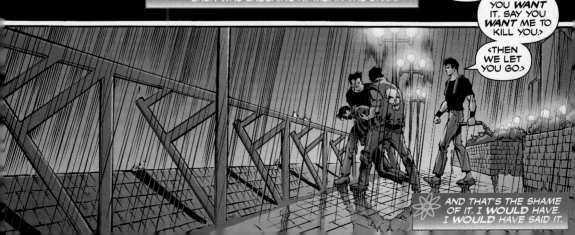

AND THAT'S THE SHAME OF IT. I *WOULD* HAVE. I *WOULD* HAVE SAID IT.

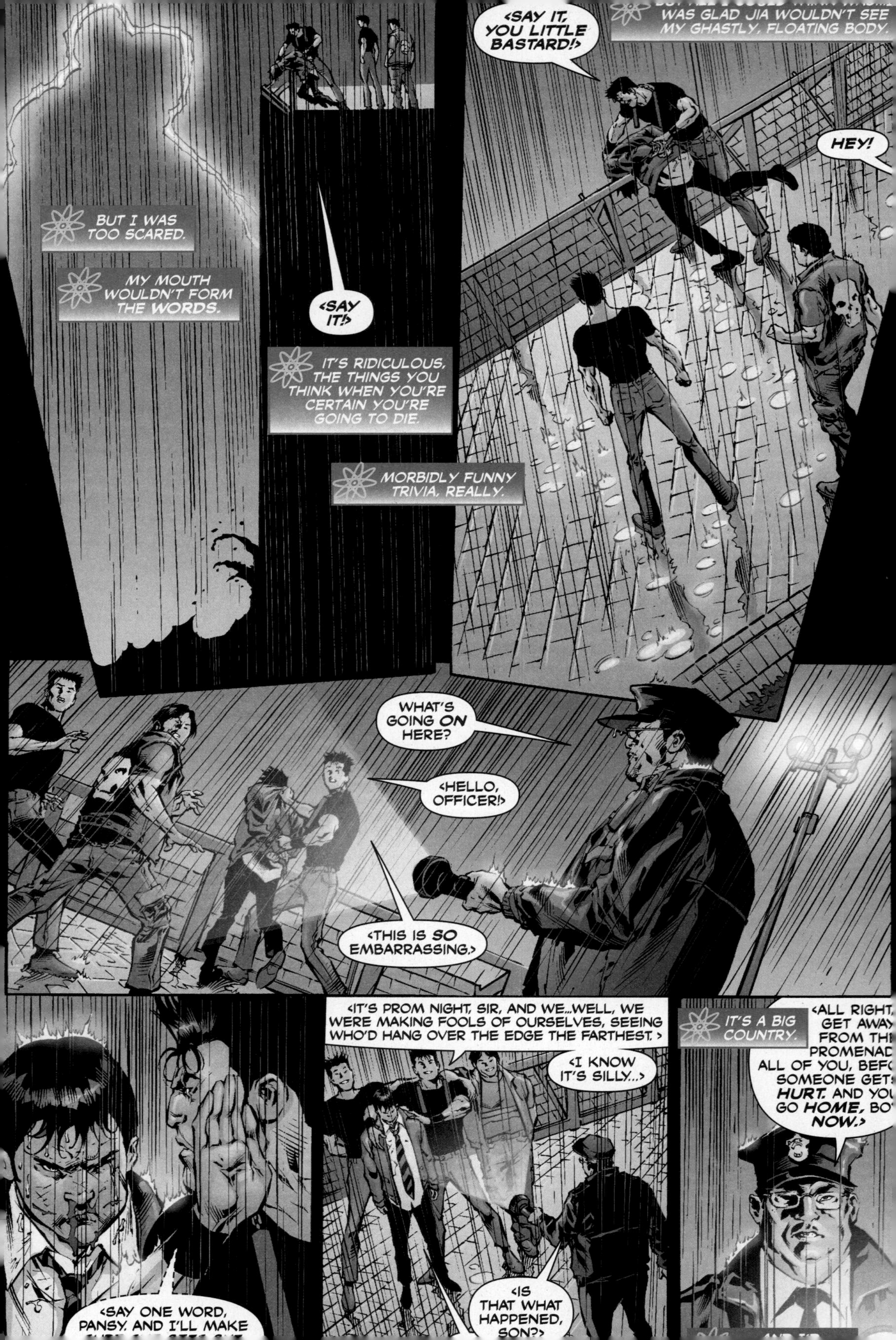
BUT I WAS TOO SCARED.
MY MOUTH WOULDN'T FORM THE WORDS.
<SAY IT!>
IT'S RIDICULOUS, THE THINGS YOU THINK WHEN YOU'RE CERTAIN YOU'RE GOING TO DIE.
MORBIDLY FUNNY TRIVIA, REALLY.
WAS GLAD JIA WOULDN'T SEE MY GHASTLY, FLOATING BODY.
<SAY IT, YOU LITTLE BASTARD!>
HEY!
WHAT'S GOING ON HERE?
<HELLO, OFFICER!>
<THIS IS SO EMBARRASSING.>
<SAY ONE WORD, PANSY. AND I'LL MAKE
<IT'S PROM NIGHT, SIR, AND WE...WELL, WE WERE MAKING FOOLS OF OURSELVES, SEEING WHO'D HANG OVER THE EDGE THE FARTHEST.>
<I KNOW IT'S SILLY...>
<IS THAT WHAT HAPPENED, SON?>
IT'S A BIG COUNTRY.
<ALL RIGHT, GET AWAY FROM TH PROMENAD ALL OF YOU, BEF SOMEONE GET HURT. AND YOU GO HOME, BO NOW.>

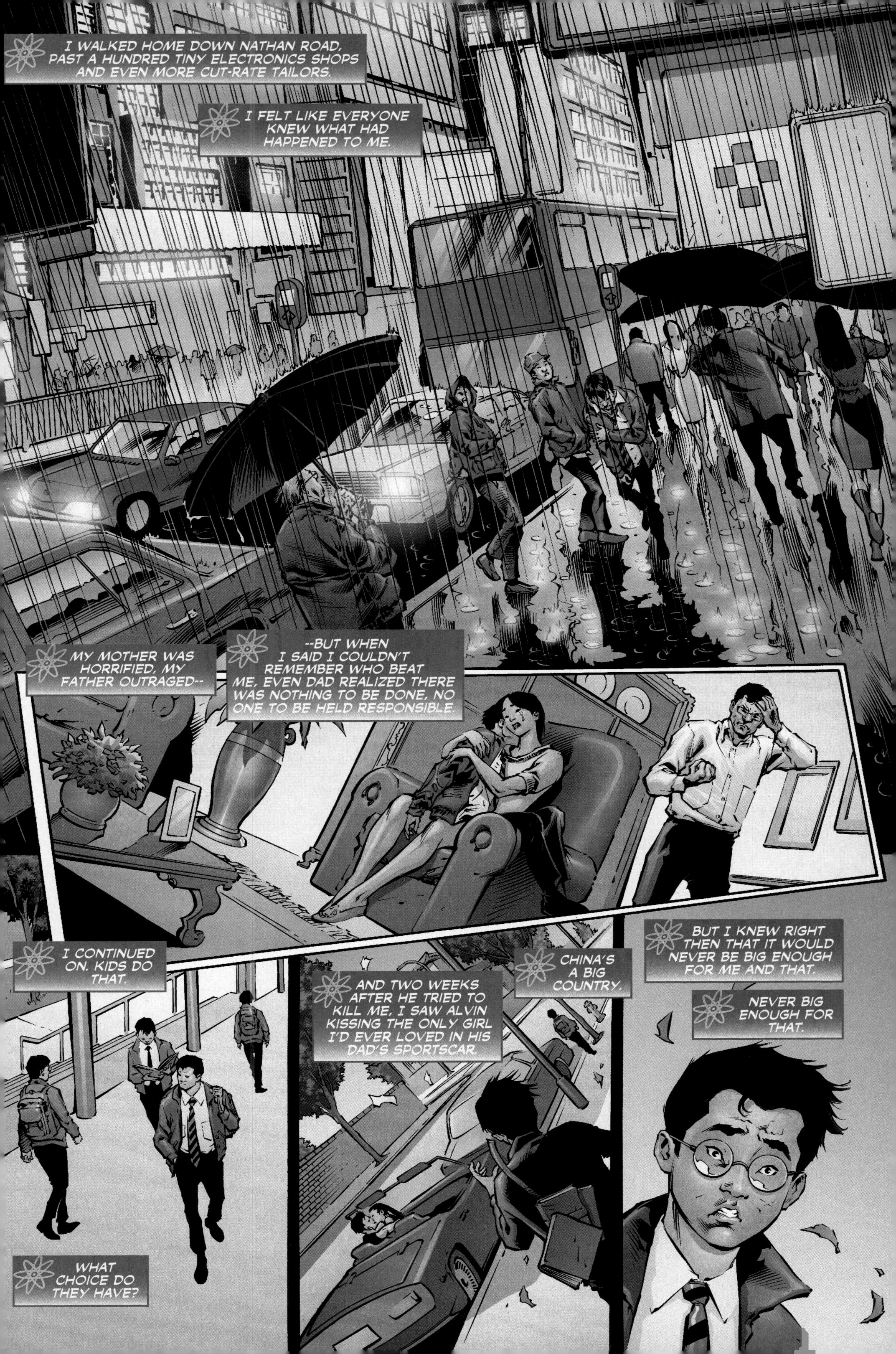
I WALKED HOME DOWN NATHAN ROAD, PAST A HUNDRED TINY ELECTRONICS SHOPS AND EVEN MORE CUT-RATE TAILORS.
I FELT LIKE EVERYONE KNEW WHAT HAD HAPPENED TO ME.
MY MOTHER WAS HORRIFIED, MY FATHER OUTRAGED--
--BUT WHEN I SAID I COULDN'T REMEMBER WHO BEAT ME, EVEN DAD REALIZED THERE WAS NOTHING TO BE DONE, NO ONE TO BE HELD RESPONSIBLE.
I CONTINUED ON. KIDS DO THAT.
WHAT CHOICE DO THEY HAVE?
AND TWO WEEKS AFTER HE TRIED TO KILL ME, I SAW ALVIN KISSING THE ONLY GIRL I'D EVER LOVED IN HIS DAD'S SPORTSCAR.
CHINA'S A BIG COUNTRY.
BUT I KNEW RIGHT THEN THAT IT WOULD NEVER BE BIG ENOUGH FOR ME AND THAT.
NEVER BIG ENOUGH FOR THAT.

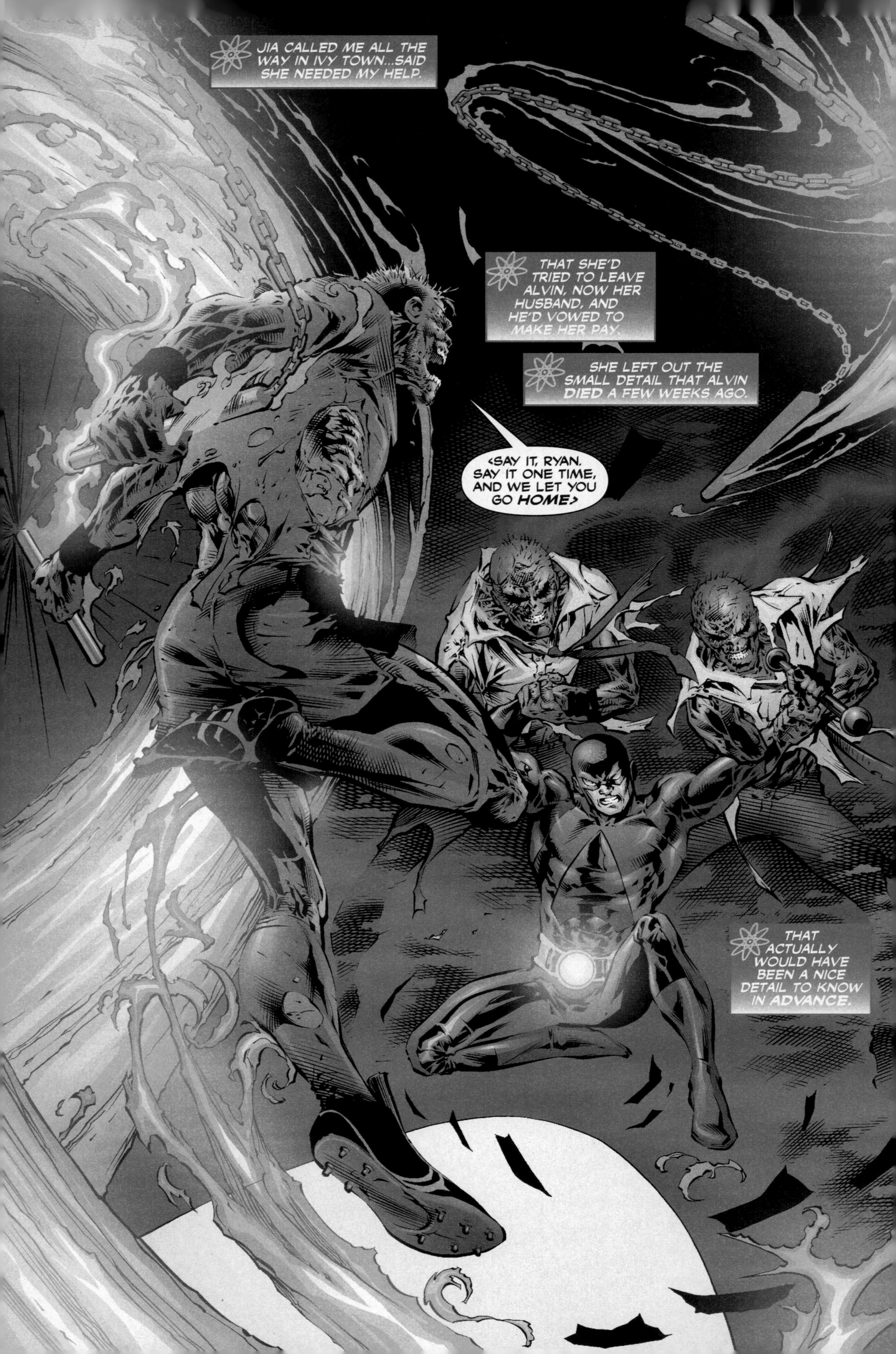
JIA CALLED ME ALL THE WAY IN IVY TOWN...SAID SHE NEEDED MY HELP.
THAT SHE'D TRIED TO LEAVE ALVIN, NOW HER HUSBAND, AND HE'D VOWED TO MAKE HER PAY.
SHE LEFT OUT THE SMALL DETAIL THAT ALVIN DIED A FEW WEEKS AGO.
<SAY IT, RYAN. SAY IT ONE TIME, AND WE LET YOU GO HOME.>
THAT ACTUALLY WOULD HAVE BEEN A NICE DETAIL TO KNOW IN ADVANCE.

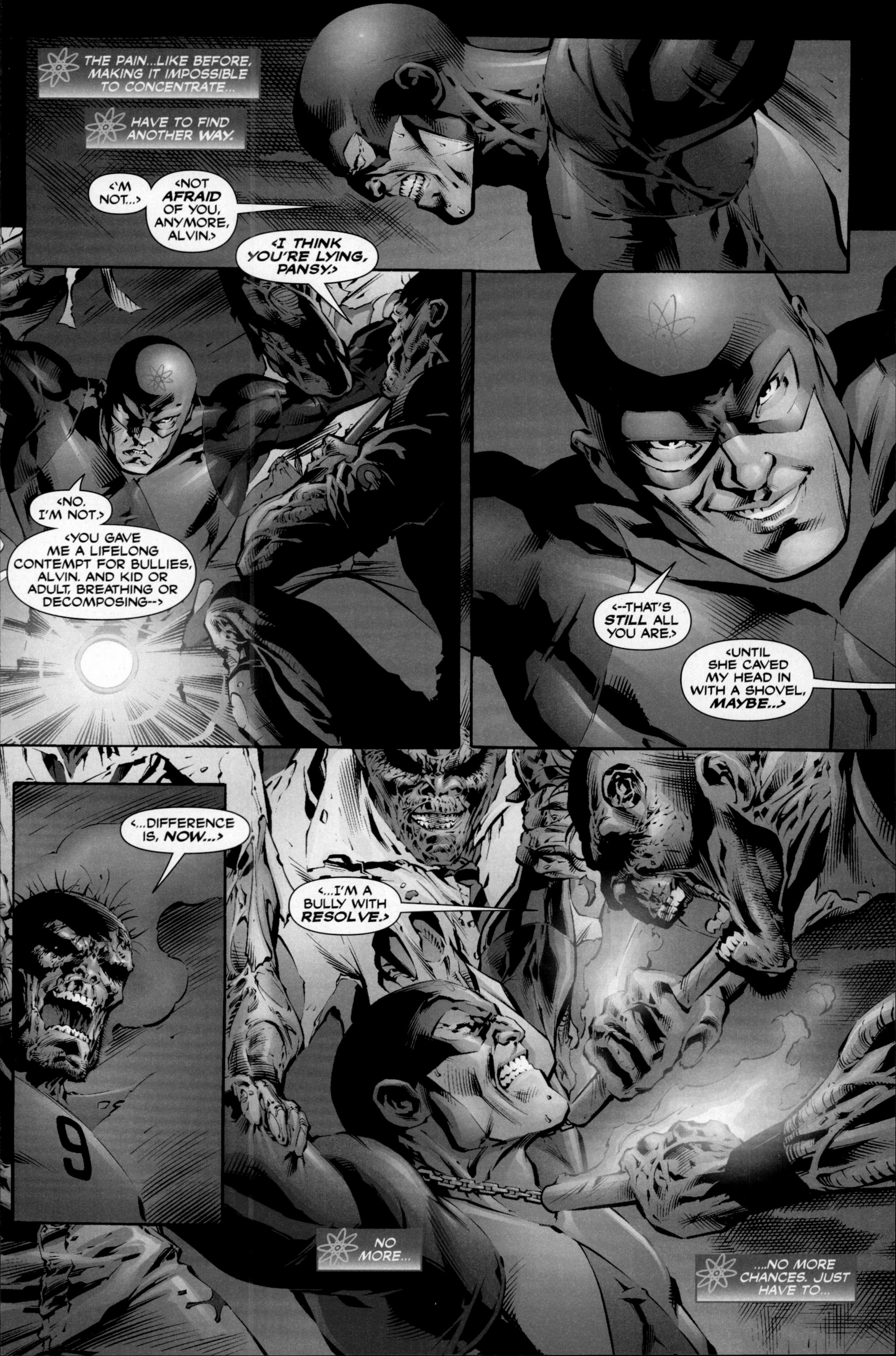
THE PAIN...LIKE BEFORE, MAKING IT IMPOSSIBLE TO CONCENTRATE...
HAVE TO FIND ANOTHER WAY.
<'M NOT...>
<NOT AFRAID OF YOU, ANYMORE, ALVIN.>
<I THINK YOU'RE LYING, PANSY.>
<NO, I'M NOT.>
<YOU GAVE ME A LIFELONG CONTEMPT FOR BULLIES, ALVIN, AND KID OR ADULT, BREATHING OR DECOMPOSING-->
<--THAT'S STILL ALL YOU ARE.>
<UNTIL SHE CAVED MY HEAD IN WITH A SHOVEL, MAYBE...>
<...DIFFERENCE IS, NOW...>
<...I'M A BULLY WITH RESOLVE.>
NO MORE...
...NO MORE CHANCES. JUST HAVE TO...

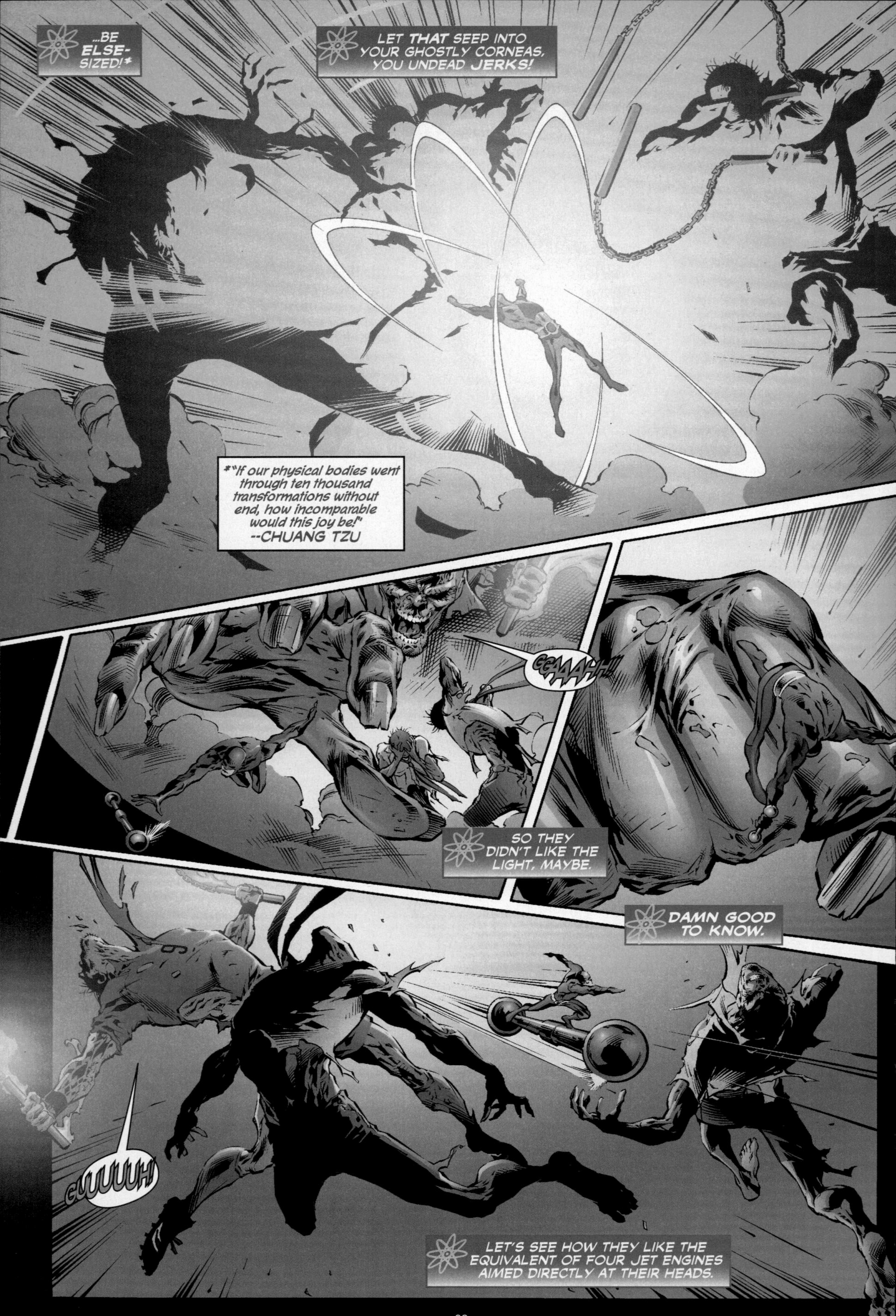
...BE ELSE-SIZED!*
LET THAT SEEP INTO YOUR GHOSTLY CORNEAS, YOU UNDEAD JERKS!
*"If our physical bodies went through ten thousand transformations without end, how incomparable would this joy be!" --CHUANG TZU
GGAAAHH!!
SO THEY DIDN'T LIKE THE LIGHT, MAYBE.
DAMN GOOD TO KNOW.
GUUUUH!
LET'S SEE HOW THEY LIKE THE EQUIVALENT OF FOUR JET ENGINES AIMED DIRECTLY AT THEIR HEADS.

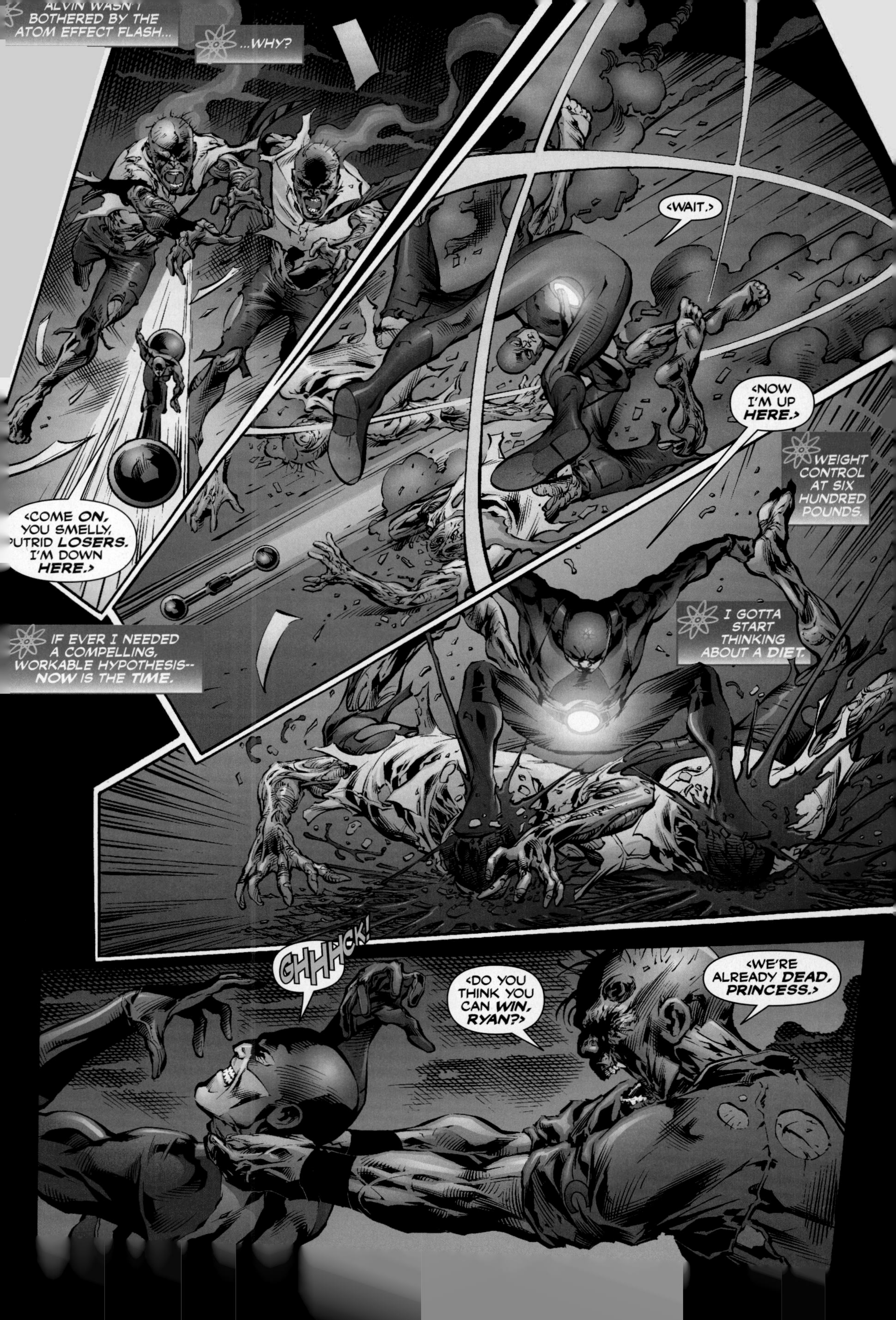
ALVIN WASN'T BOTHERED BY THE ATOM EFFECT FLASH...
...WHY?
<WAIT.>
<COME ON, YOU SMELLY, PUTRID LOSERS. I'M DOWN HERE.>
<NOW I'M UP HERE.>
WEIGHT CONTROL AT SIX HUNDRED POUNDS.
IF EVER I NEEDED A COMPELLING, WORKABLE HYPOTHESIS-- NOW IS THE TIME.
I GOTTA START THINKING ABOUT A DIET.
GHHHCK!
<DO YOU THINK YOU CAN WIN, RYAN?>
<WE'RE ALREADY DEAD, PRINCESS.>

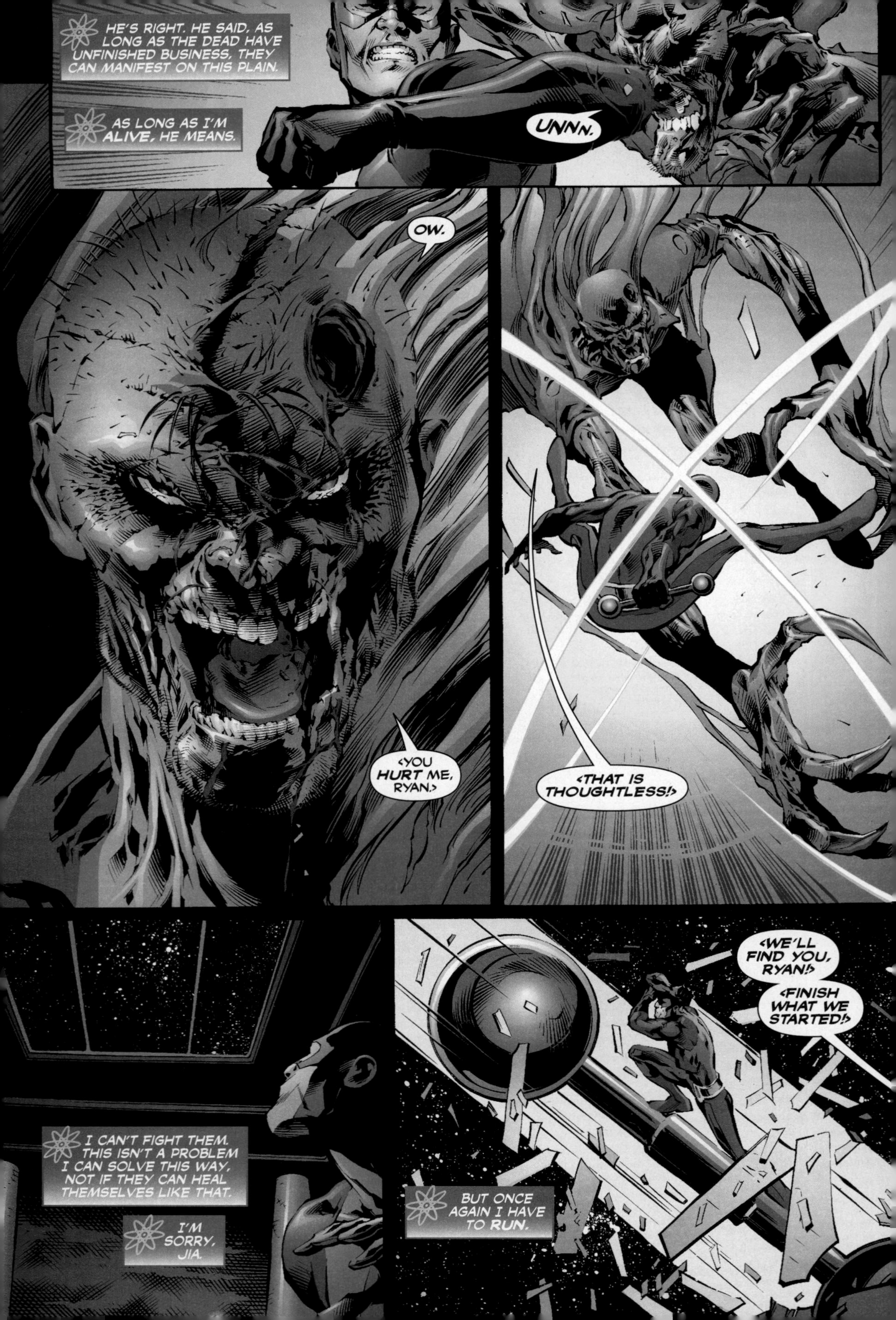

HE'S RIGHT. HE SAID, AS LONG AS THE DEAD HAVE UNFINISHED BUSINESS, THEY CAN MANIFEST ON THIS PLAIN.
AS LONG AS I'M ALIVE, HE MEANS.
UNNN.
OW.
‹YOU HURT ME, RYAN.›
‹THAT IS THOUGHTLESS!›
I CAN'T FIGHT THEM. THIS ISN'T A PROBLEM I CAN SOLVE THIS WAY, NOT IF THEY CAN HEAL THEMSELVES LIKE THAT.
I'M SORRY, JIA.
‹WE'LL FIND YOU, RYAN!›
‹FINISH WHAT WE STARTED!›
BUT ONCE AGAIN I HAVE TO RUN.

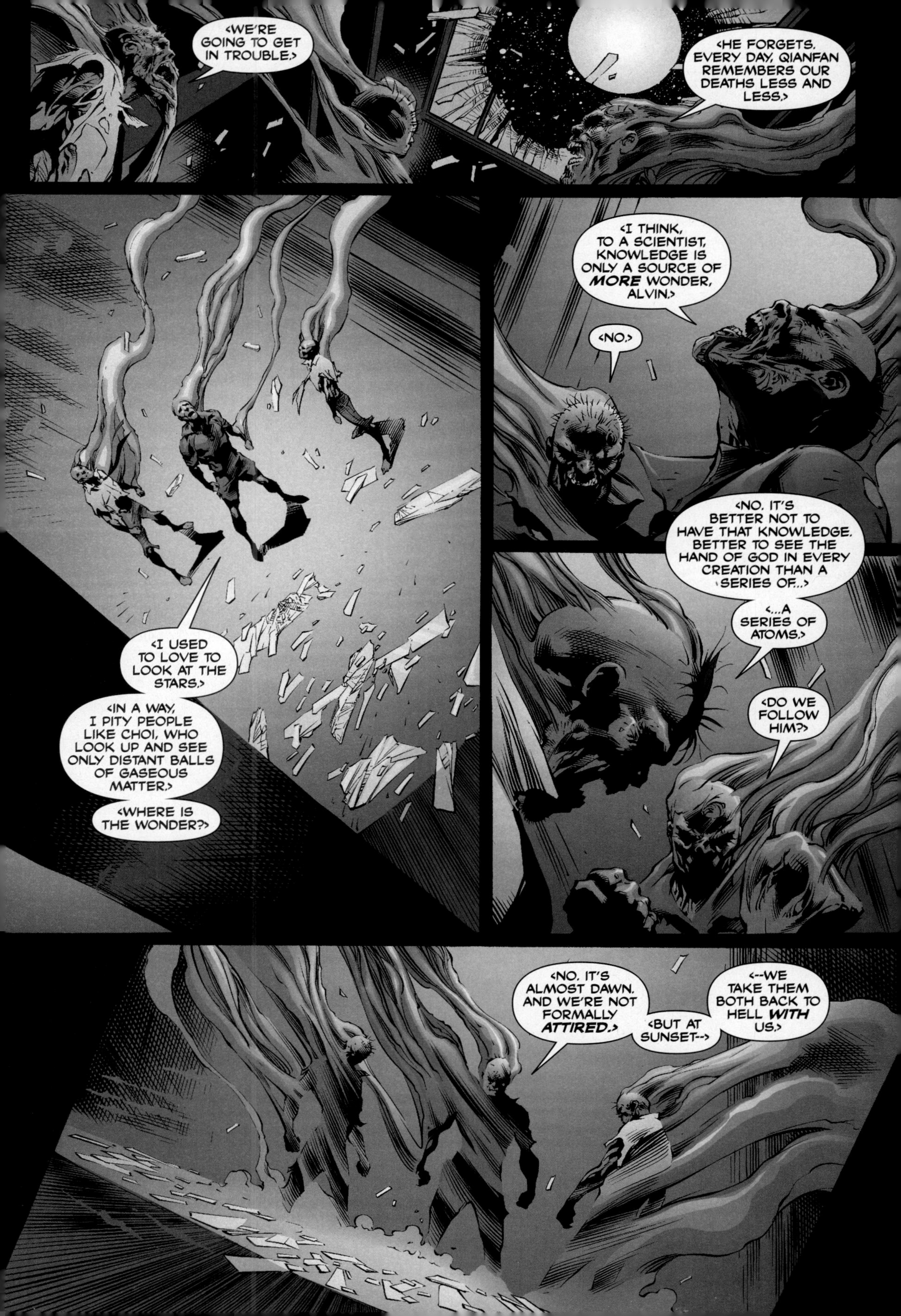

<WE'RE GOING TO GET IN TROUBLE.>
<HE FORGETS. EVERY DAY, QIANFAN REMEMBERS OUR DEATHS LESS AND LESS.>
<I USED TO LOVE TO LOOK AT THE STARS.>
<IN A WAY, I PITY PEOPLE LIKE CHOI, WHO LOOK UP AND SEE ONLY DISTANT BALLS OF GASEOUS MATTER.>
<WHERE IS THE WONDER?>
<I THINK, TO A SCIENTIST, KNOWLEDGE IS ONLY A SOURCE OF MORE WONDER, ALVIN.>
<NO.>
<NO, IT'S BETTER NOT TO HAVE THAT KNOWLEDGE. BETTER TO SEE THE HAND OF GOD IN EVERY CREATION THAN A SERIES OF...>
<...A SERIES OF ATOMS.>
<DO WE FOLLOW HIM?>
<NO, IT'S ALMOST DAWN, AND WE'RE NOT FORMALLY ATTIRED.>
<BUT AT SUNSET-->
<--WE TAKE THEM BOTH BACK TO HELL WITH US.>

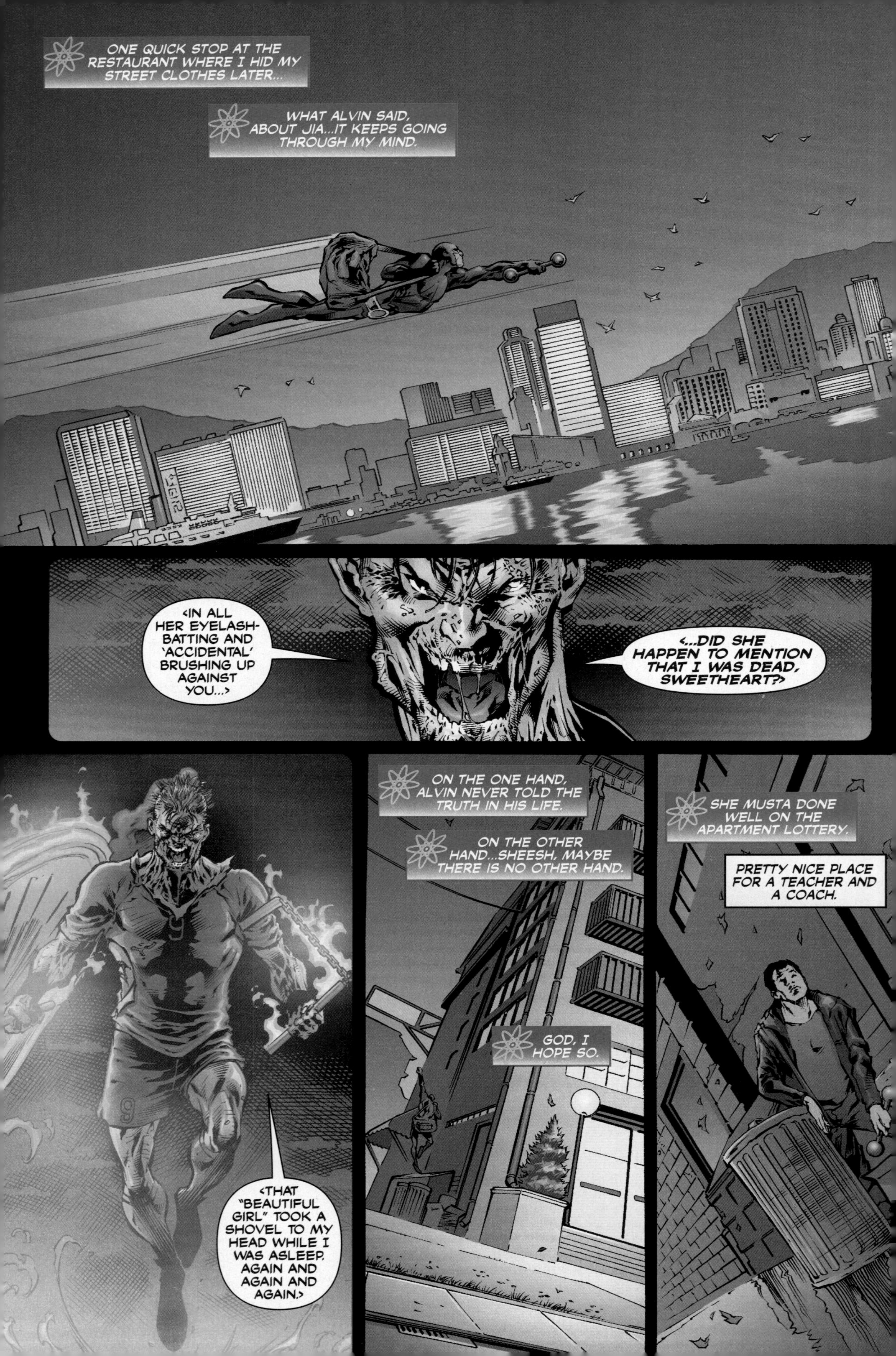
ONE QUICK STOP AT THE RESTAURANT WHERE I HID MY STREET CLOTHES LATER...
WHAT ALVIN SAID, ABOUT JIA...IT KEEPS GOING THROUGH MY MIND.
<IN ALL HER EYELASH-BATTING AND 'ACCIDENTAL' BRUSHING UP AGAINST YOU...>
<...DID SHE HAPPEN TO MENTION THAT I WAS DEAD, SWEETHEART?>
<THAT "BEAUTIFUL GIRL" TOOK A SHOVEL TO MY HEAD WHILE I WAS ASLEEP. AGAIN AND AGAIN AND AGAIN.>
ON THE ONE HAND, ALVIN NEVER TOLD THE TRUTH IN HIS LIFE.
ON THE OTHER HAND...SHEESH, MAYBE THERE IS NO OTHER HAND.
GOD, I HOPE SO.
SHE MUSTA DONE WELL ON THE APARTMENT LOTTERY.
PRETTY NICE PLACE FOR A TEACHER AND A COACH.

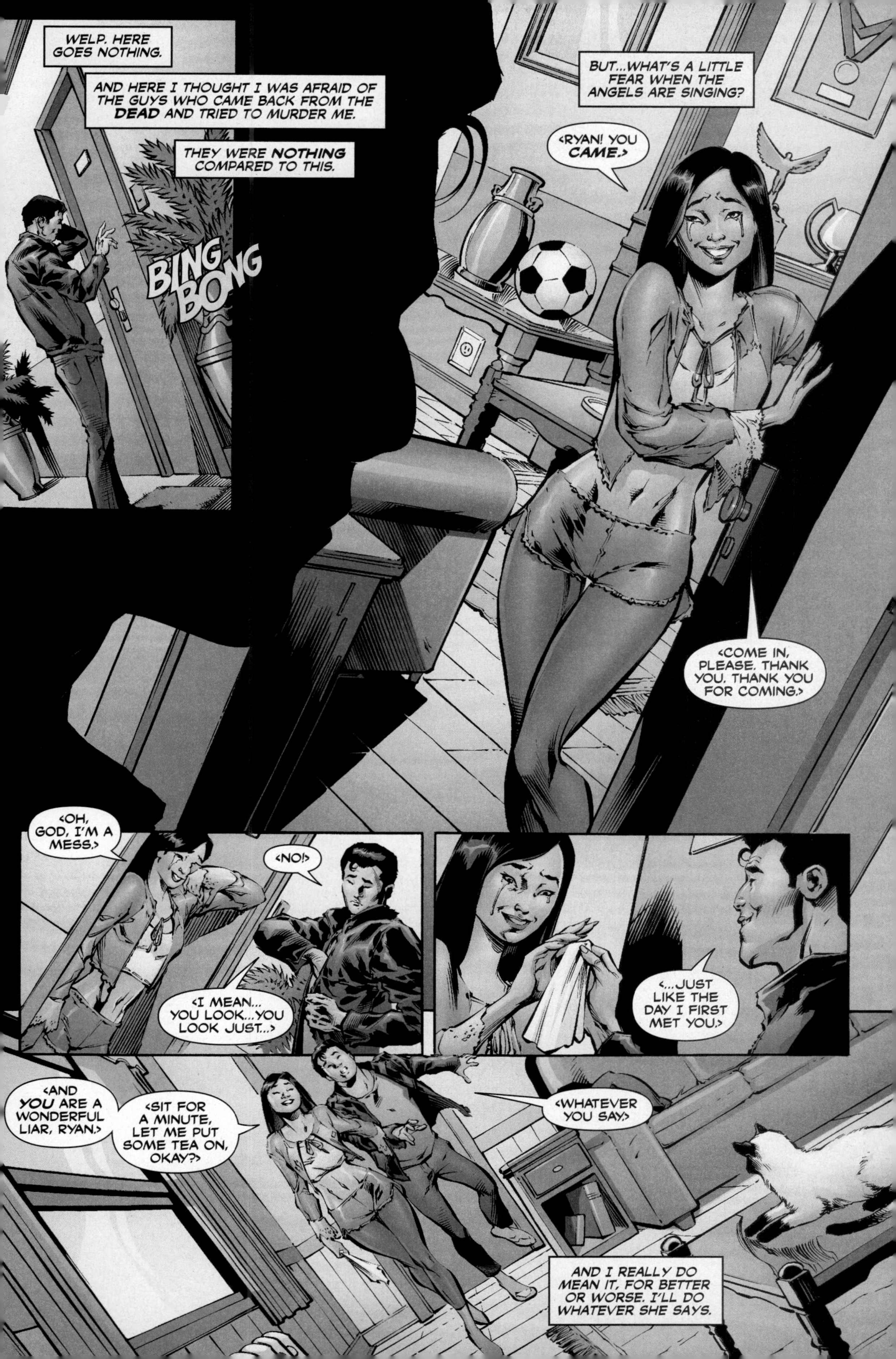
WELP. HERE GOES NOTHING.
AND HERE I THOUGHT I WAS AFRAID OF THE GUYS WHO CAME BACK FROM THE DEAD AND TRIED TO MURDER ME.
THEY WERE NOTHING COMPARED TO THIS.
BING BONG
BUT...WHAT'S A LITTLE FEAR WHEN THE ANGELS ARE SINGING?
‹RYAN! YOU CAME.›
‹COME IN, PLEASE. THANK YOU. THANK YOU FOR COMING.›
‹OH, GOD, I'M A MESS.›
‹NO!›
‹I MEAN... YOU LOOK...YOU LOOK JUST...›
‹...JUST LIKE THE DAY I FIRST MET YOU.›
‹AND YOU ARE A WONDERFUL LIAR, RYAN.›
‹SIT FOR A MINUTE, LET ME PUT SOME TEA ON, OKAY?›
‹WHATEVER YOU SAY.›
AND I REALLY DO MEAN IT, FOR BETTER OR WORSE. I'LL DO WHATEVER SHE SAYS.

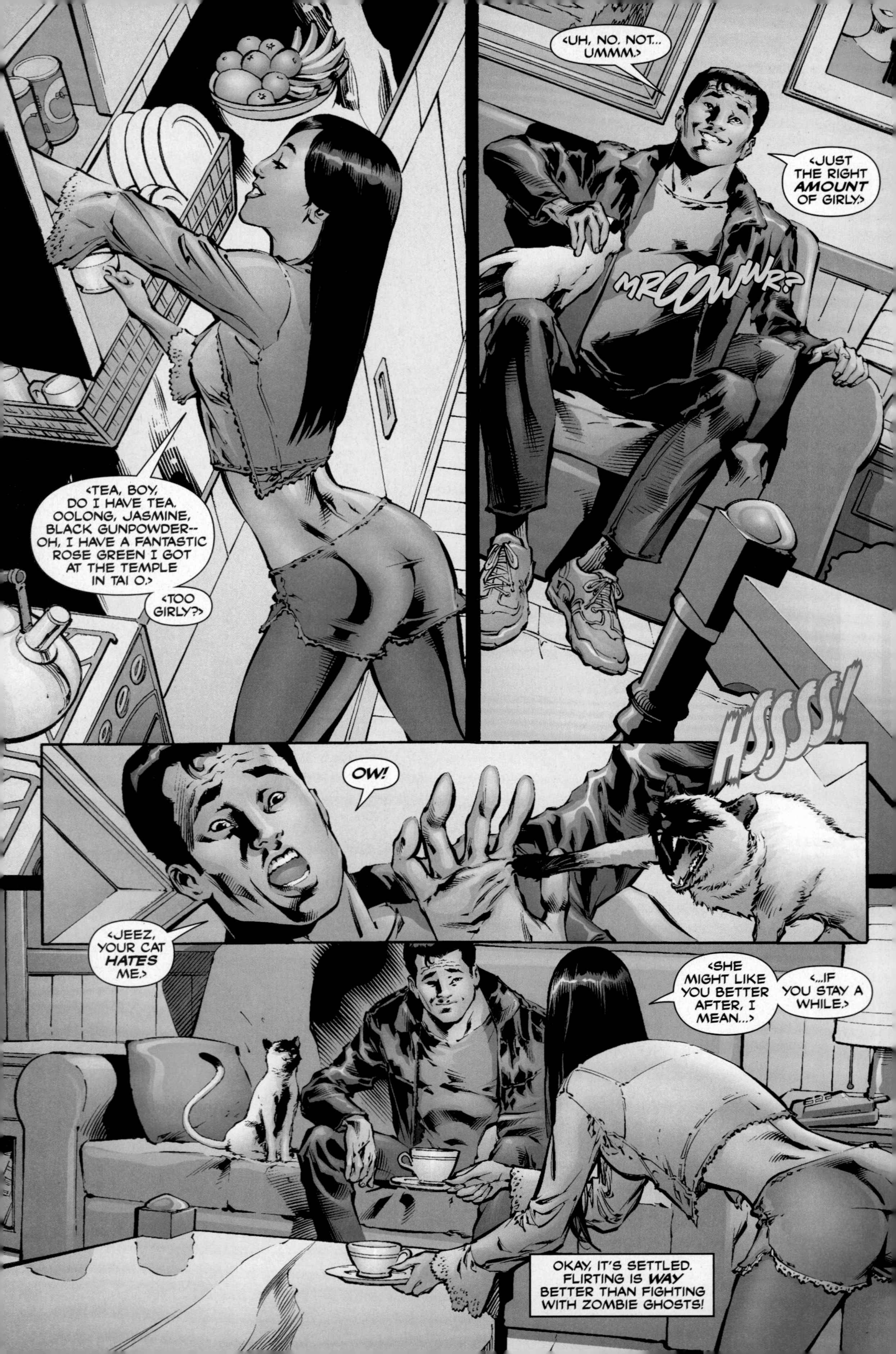
<TEA, BOY, DO I HAVE TEA. OOLONG, JASMINE, BLACK GUNPOWDER-- OH, I HAVE A FANTASTIC ROSE GREEN I GOT AT THE TEMPLE IN TAI O.>
<TOO GIRLY?>
<UH, NO. NOT... UMMM.>
<JUST THE RIGHT AMOUNT OF GIRLY.>
MROOWWR?
HSSSS!
OW!
<JEEZ, YOUR CAT HATES ME.>
<SHE MIGHT LIKE YOU BETTER AFTER, I MEAN...>
<...IF YOU STAY A WHILE.>
OKAY, IT'S SETTLED. FLIRTING IS WAY BETTER THAN FIGHTING WITH ZOMBIE GHOSTS!

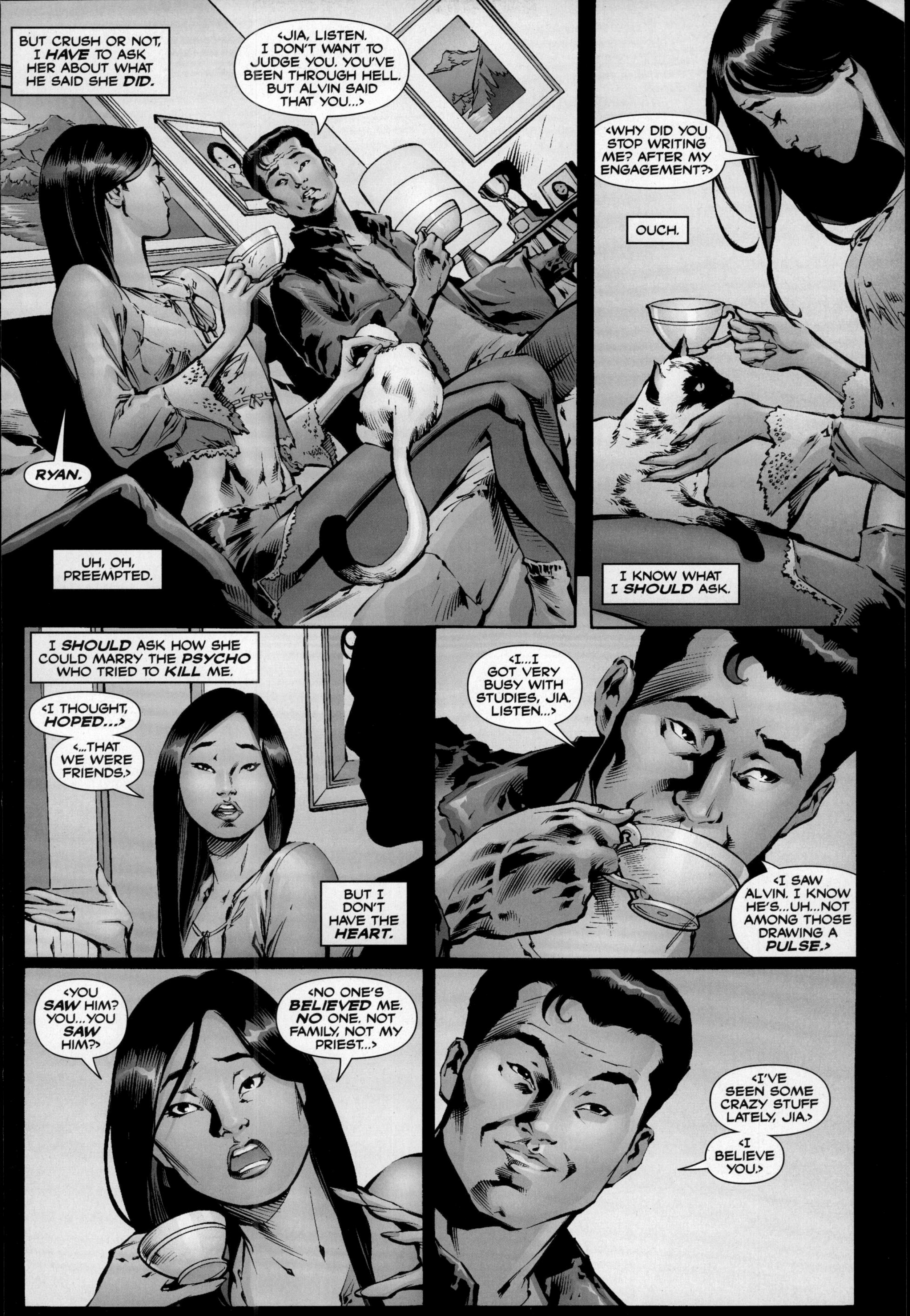
BUT CRUSH OR NOT, I HAVE TO ASK HER ABOUT WHAT HE SAID SHE DID.
<JIA, LISTEN. I DON'T WANT TO JUDGE YOU. YOU'VE BEEN THROUGH HELL. BUT ALVIN SAID THAT YOU...>
RYAN.
UH, OH, PREEMPTED.
<WHY DID YOU STOP WRITING ME? AFTER MY ENGAGEMENT?>
OUCH.
I KNOW WHAT I SHOULD ASK.
I SHOULD ASK HOW SHE COULD MARRY THE PSYCHO WHO TRIED TO KILL ME.
<I THOUGHT, HOPED...>
<...THAT WE WERE FRIENDS.>
BUT I DON'T HAVE THE HEART.
<I...I GOT VERY BUSY WITH STUDIES, JIA. LISTEN...>
<I SAW ALVIN. I KNOW HE'S...UH...NOT AMONG THOSE DRAWING A PULSE.>
<YOU SAW HIM? YOU...YOU SAW HIM?>
<NO ONE'S BELIEVED ME. NO ONE. NOT FAMILY, NOT MY PRIEST...>
<I'VE SEEN SOME CRAZY STUFF LATELY, JIA.>
<I BELIEVE YOU.>

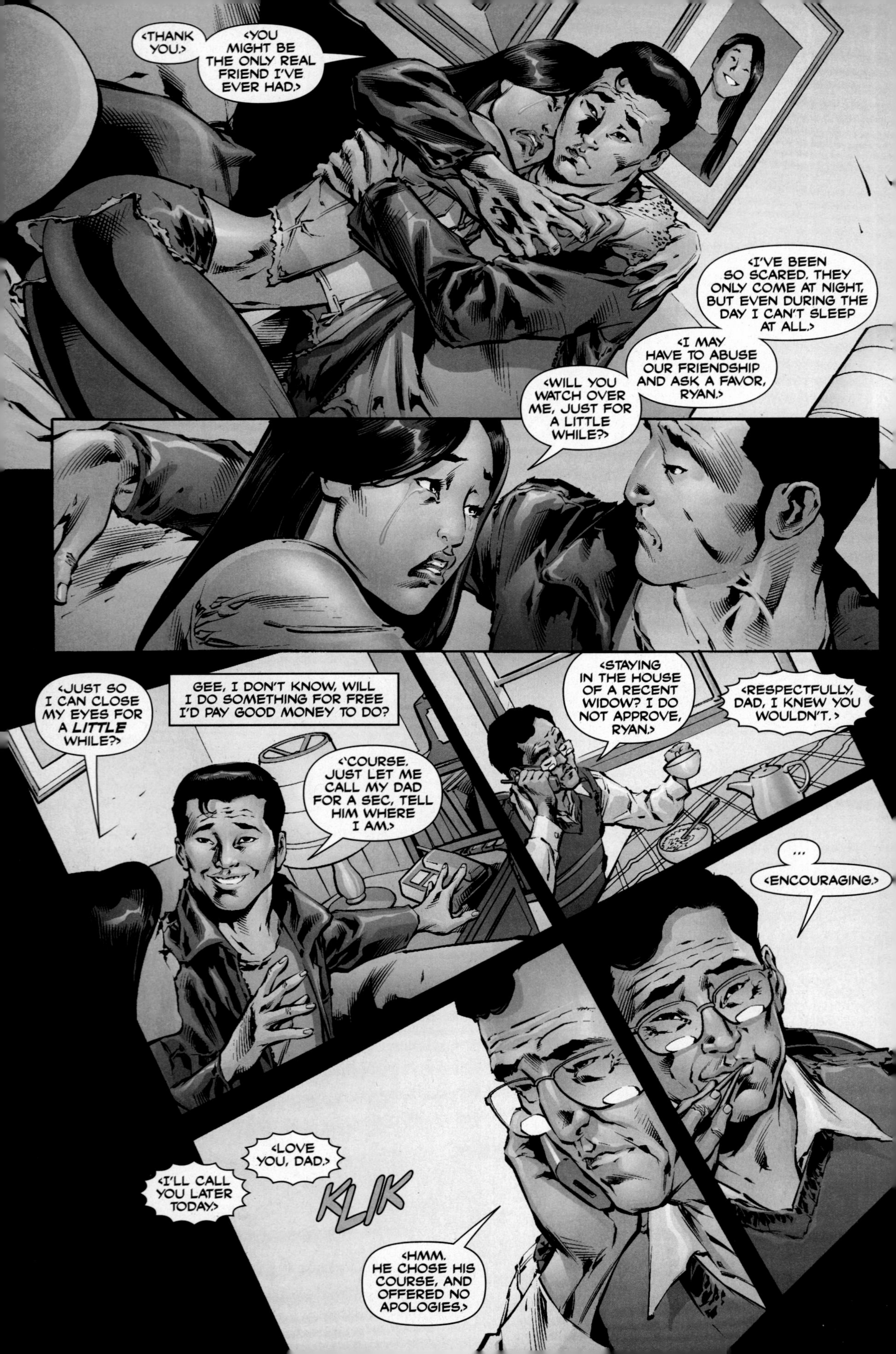

‹THANK YOU.›
‹YOU MIGHT BE THE ONLY REAL FRIEND I'VE EVER HAD.›
‹I'VE BEEN SO SCARED. THEY ONLY COME AT NIGHT, BUT EVEN DURING THE DAY I CAN'T SLEEP AT ALL.›
‹I MAY HAVE TO ABUSE OUR FRIENDSHIP AND ASK A FAVOR, RYAN.›
‹WILL YOU WATCH OVER ME, JUST FOR A LITTLE WHILE?›
‹JUST SO I CAN CLOSE MY EYES FOR A *LITTLE* WHILE?›
GEE, I DON'T KNOW, WILL I DO SOMETHING FOR FREE I'D PAY GOOD MONEY TO DO?
‹'COURSE. JUST LET ME CALL MY DAD FOR A SEC, TELL HIM WHERE I AM.›
‹STAYING IN THE HOUSE OF A RECENT WIDOW? I DO NOT APPROVE, RYAN.›
‹RESPECTFULLY, DAD, I KNEW YOU WOULDN'T.›
...
‹ENCOURAGING.›
‹LOVE YOU, DAD.›
‹I'LL CALL YOU LATER TODAY›
KLIK
‹HMM. HE CHOSE HIS COURSE, AND OFFERED NO APOLOGIES.›

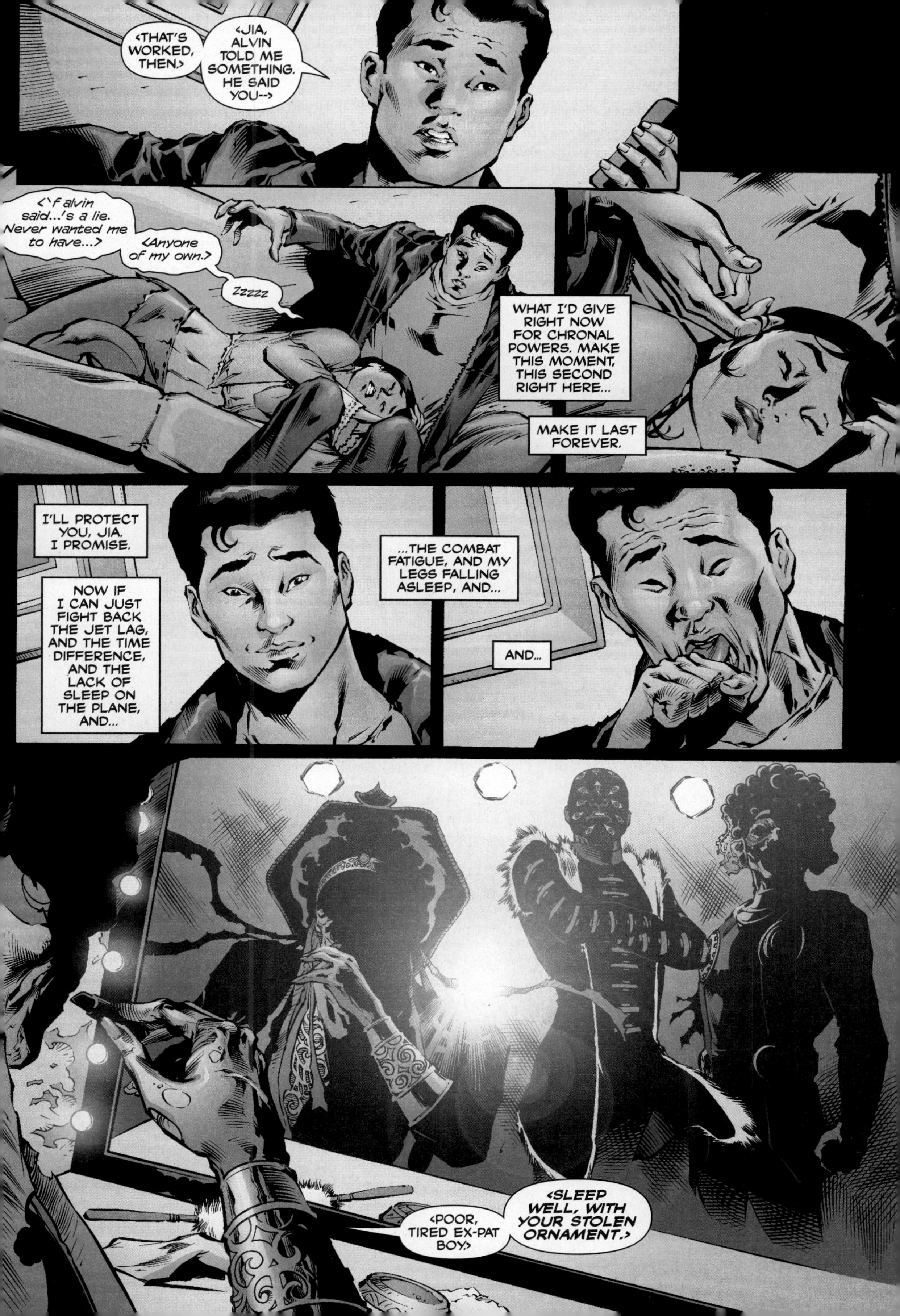

<THAT'S WORKED, THEN.>
<JIA, ALVIN TOLD ME SOMETHING. HE SAID YOU-->
<'f alvin said...'s a lie. Never wanted me to have...>
<Anyone of my own.>
Zzzzz
WHAT I'D GIVE RIGHT NOW FOR CHRONAL POWERS. MAKE THIS MOMENT, THIS SECOND RIGHT HERE...
MAKE IT LAST FOREVER.
I'LL PROTECT YOU, JIA. I PROMISE.
NOW IF I CAN JUST FIGHT BACK THE JET LAG, AND THE TIME DIFFERENCE, AND THE LACK OF SLEEP ON THE PLANE, AND...
...THE COMBAT FATIGUE, AND MY LEGS FALLING ASLEEP, AND...
AND...
<POOR, TIRED EX-PAT BOY.>
<SLEEP WELL, WITH YOUR STOLEN ORNAMENT.>

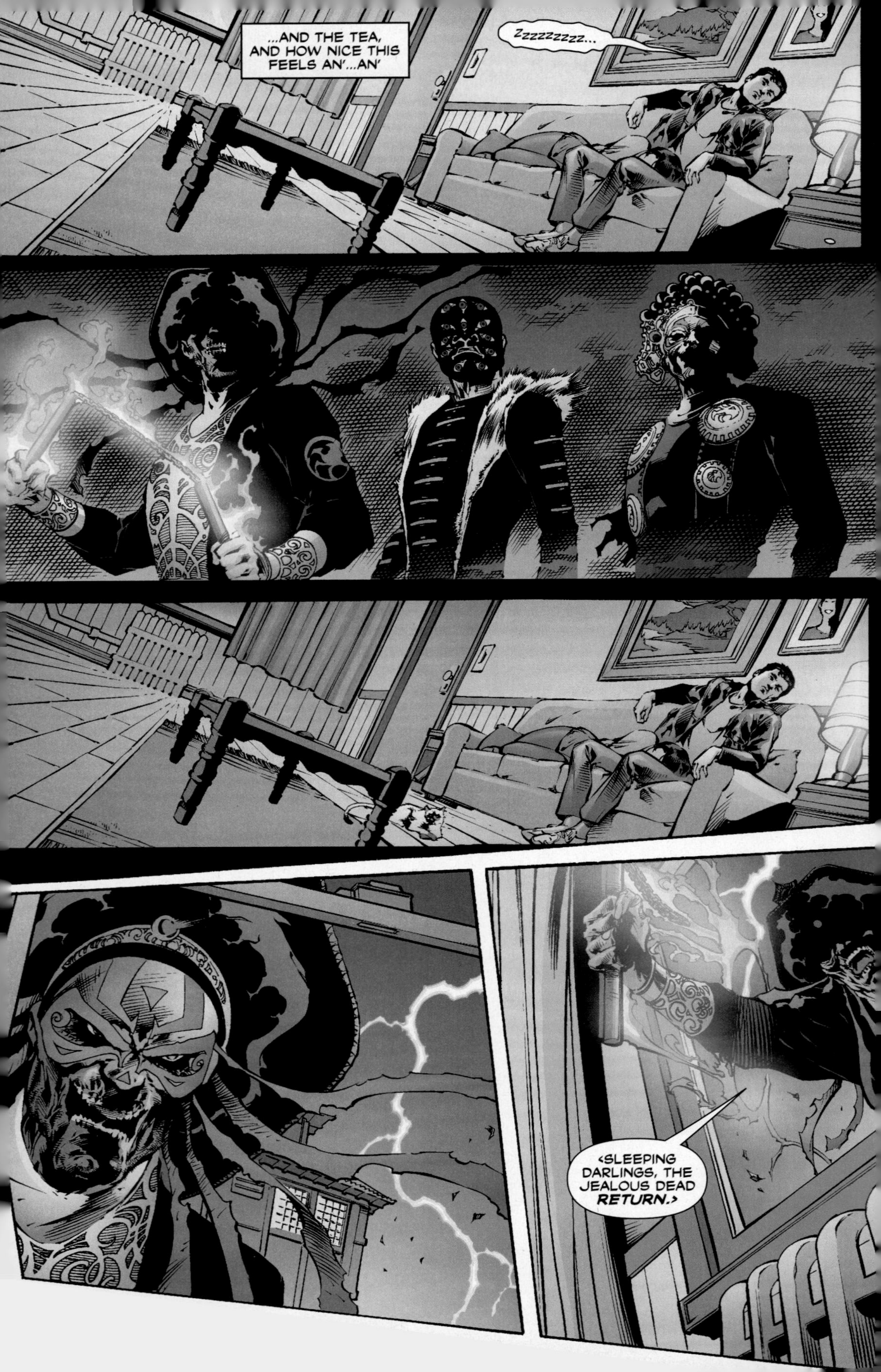

...AND THE TEA, AND HOW NICE THIS FEELS AN'...AN'
Zzzzzzzzz...
‹SLEEPING DARLINGS, THE JEALOUS DEAD **RETURN.**›

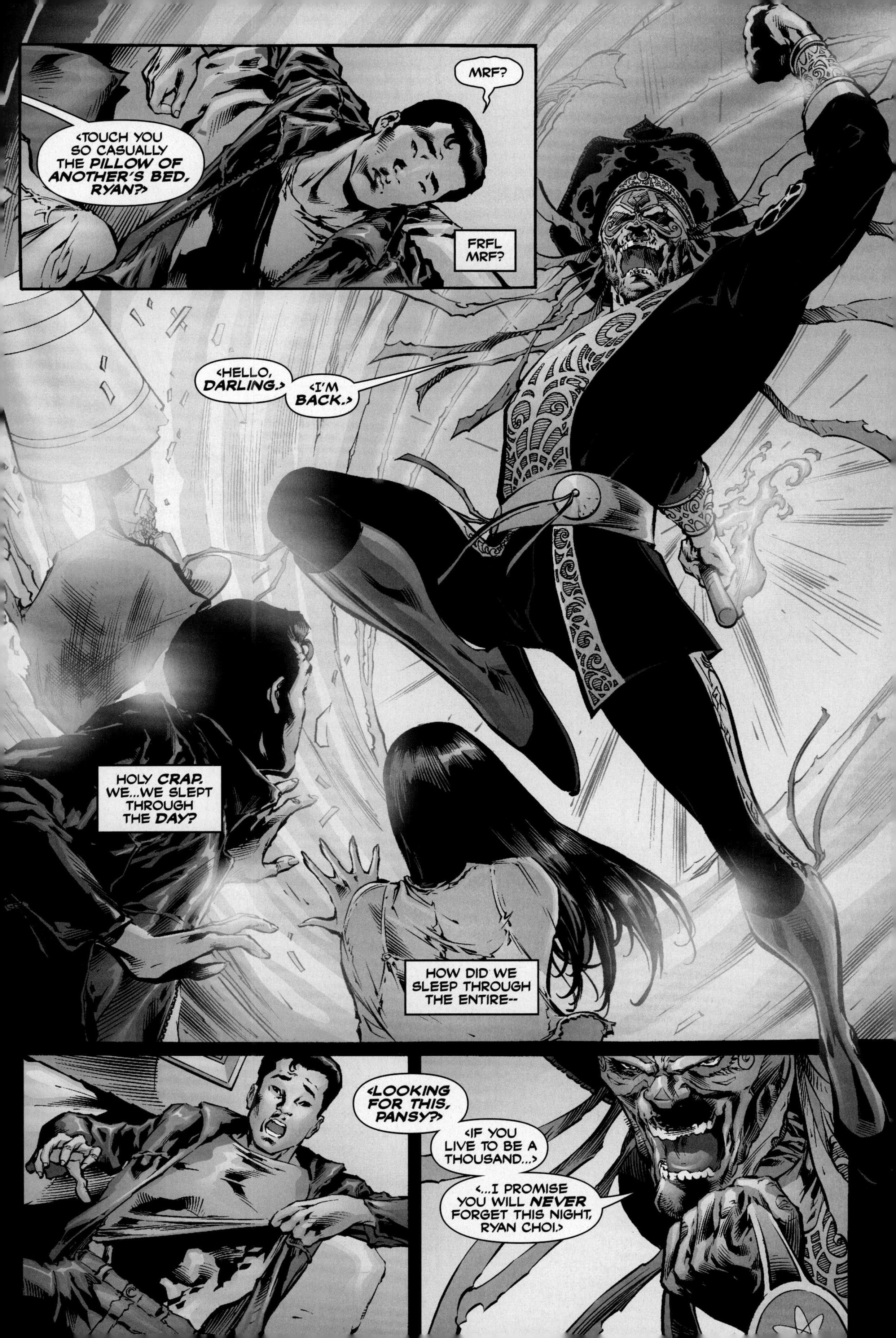

MRF?
<TOUCH YOU SO CASUALLY THE PILLOW OF ANOTHER'S BED, RYAN?>
FRFL MRF?
<HELLO, DARLING.>
<I'M BACK.>
HOLY CRAP. WE...WE SLEPT THROUGH THE DAY?
HOW DID WE SLEEP THROUGH THE ENTIRE--
<LOOKING FOR THIS, PANSY?>
<IF YOU LIVE TO BE A THOUSAND...>
<...I PROMISE YOU WILL NEVER FORGET THIS NIGHT, RYAN CHOI.>

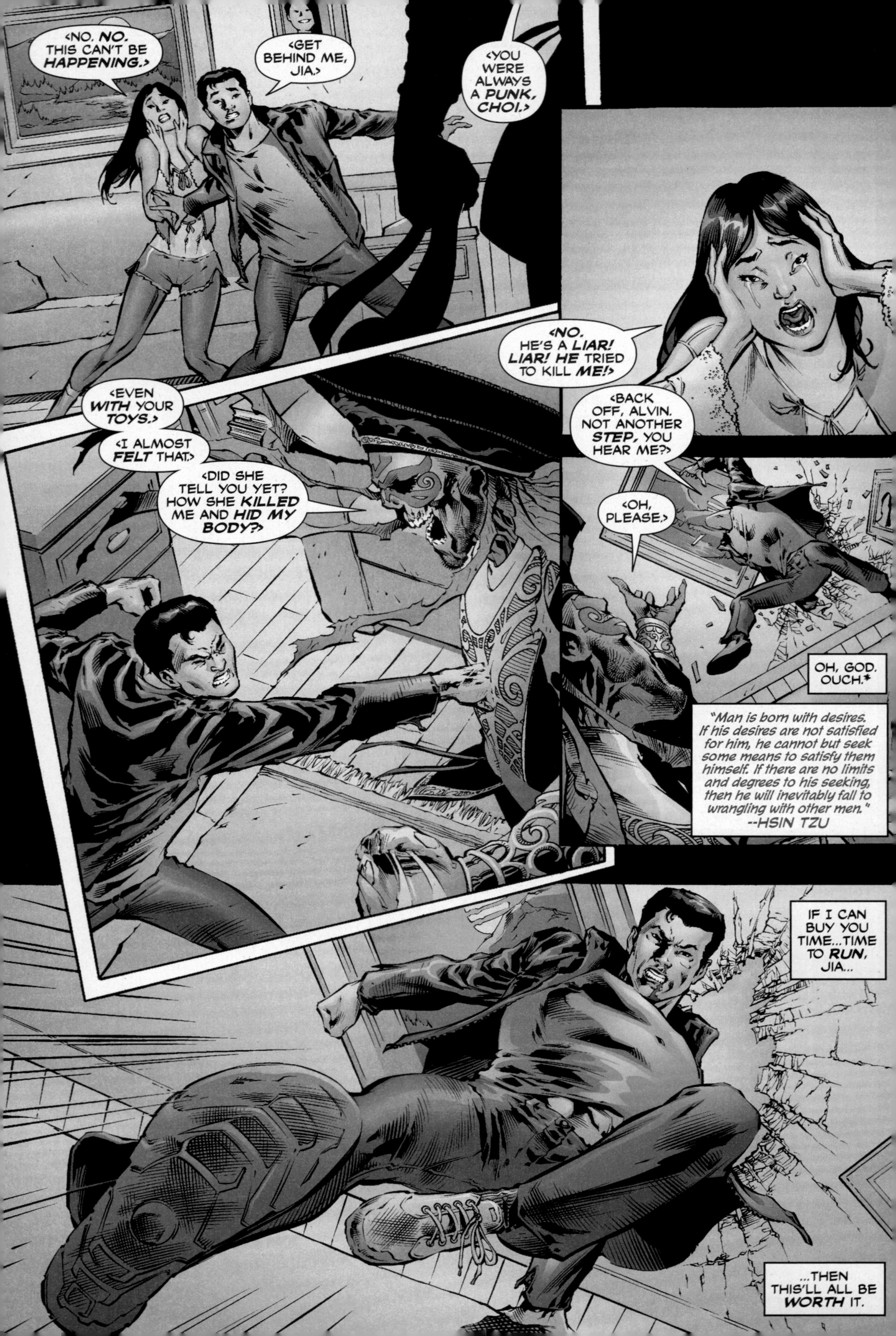
<NO, NO. THIS CAN'T BE HAPPENING.>
<GET BEHIND ME, JIA.>
<YOU WERE ALWAYS A PUNK, CHOI.>
<NO. HE'S A LIAR! LIAR! HE TRIED TO KILL ME!>
<BACK OFF, ALVIN. NOT ANOTHER STEP, YOU HEAR ME?>
<OH, PLEASE.>
OH, GOD. OUCH.*
"Man is born with desires. If his desires are not satisfied for him, he cannot but seek some means to satisfy them himself. If there are no limits and degrees to his seeking, then he will inevitably fall to wrangling with other men." --HSIN TZU
<EVEN WITH YOUR TOYS.>
<I ALMOST FELT THAT.>
<DID SHE TELL YOU YET? HOW SHE KILLED ME AND HID MY BODY?>
IF I CAN BUY YOU TIME...TIME TO RUN, JIA...
...THEN THIS'LL ALL BE WORTH IT.

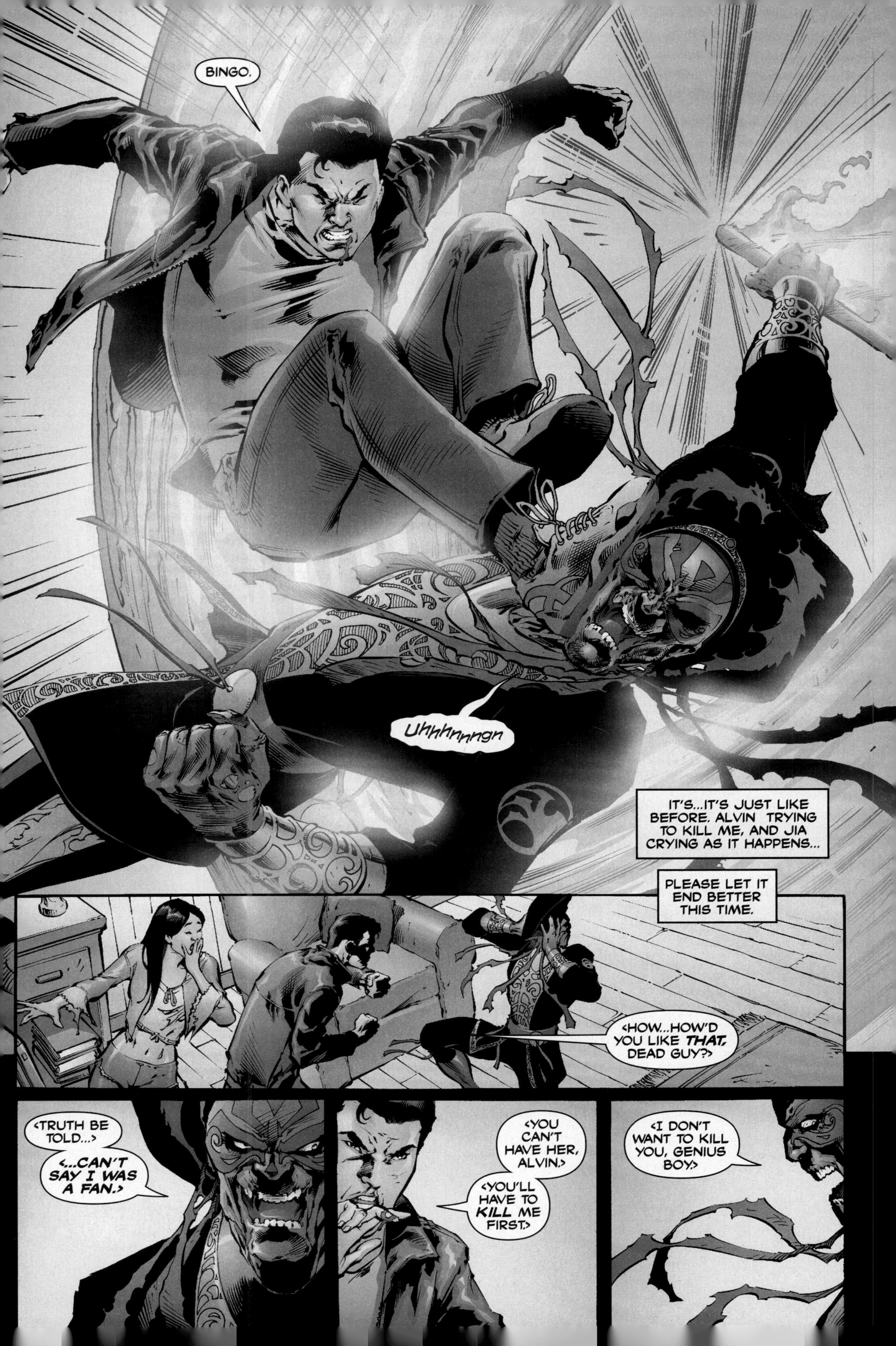
BINGO.
Uhhhnnngn
IT'S...IT'S JUST LIKE BEFORE. ALVIN TRYING TO KILL ME, AND JIA CRYING AS IT HAPPENS...
PLEASE LET IT END BETTER THIS TIME.
<HOW...HOW'D YOU LIKE THAT, DEAD GUY?>
<TRUTH BE TOLD...>
<...CAN'T SAY I WAS A FAN.>
<YOU CAN'T HAVE HER, ALVIN.>
<YOU'LL HAVE TO KILL ME FIRST.>
<I DON'T WANT TO KILL YOU, GENIUS BOY.>

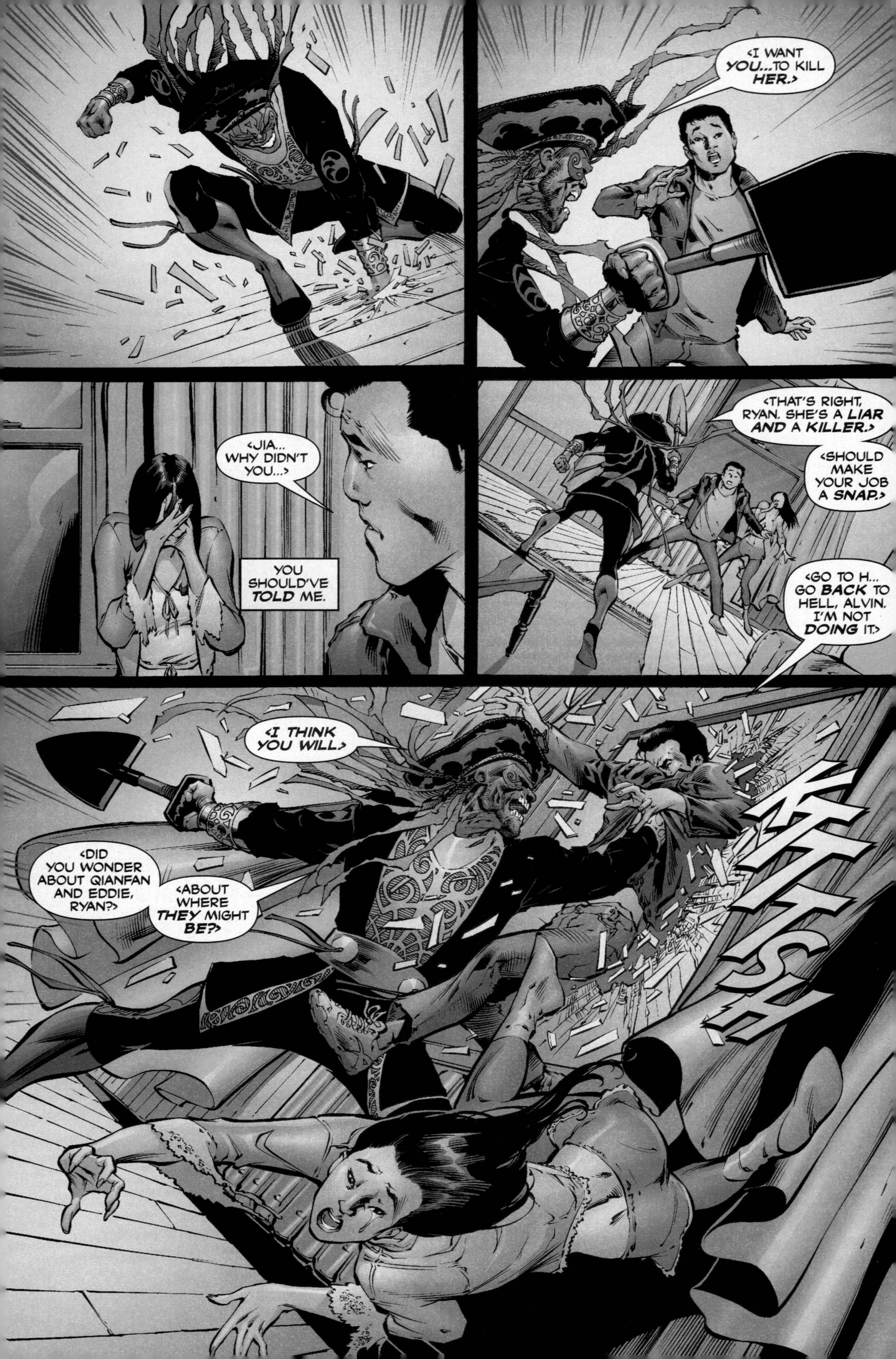

<I WANT YOU...TO KILL HER.>
<JIA... WHY DIDN'T YOU...>
YOU SHOULD'VE TOLD ME.
<THAT'S RIGHT, RYAN. SHE'S A LIAR AND A KILLER.>
<SHOULD MAKE YOUR JOB A SNAP.>
<GO TO H... GO BACK TO HELL, ALVIN. I'M NOT DOING IT.>
<I THINK YOU WILL.>
<DID YOU WONDER ABOUT QIANFAN AND EDDIE, RYAN?>
<ABOUT WHERE THEY MIGHT BE?>
KTTTSSH

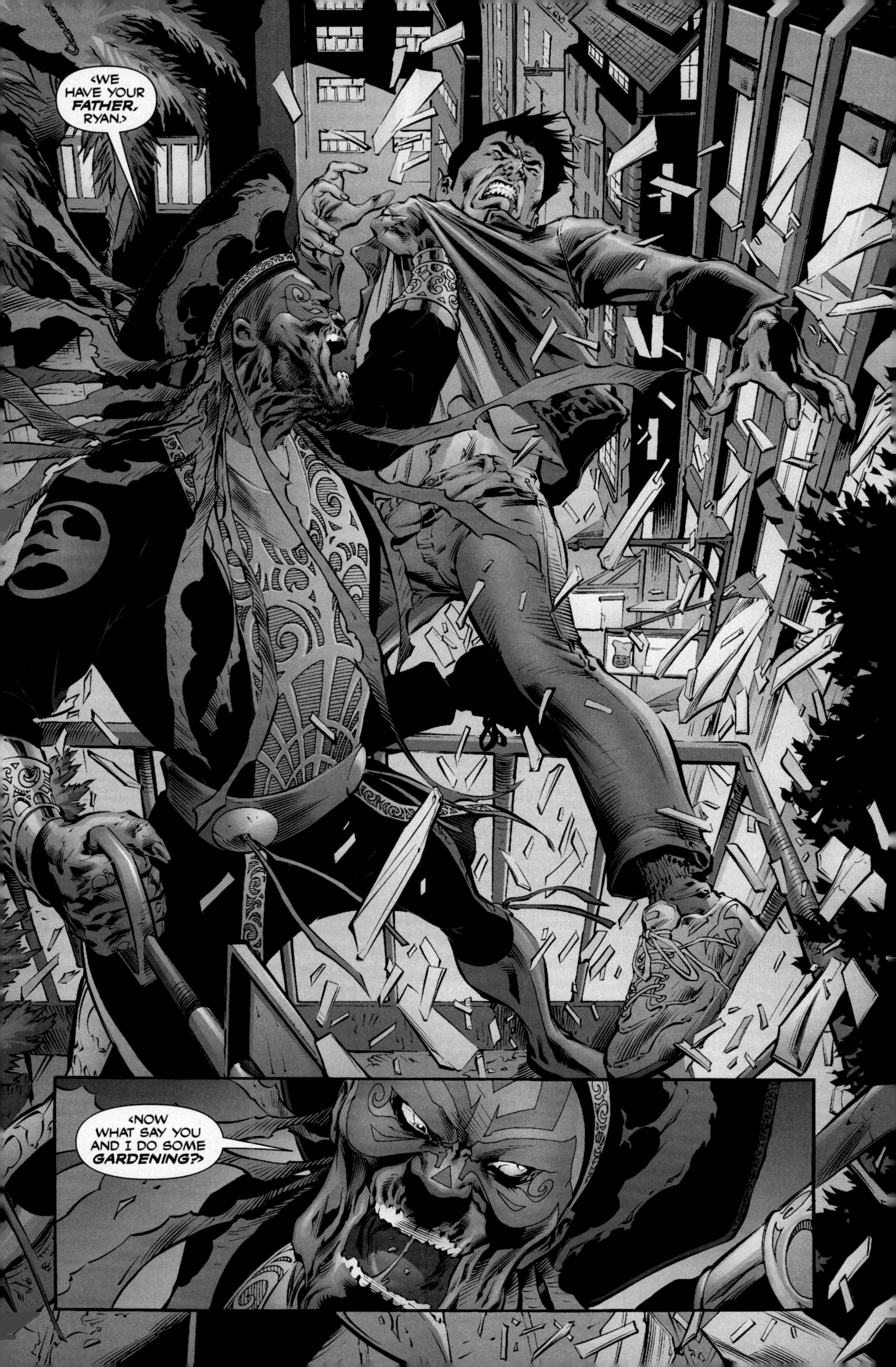
<WE HAVE YOUR FATHER, RYAN.>
<NOW WHAT SAY YOU AND I DO SOME GARDENING?>

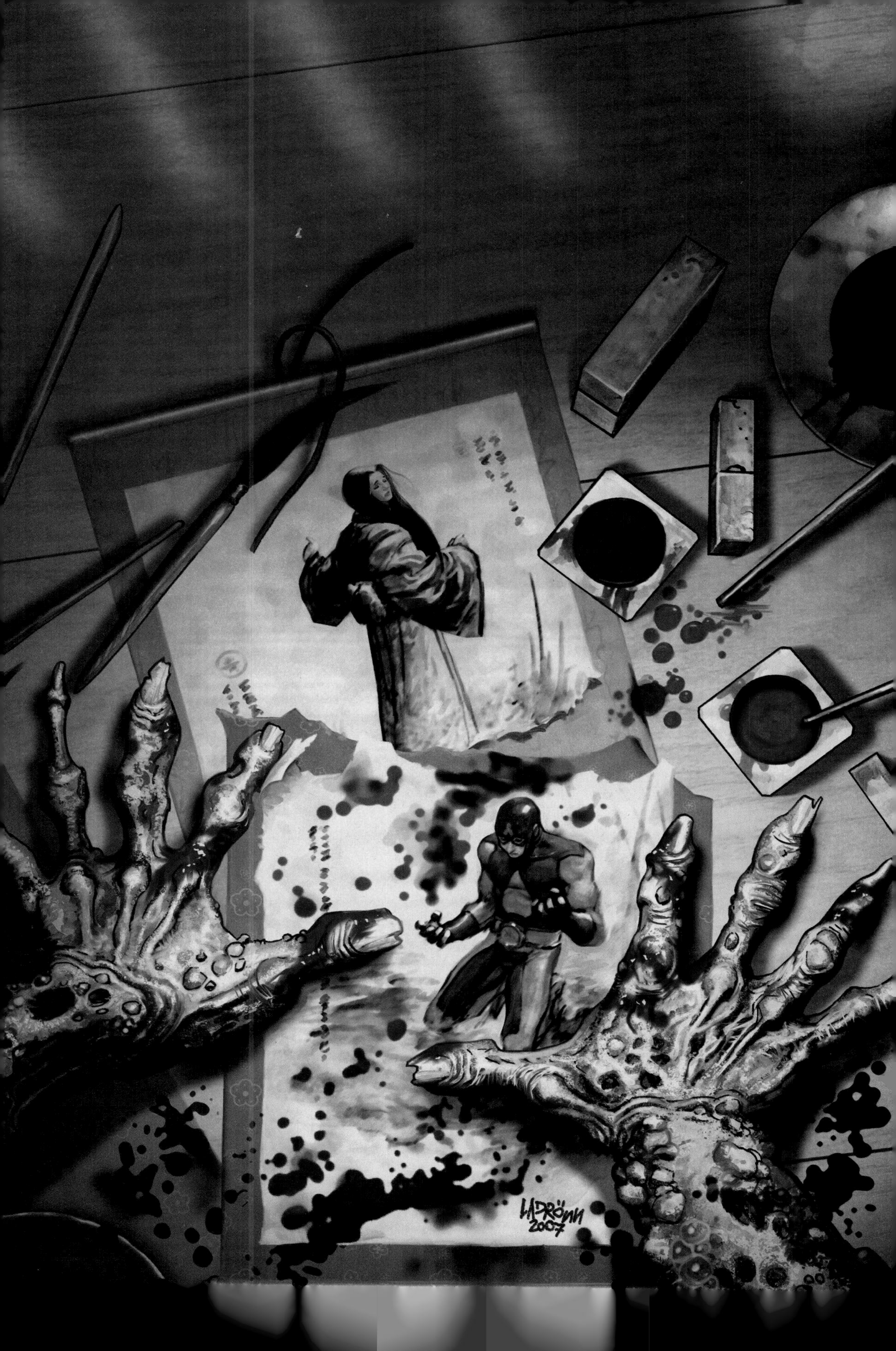
LAPRÖNN
2007

JIA: PART THREE
THE BORDER BETWEEN

from **THE ALL NEW ATOM #11**

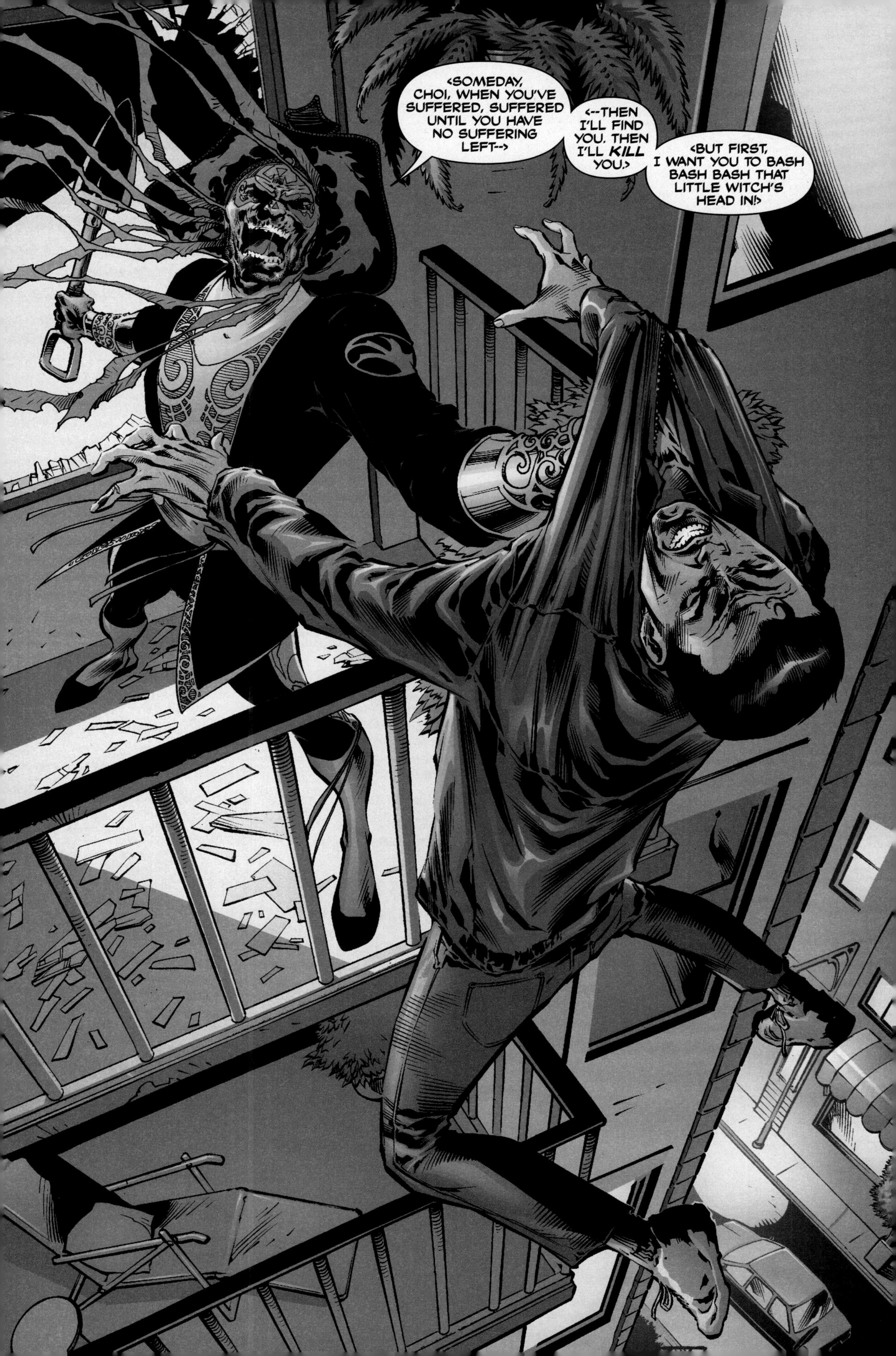
<SOMEDAY, CHOI, WHEN YOU'VE SUFFERED, SUFFERED UNTIL YOU HAVE NO SUFFERING LEFT-->
<--THEN I'LL FIND YOU. THEN I'LL **KILL** YOU.>
<BUT FIRST, I WANT YOU TO BASH BASH BASH THAT LITTLE WITCH'S HEAD IN!>

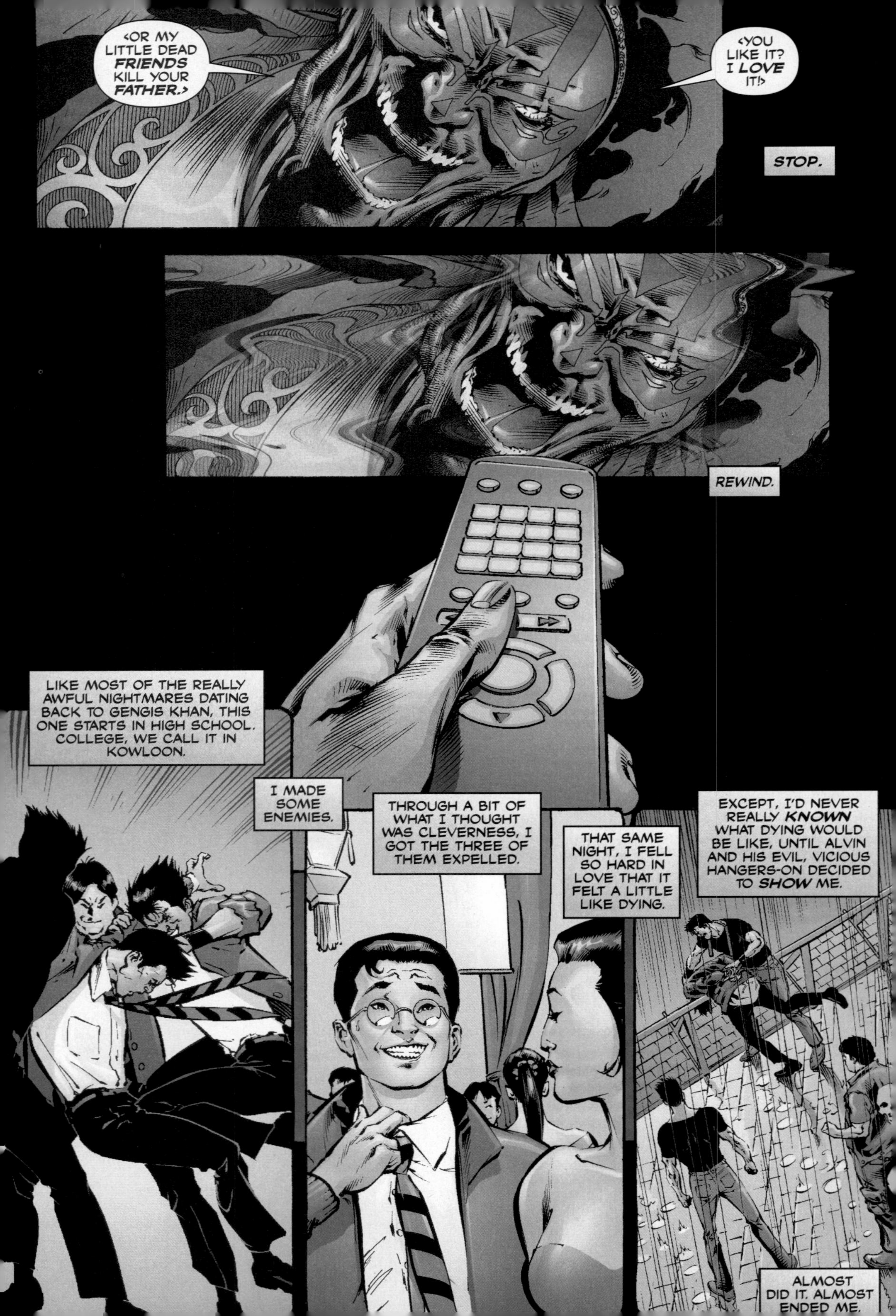

‹OR MY LITTLE DEAD **FRIENDS** KILL YOUR **FATHER.**›
‹YOU LIKE IT? I **LOVE** IT!›
STOP.
REWIND.
LIKE MOST OF THE REALLY AWFUL NIGHTMARES DATING BACK TO GENGIS KHAN, THIS ONE STARTS IN HIGH SCHOOL. COLLEGE, WE CALL IT IN KOWLOON.
I MADE SOME ENEMIES.
THROUGH A BIT OF WHAT I THOUGHT WAS CLEVERNESS, I GOT THE THREE OF THEM EXPELLED.
THAT SAME NIGHT, I FELL SO HARD IN LOVE THAT IT FELT A LITTLE LIKE DYING.
EXCEPT, I'D NEVER REALLY **KNOWN** WHAT DYING WOULD BE LIKE, UNTIL ALVIN AND HIS EVIL, VICIOUS HANGERS-ON DECIDED TO **SHOW** ME.
ALMOST DID IT. ALMOST ENDED ME.

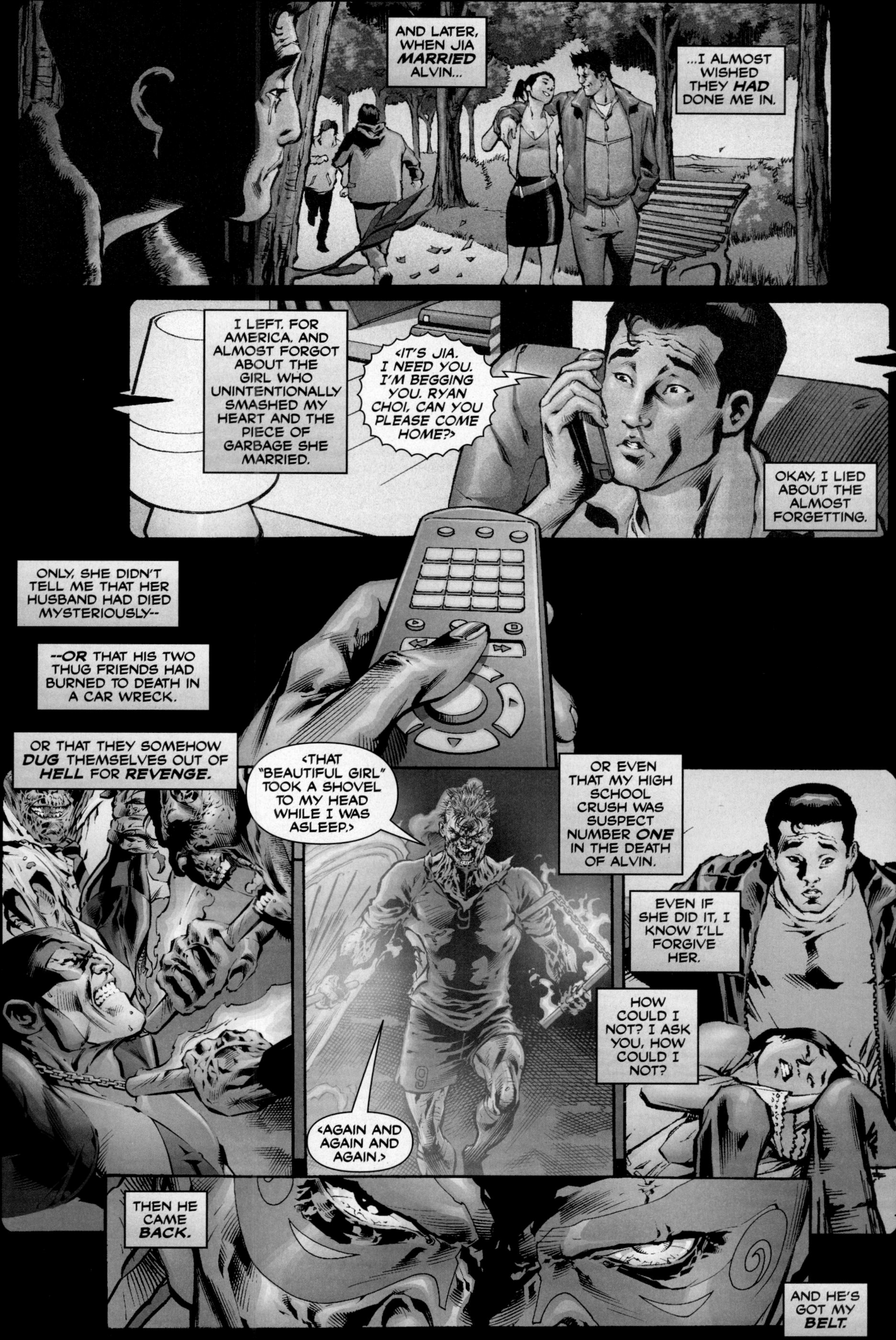
AND LATER, WHEN JIA MARRIED ALVIN...
...I ALMOST WISHED THEY HAD DONE ME IN.
I LEFT. FOR AMERICA. AND ALMOST FORGOT ABOUT THE GIRL WHO UNINTENTIONALLY SMASHED MY HEART AND THE PIECE OF GARBAGE SHE MARRIED.
<IT'S JIA. I NEED YOU. I'M BEGGING YOU. RYAN CHOI, CAN YOU PLEASE COME HOME?>
OKAY, I LIED ABOUT THE ALMOST FORGETTING.
ONLY, SHE DIDN'T TELL ME THAT HER HUSBAND HAD DIED MYSTERIOUSLY--
--OR THAT HIS TWO THUG FRIENDS HAD BURNED TO DEATH IN A CAR WRECK.
OR THAT THEY SOMEHOW DUG THEMSELVES OUT OF HELL FOR REVENGE.
<THAT "BEAUTIFUL GIRL" TOOK A SHOVEL TO MY HEAD WHILE I WAS ASLEEP.>
<AGAIN AND AGAIN AND AGAIN.>
OR EVEN THAT MY HIGH SCHOOL CRUSH WAS SUSPECT NUMBER ONE IN THE DEATH OF ALVIN.
EVEN IF SHE DID IT, I KNOW I'LL FORGIVE HER.
HOW COULD I NOT? I ASK YOU, HOW COULD I NOT?
THEN HE CAME BACK.
AND HE'S GOT MY BELT.

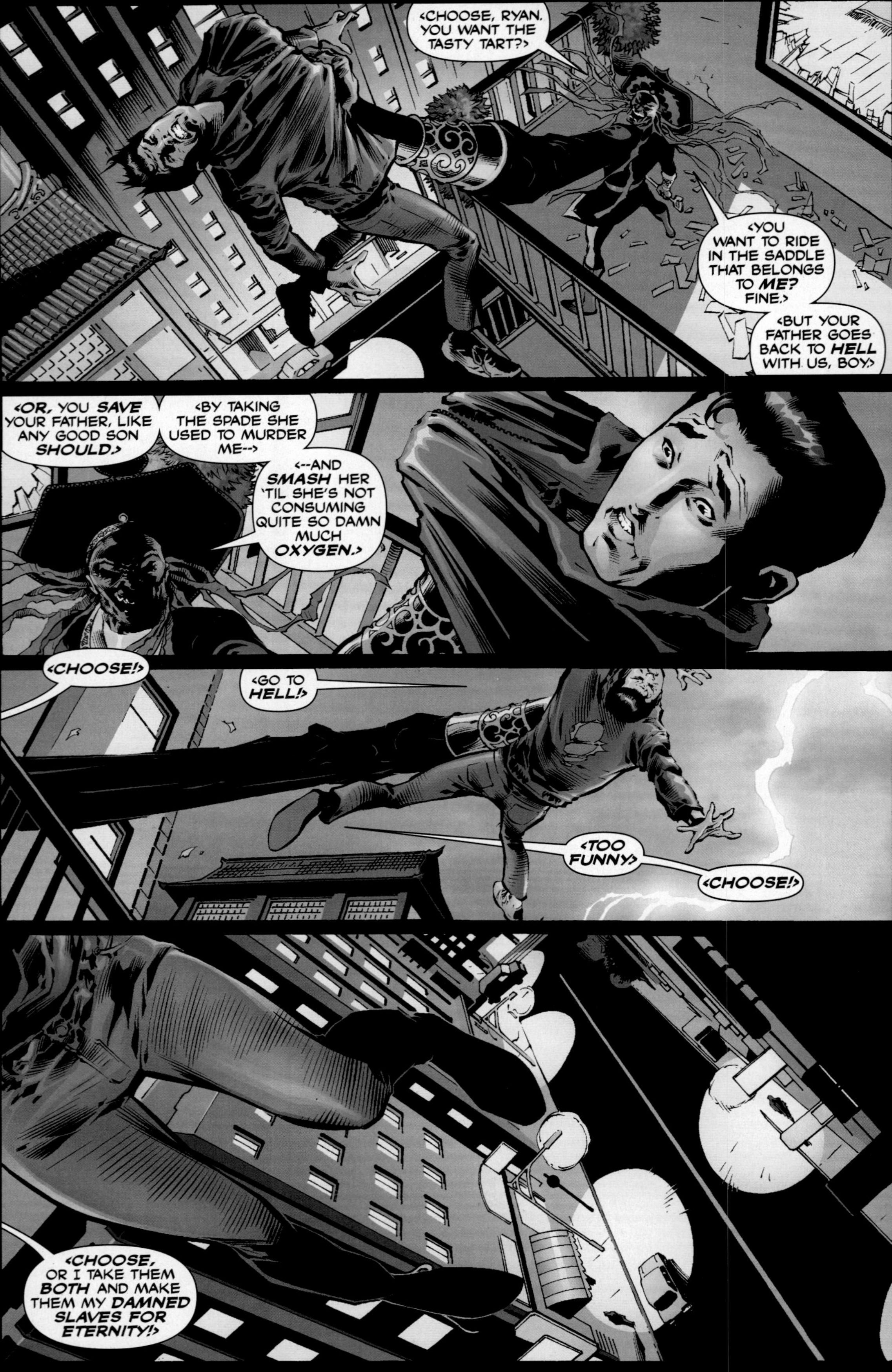
‹CHOOSE, RYAN. YOU WANT THE TASTY TART?›
‹YOU WANT TO RIDE IN THE SADDLE THAT BELONGS TO ***ME?*** FINE.›
‹BUT YOUR FATHER GOES BACK TO ***HELL*** WITH US, BOY.›
‹***OR,*** YOU ***SAVE*** YOUR FATHER, LIKE ANY GOOD SON ***SHOULD.***›
‹BY TAKING THE SPADE SHE USED TO MURDER ME--›
‹--AND ***SMASH*** HER 'TIL SHE'S NOT CONSUMING QUITE SO DAMN MUCH ***OXYGEN.***›
‹CHOOSE!›
‹GO TO ***HELL!***›
‹TOO FUNNY.›
‹CHOOSE!›
‹***CHOOSE,*** OR I TAKE THEM ***BOTH*** AND MAKE THEM MY ***DAMNED SLAVES FOR ETERNITY!***›

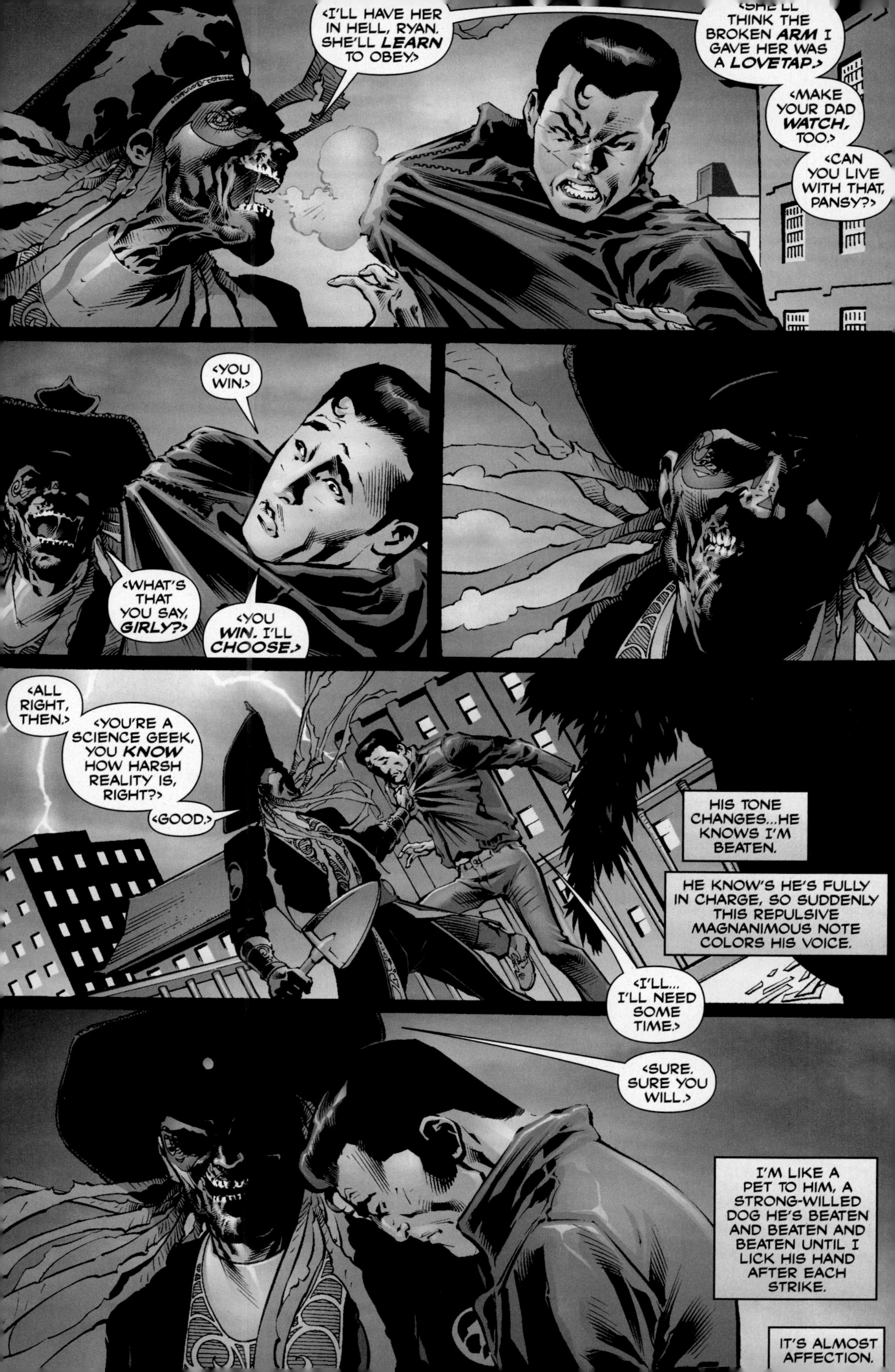

<I'LL HAVE HER IN HELL, RYAN. SHE'LL LEARN TO OBEY.>
<SHE'LL THINK THE BROKEN ARM I GAVE HER WAS A LOVETAP.>
<MAKE YOUR DAD WATCH, TOO.>
<CAN YOU LIVE WITH THAT, PANSY?>
<YOU WIN.>
<WHAT'S THAT YOU SAY, GIRLY?>
<YOU WIN. I'LL CHOOSE.>
<ALL RIGHT, THEN.>
<YOU'RE A SCIENCE GEEK, YOU KNOW HOW HARSH REALITY IS, RIGHT?>
<GOOD.>
HIS TONE CHANGES...HE KNOWS I'M BEATEN.
HE KNOW'S HE'S FULLY IN CHARGE, SO SUDDENLY THIS REPULSIVE MAGNANIMOUS NOTE COLORS HIS VOICE.
<I'LL... I'LL NEED SOME TIME.>
<SURE. SURE YOU WILL.>
I'M LIKE A PET TO HIM, A STRONG-WILLED DOG HE'S BEATEN AND BEATEN AND BEATEN UNTIL I LICK HIS HAND AFTER EACH STRIKE.
IT'S ALMOST AFFECTION.

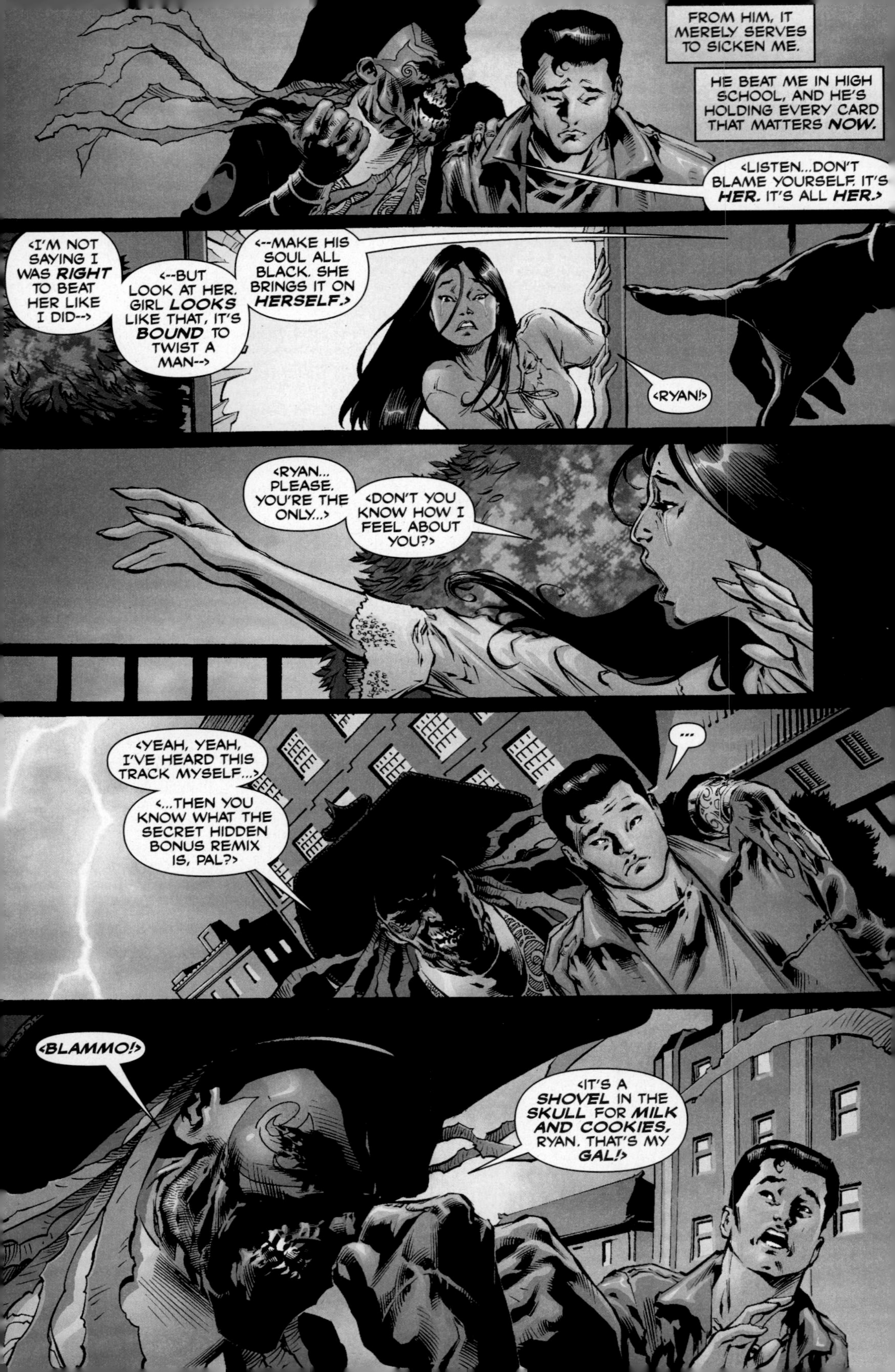
FROM HIM, IT MERELY SERVES TO SICKEN ME.
HE BEAT ME IN HIGH SCHOOL, AND HE'S HOLDING EVERY CARD THAT MATTERS NOW.
<LISTEN...DON'T BLAME YOURSELF. IT'S HER. IT'S ALL HER.>
<I'M NOT SAYING I WAS RIGHT TO BEAT HER LIKE I DID-->
<--BUT LOOK AT HER. GIRL LOOKS LIKE THAT, IT'S BOUND TO TWIST A MAN-->
<--MAKE HIS SOUL ALL BLACK. SHE BRINGS IT ON HERSELF.>
<RYAN!>
<RYAN... PLEASE. YOU'RE THE ONLY...>
<DON'T YOU KNOW HOW I FEEL ABOUT YOU?>
<YEAH, YEAH, I'VE HEARD THIS TRACK MYSELF...>
<...THEN YOU KNOW WHAT THE SECRET HIDDEN BONUS REMIX IS, PAL?>
...
<BLAMMO!>
<IT'S A SHOVEL IN THE SKULL FOR MILK AND COOKIES, RYAN. THAT'S MY GAL!>

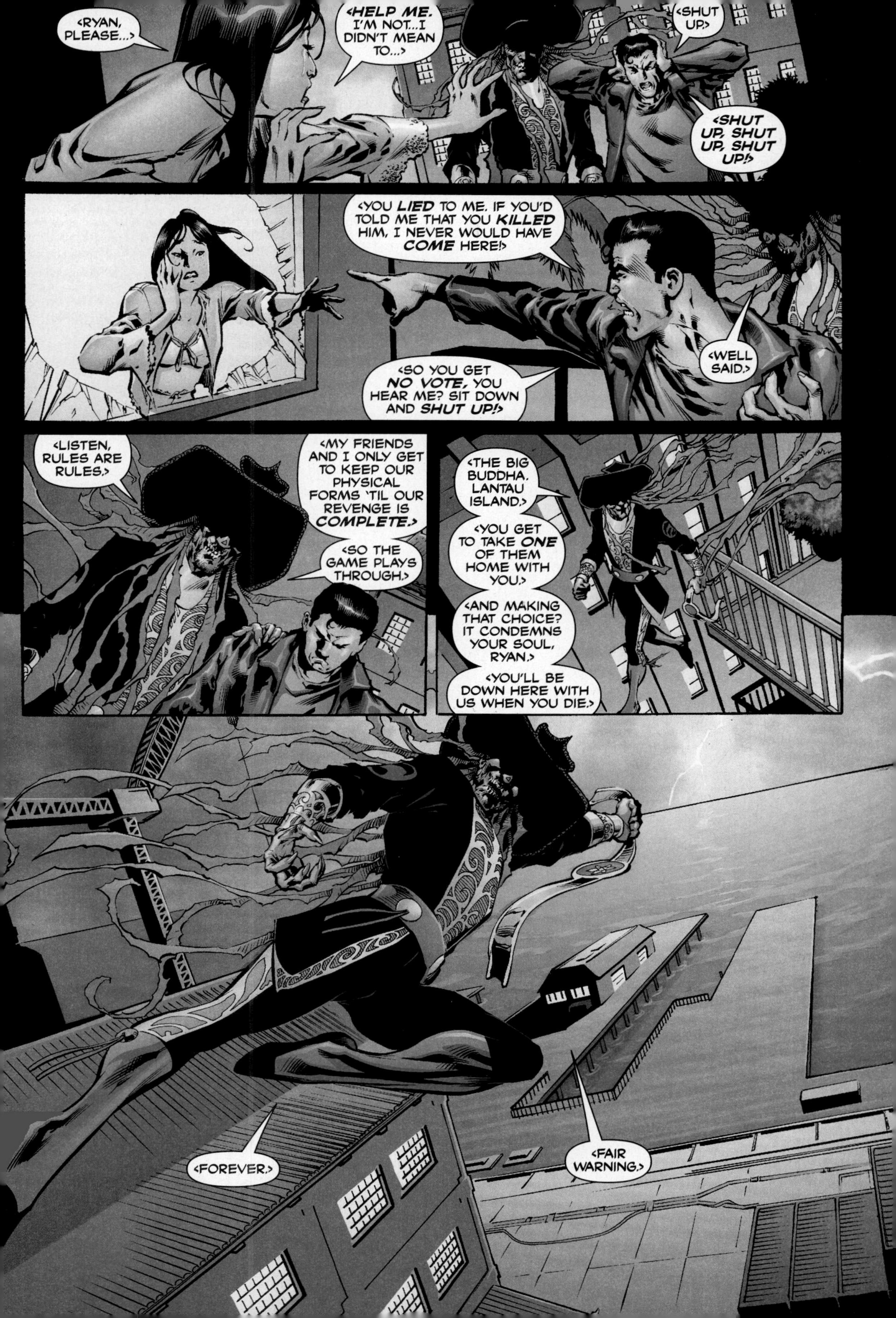

<RYAN, PLEASE...>
<HELP ME. I'M NOT...I DIDN'T MEAN TO...>
<SHUT UP.>
<SHUT UP, SHUT UP, SHUT UP!>
<YOU LIED TO ME. IF YOU'D TOLD ME THAT YOU KILLED HIM, I NEVER WOULD HAVE COME HERE!>
<SO YOU GET NO VOTE, YOU HEAR ME? SIT DOWN AND SHUT UP!>
<WELL SAID.>
<LISTEN, RULES ARE RULES.>
<MY FRIENDS AND I ONLY GET TO KEEP OUR PHYSICAL FORMS 'TIL OUR REVENGE IS COMPLETE.>
<SO THE GAME PLAYS THROUGH.>
<THE BIG BUDDHA, LANTAU ISLAND.>
<YOU GET TO TAKE ONE OF THEM HOME WITH YOU.>
<AND MAKING THAT CHOICE? IT CONDEMNS YOUR SOUL, RYAN.>
<YOU'LL BE DOWN HERE WITH US WHEN YOU DIE.>
<FAIR WARNING.>
<FOREVER.>

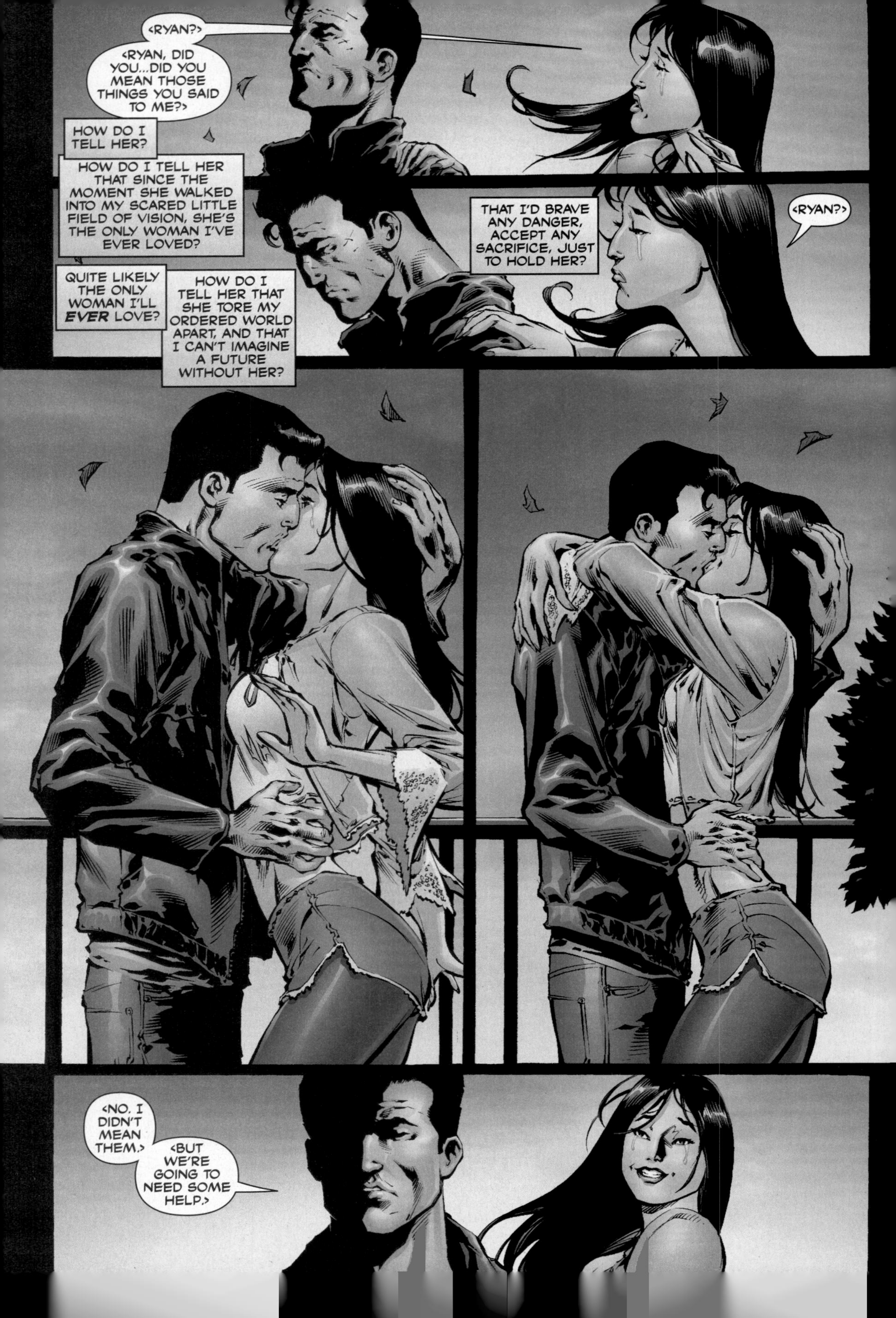

<RYAN?>
<RYAN, DID YOU...DID YOU MEAN THOSE THINGS YOU SAID TO ME?>
HOW DO I TELL HER?
HOW DO I TELL HER THAT SINCE THE MOMENT SHE WALKED INTO MY SCARED LITTLE FIELD OF VISION, SHE'S THE ONLY WOMAN I'VE EVER LOVED?
THAT I'D BRAVE ANY DANGER, ACCEPT ANY SACRIFICE, JUST TO HOLD HER?
<RYAN?>
QUITE LIKELY THE ONLY WOMAN I'LL EVER LOVE?
HOW DO I TELL HER THAT SHE TORE MY ORDERED WORLD APART, AND THAT I CAN'T IMAGINE A FUTURE WITHOUT HER?
<NO. I DIDN'T MEAN THEM.>
<BUT WE'RE GOING TO NEED SOME HELP.>

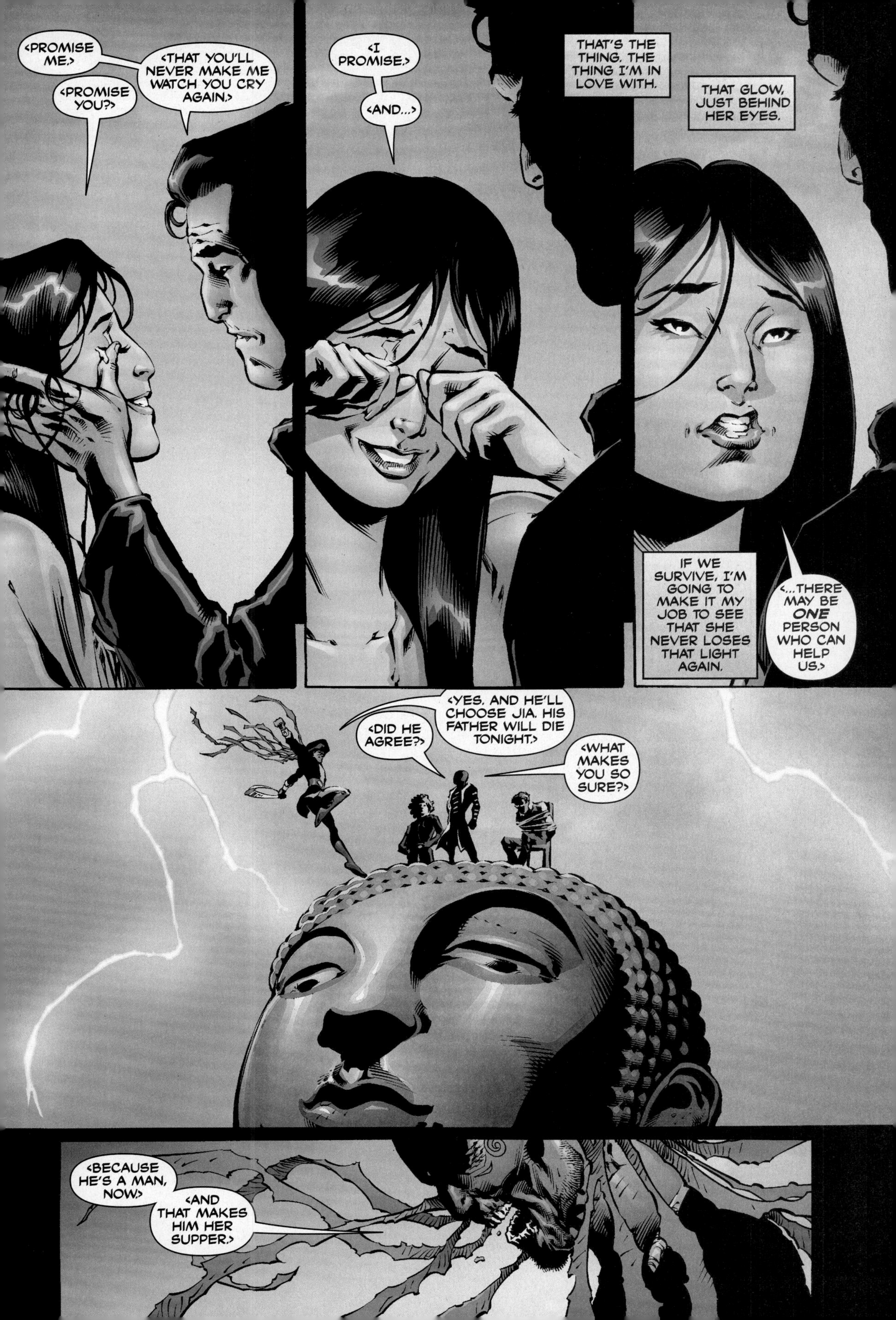
<PROMISE ME.>
<PROMISE YOU?>
<THAT YOU'LL NEVER MAKE ME WATCH YOU CRY AGAIN.>
<I PROMISE.>
<AND...>
THAT'S THE THING. THE THING I'M IN LOVE WITH.
THAT GLOW, JUST BEHIND HER EYES.
IF WE SURVIVE, I'M GOING TO MAKE IT MY JOB TO SEE THAT SHE NEVER LOSES THAT LIGHT AGAIN.
<...THERE MAY BE ONE PERSON WHO CAN HELP US.>
<DID HE AGREE?>
<YES. AND HE'LL CHOOSE JIA. HIS FATHER WILL DIE TONIGHT.>
<WHAT MAKES YOU SO SURE?>
<BECAUSE HE'S A MAN, NOW.>
<AND THAT MAKES HIM HER SUPPER.>

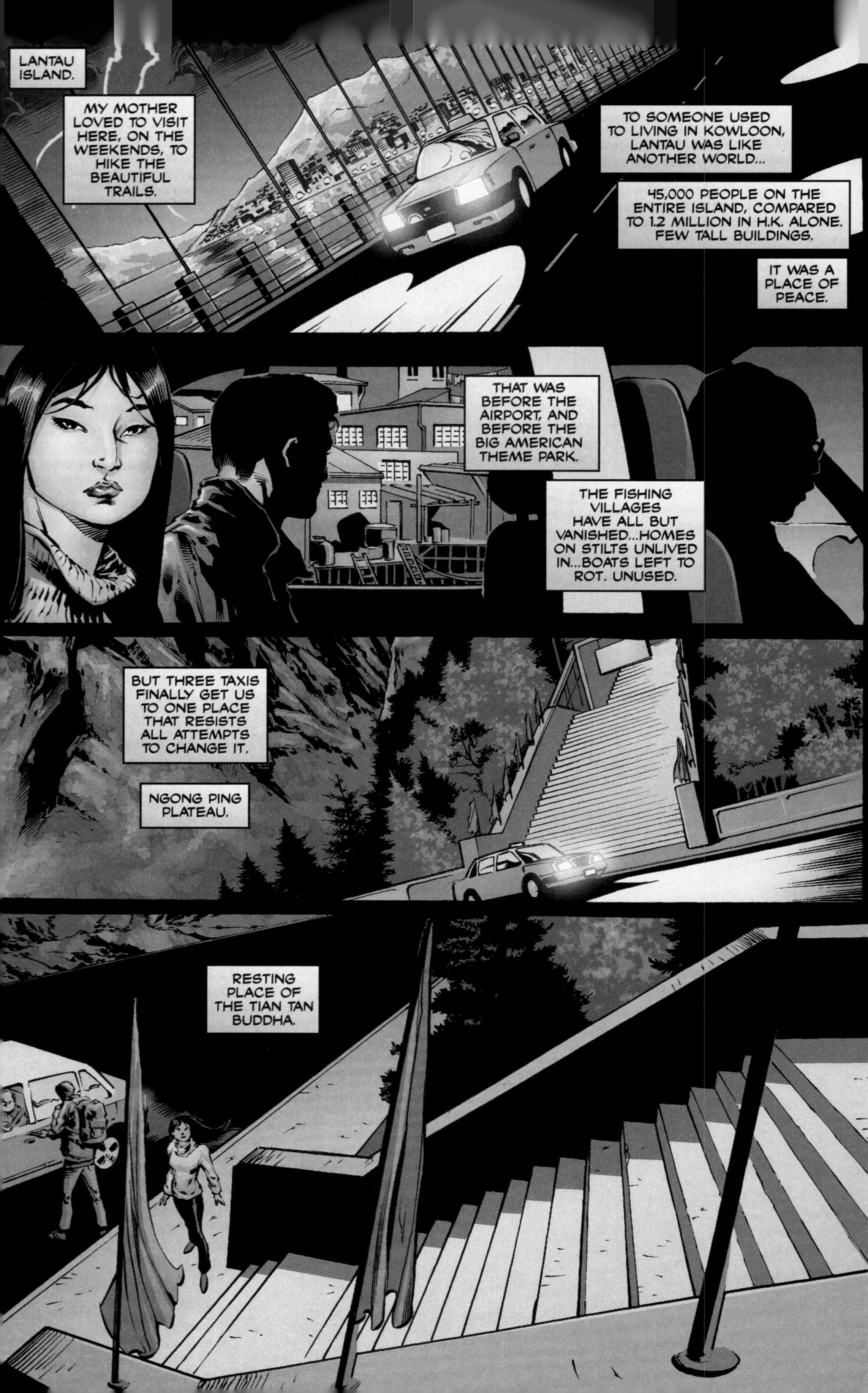
LANTAU ISLAND.
MY MOTHER LOVED TO VISIT HERE, ON THE WEEKENDS, TO HIKE THE BEAUTIFUL TRAILS.
TO SOMEONE USED TO LIVING IN KOWLOON, LANTAU WAS LIKE ANOTHER WORLD...
45,000 PEOPLE ON THE ENTIRE ISLAND, COMPARED TO 1.2 MILLION IN H.K. ALONE. FEW TALL BUILDINGS.
IT WAS A PLACE OF PEACE.
THAT WAS BEFORE THE AIRPORT, AND BEFORE THE BIG AMERICAN THEME PARK.
THE FISHING VILLAGES HAVE ALL BUT VANISHED...HOMES ON STILTS UNLIVED IN...BOATS LEFT TO ROT, UNUSED.
BUT THREE TAXIS FINALLY GET US TO ONE PLACE THAT RESISTS ALL ATTEMPTS TO CHANGE IT.
NGONG PING PLATEAU.
RESTING PLACE OF THE TIAN TAN BUDDHA.

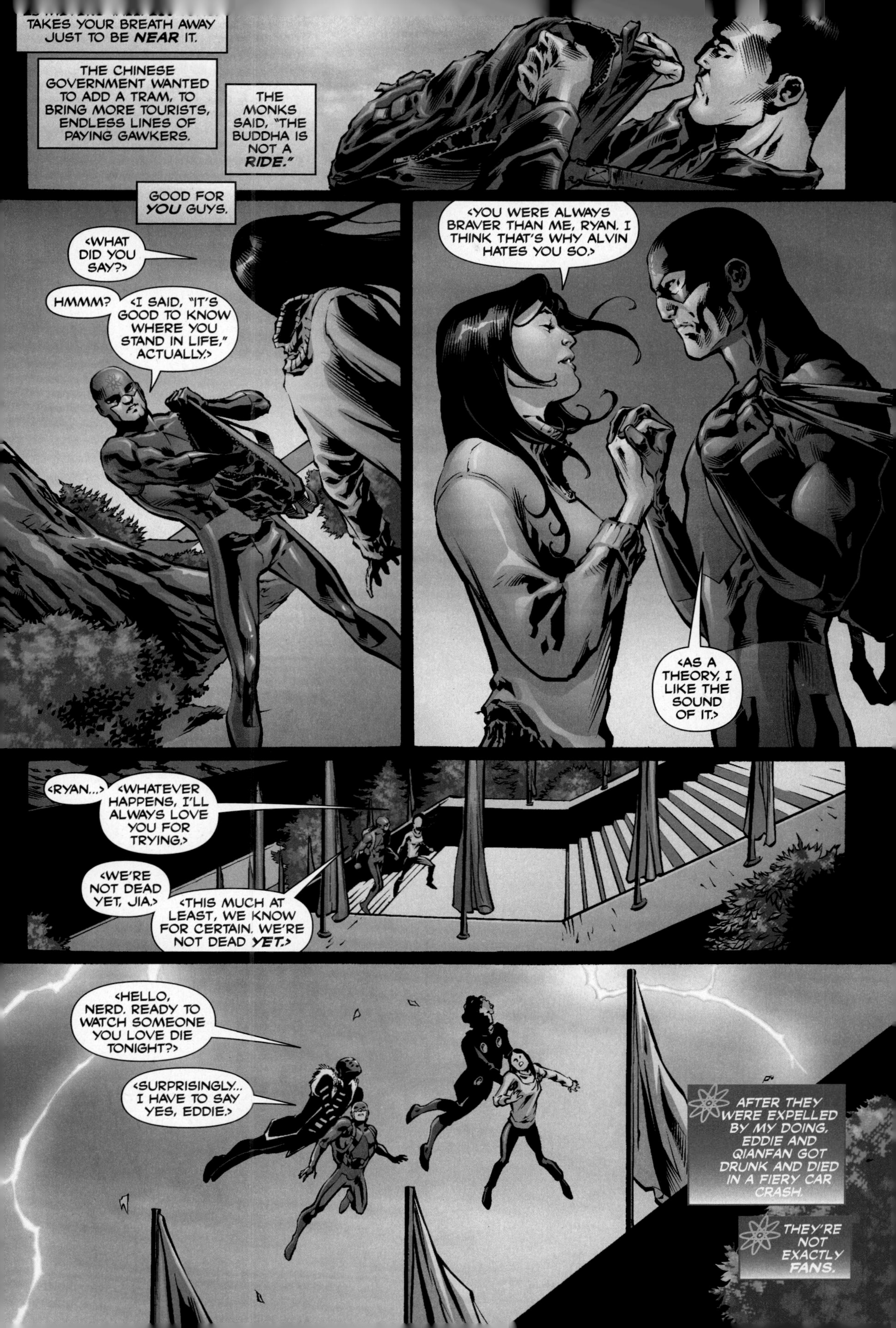
TAKES YOUR BREATH AWAY JUST TO BE NEAR IT.
THE CHINESE GOVERNMENT WANTED TO ADD A TRAM, TO BRING MORE TOURISTS, ENDLESS LINES OF PAYING GAWKERS.
THE MONKS SAID, "THE BUDDHA IS NOT A RIDE."
GOOD FOR YOU GUYS.
‹WHAT DID YOU SAY?›
HMMM?
‹I SAID, "IT'S GOOD TO KNOW WHERE YOU STAND IN LIFE," ACTUALLY.›
‹YOU WERE ALWAYS BRAVER THAN ME, RYAN. I THINK THAT'S WHY ALVIN HATES YOU SO.›
‹AS A THEORY, I LIKE THE SOUND OF IT.›
‹RYAN...›
‹WHATEVER HAPPENS, I'LL ALWAYS LOVE YOU FOR TRYING.›
‹WE'RE NOT DEAD YET, JIA.›
‹THIS MUCH AT LEAST, WE KNOW FOR CERTAIN. WE'RE NOT DEAD YET.›
‹HELLO, NERD. READY TO WATCH SOMEONE YOU LOVE DIE TONIGHT?›
‹SURPRISINGLY... I HAVE TO SAY YES, EDDIE.›
AFTER THEY WERE EXPELLED BY MY DOING, EDDIE AND QIANFAN GOT DRUNK AND DIED IN A FIERY CAR CRASH.
THEY'RE NOT EXACTLY FANS.

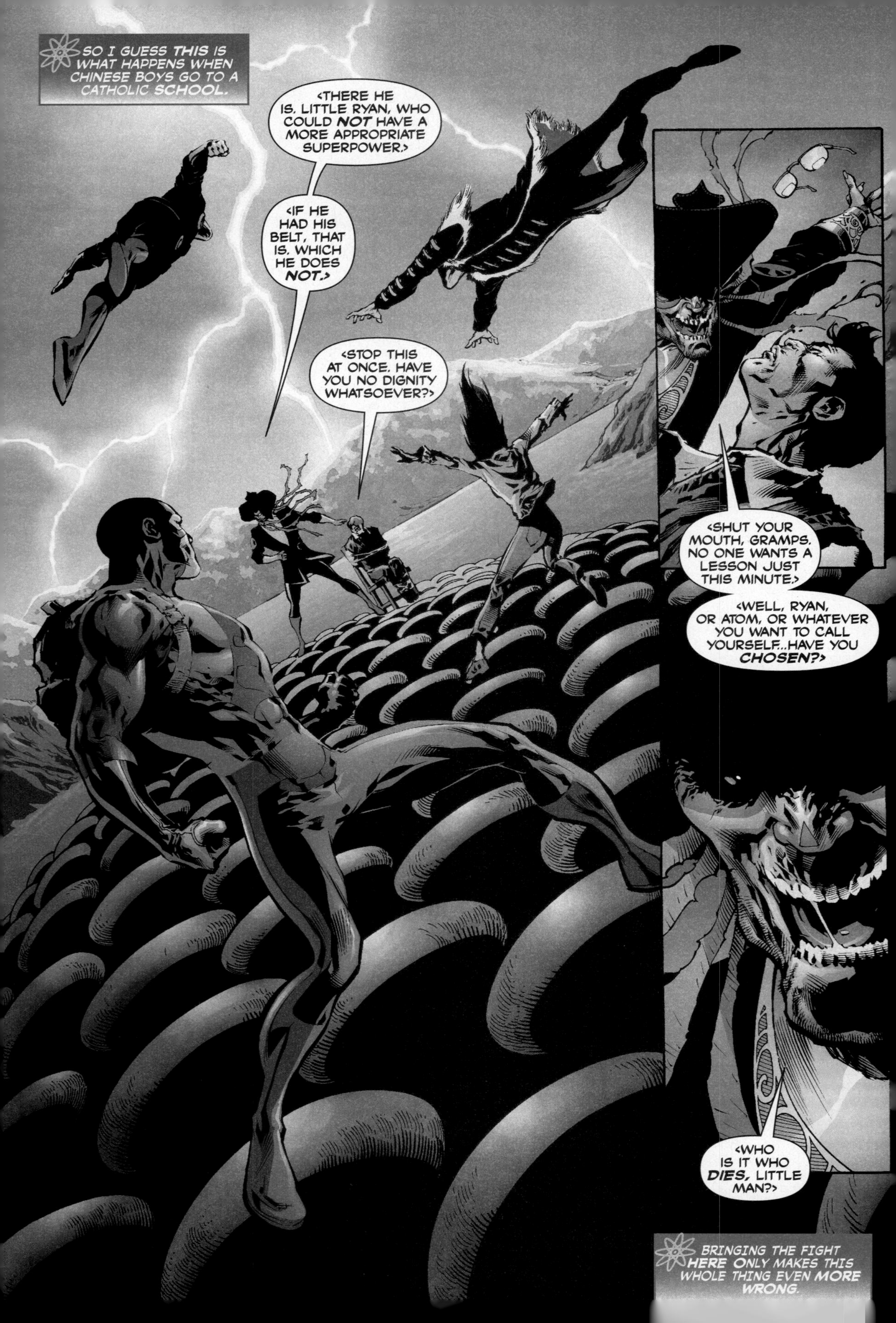
SO I GUESS THIS IS WHAT HAPPENS WHEN CHINESE BOYS GO TO A CATHOLIC SCHOOL.
<THERE HE IS. LITTLE RYAN, WHO COULD NOT HAVE A MORE APPROPRIATE SUPERPOWER.>
<IF HE HAD HIS BELT, THAT IS. WHICH HE DOES NOT.>
<STOP THIS AT ONCE. HAVE YOU NO DIGNITY WHATSOEVER?>
<SHUT YOUR MOUTH, GRAMPS. NO ONE WANTS A LESSON JUST THIS MINUTE.>
<WELL, RYAN, OR ATOM, OR WHATEVER YOU WANT TO CALL YOURSELF...HAVE YOU CHOSEN?>
<WHO IS IT WHO DIES, LITTLE MAN?>
BRINGING THE FIGHT HERE ONLY MAKES THIS WHOLE THING EVEN MORE WRONG.

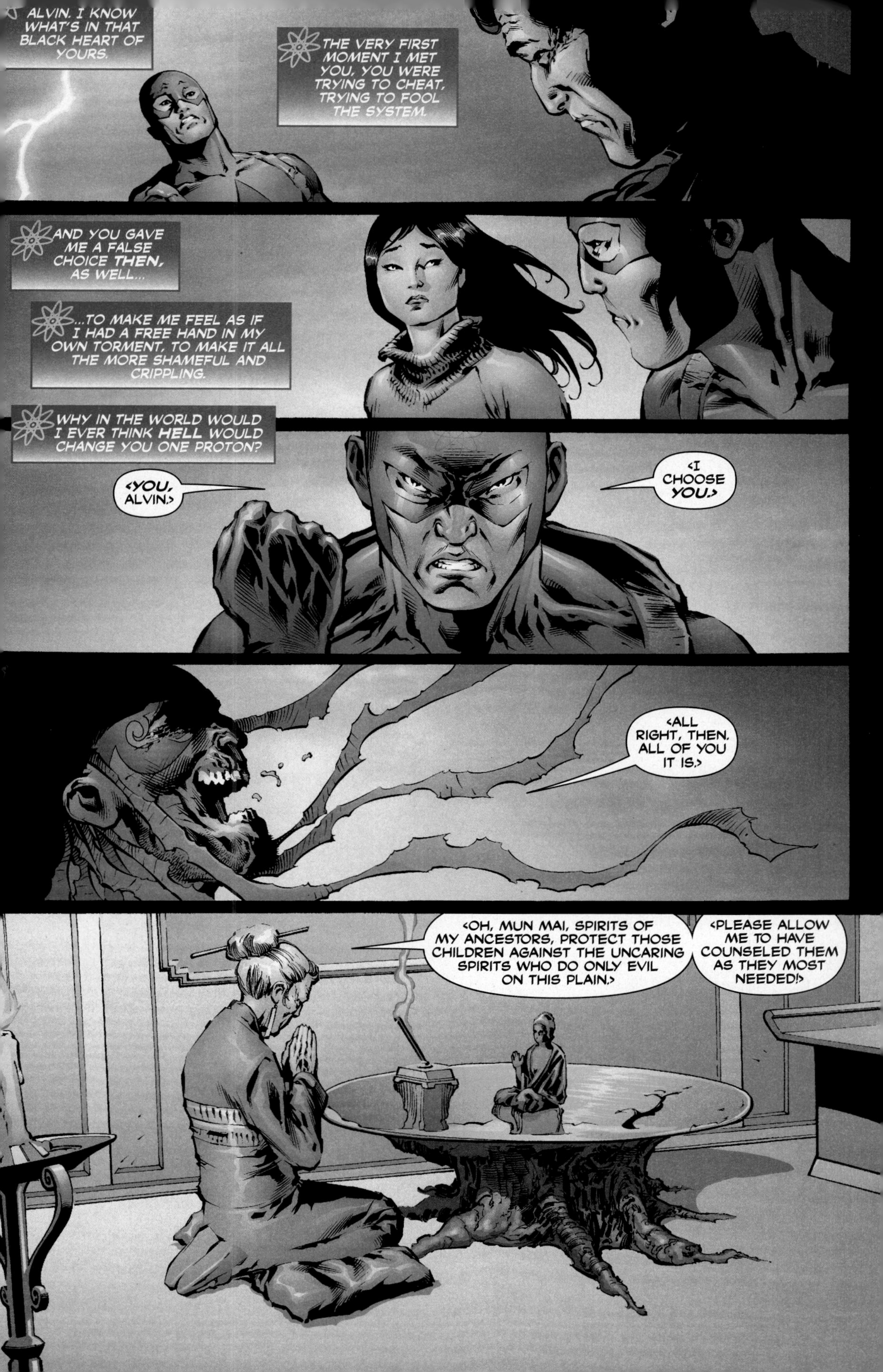
ALVIN. I KNOW WHAT'S IN THAT BLACK HEART OF YOURS.
THE VERY FIRST MOMENT I MET YOU, YOU WERE TRYING TO CHEAT, TRYING TO FOOL THE SYSTEM.
AND YOU GAVE ME A FALSE CHOICE THEN, AS WELL...
...TO MAKE ME FEEL AS IF I HAD A FREE HAND IN MY OWN TORMENT, TO MAKE IT ALL THE MORE SHAMEFUL AND CRIPPLING.
WHY IN THE WORLD WOULD I EVER THINK HELL WOULD CHANGE YOU ONE PROTON?
<YOU, ALVIN.>
<I CHOOSE YOU.>
<ALL RIGHT, THEN. ALL OF YOU IT IS.>
<OH, MUN MAI, SPIRITS OF MY ANCESTORS, PROTECT THOSE CHILDREN AGAINST THE UNCARING SPIRITS WHO DO ONLY EVIL ON THIS PLAIN.>
<PLEASE ALLOW ME TO HAVE COUNSELED THEM AS THEY MOST NEEDED!>

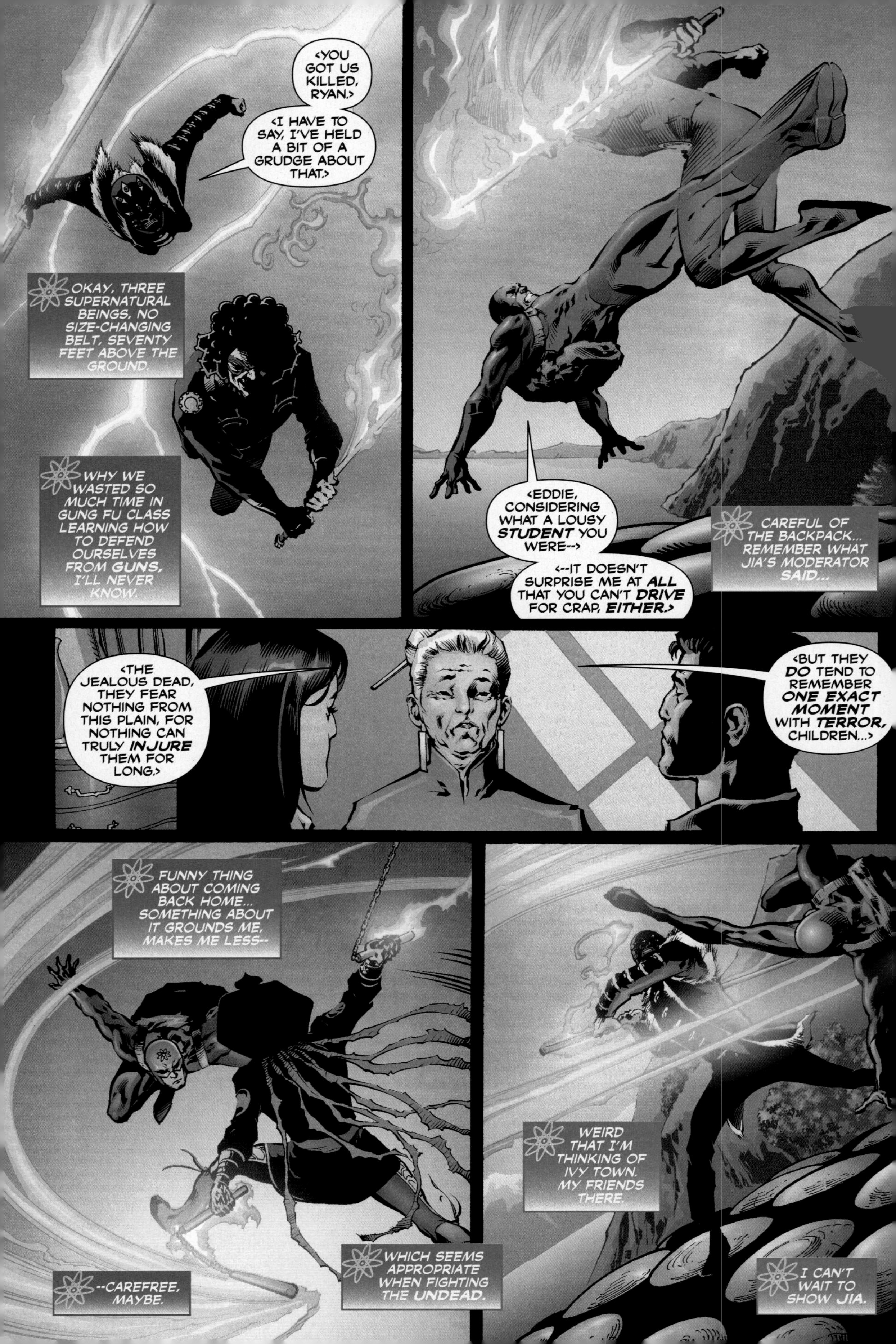
<YOU GOT US KILLED, RYAN.>
<I HAVE TO SAY, I'VE HELD A BIT OF A GRUDGE ABOUT THAT.>
OKAY, THREE SUPERNATURAL BEINGS, NO SIZE-CHANGING BELT, SEVENTY FEET ABOVE THE GROUND.
WHY WE WASTED SO MUCH TIME IN GUNG FU CLASS LEARNING HOW TO DEFEND OURSELVES FROM GUNS, I'LL NEVER KNOW.
<EDDIE, CONSIDERING WHAT A LOUSY STUDENT YOU WERE-->
<--IT DOESN'T SURPRISE ME AT ALL THAT YOU CAN'T DRIVE FOR CRAP, EITHER.>
CAREFUL OF THE BACKPACK... REMEMBER WHAT JIA'S MODERATOR SAID...
<THE JEALOUS DEAD, THEY FEAR NOTHING FROM THIS PLAIN, FOR NOTHING CAN TRULY INJURE THEM FOR LONG.>
<BUT THEY DO TEND TO REMEMBER ONE EXACT MOMENT WITH TERROR, CHILDREN...>
FUNNY THING ABOUT COMING BACK HOME... SOMETHING ABOUT IT GROUNDS ME, MAKES ME LESS--
--CAREFREE, MAYBE.
WHICH SEEMS APPROPRIATE WHEN FIGHTING THE UNDEAD.
WEIRD THAT I'M THINKING OF IVY TOWN. MY FRIENDS THERE.
I CAN'T WAIT TO SHOW JIA.

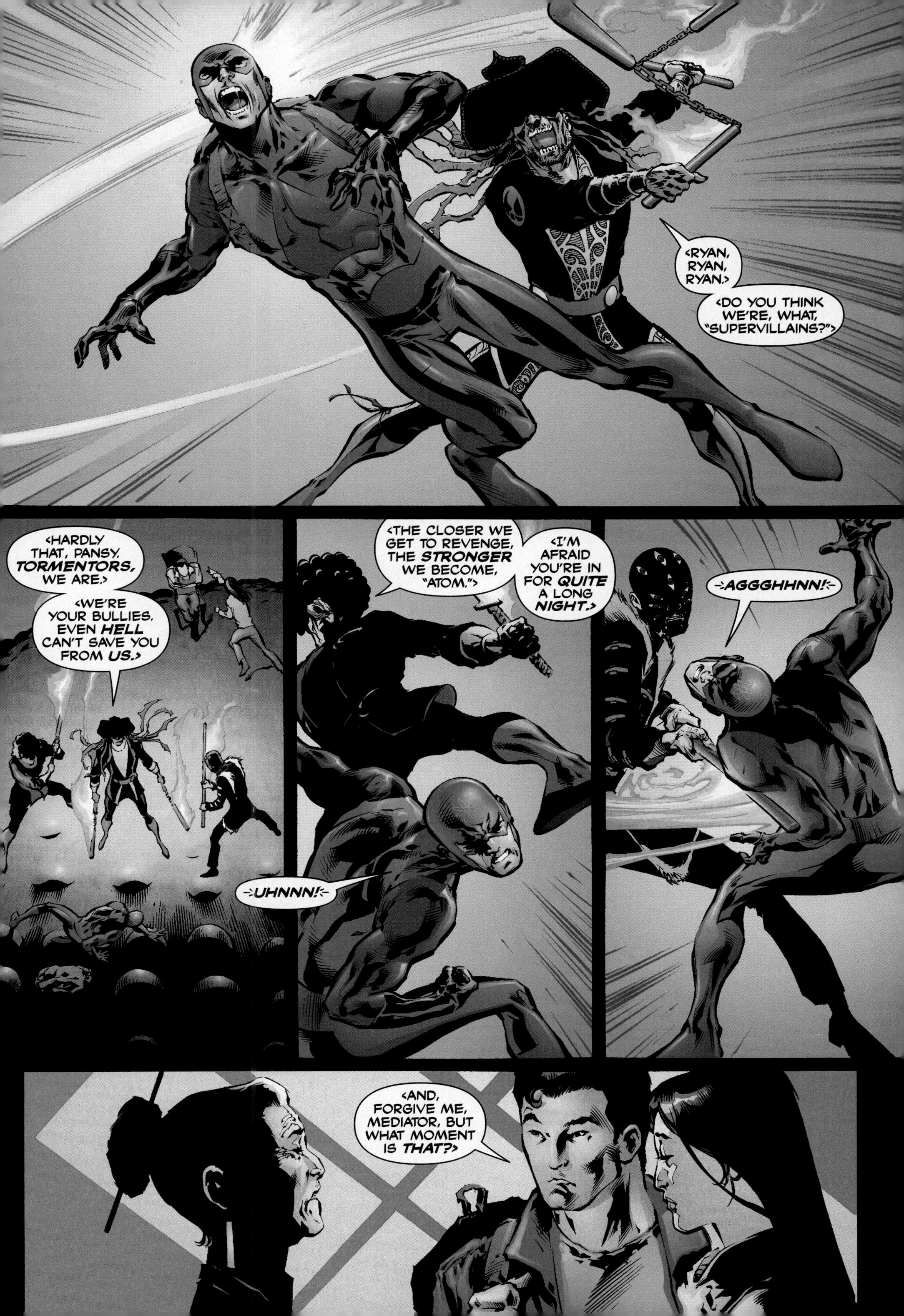

<RYAN, RYAN, RYAN.>
<DO YOU THINK WE'RE, WHAT, "SUPERVILLAINS?">
<HARDLY THAT, PANSY. TORMENTORS, WE ARE.>
<WE'RE YOUR BULLIES. EVEN HELL CAN'T SAVE YOU FROM US.>
<THE CLOSER WE GET TO REVENGE, THE STRONGER WE BECOME, "ATOM.">
<I'M AFRAID YOU'RE IN FOR QUITE A LONG NIGHT.>
->UHNNN!<-
->AGGGHHNN!<-
<AND, FORGIVE ME, MEDIATOR, BUT WHAT MOMENT IS THAT?>

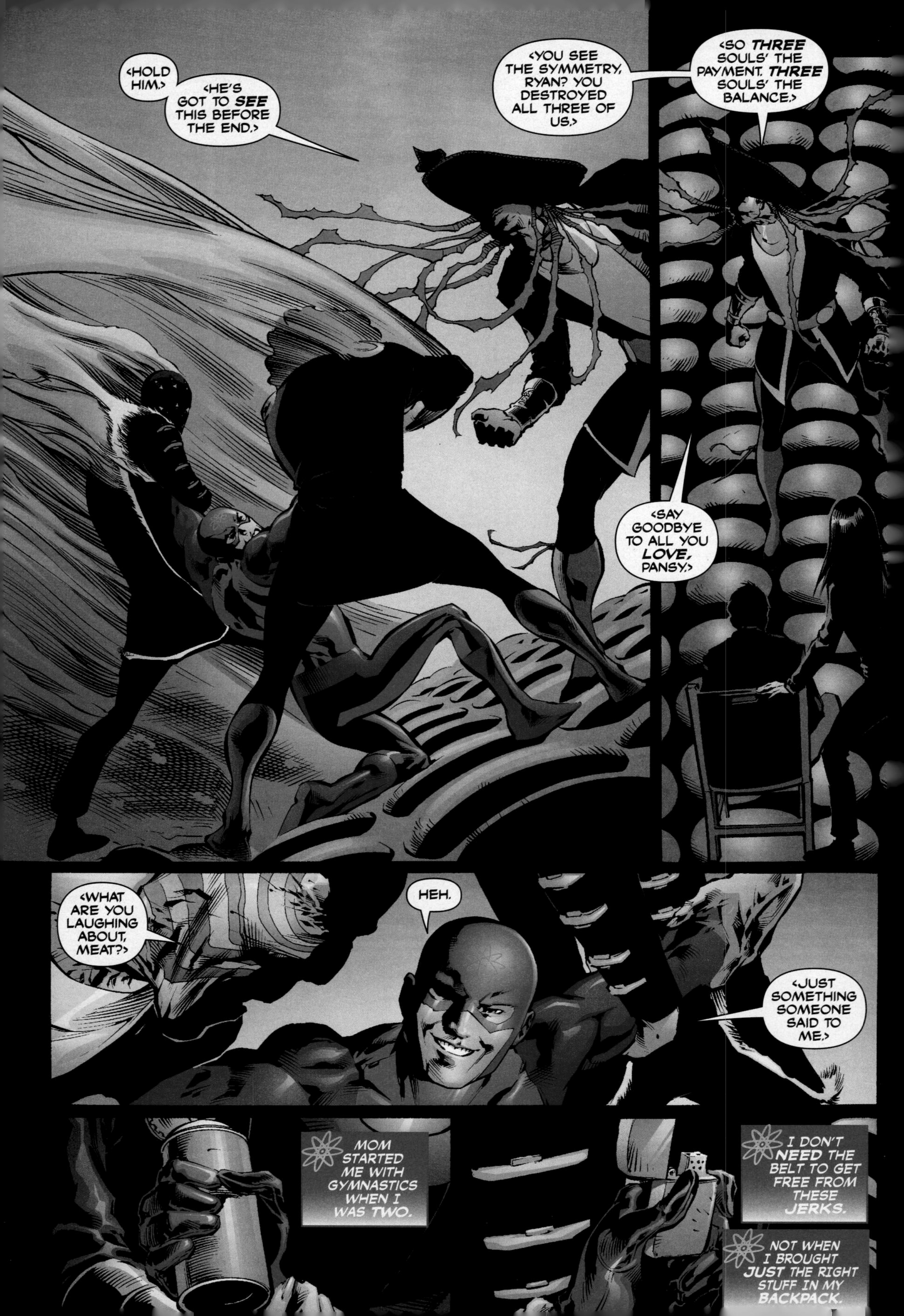
<HOLD HIM.>
<HE'S GOT TO SEE THIS BEFORE THE END.>
<YOU SEE THE SYMMETRY, RYAN? YOU DESTROYED ALL THREE OF US.>
<SO THREE SOULS' THE PAYMENT. THREE SOULS' THE BALANCE.>
<SAY GOODBYE TO ALL YOU LOVE, PANSY.>
<WHAT ARE YOU LAUGHING ABOUT, MEAT?>
HEH.
<JUST SOMETHING SOMEONE SAID TO ME.>
MOM STARTED ME WITH GYMNASTICS WHEN I WAS TWO.
I DON'T NEED THE BELT TO GET FREE FROM THESE JERKS.
NOT WHEN I BROUGHT JUST THE RIGHT STUFF IN MY BACKPACK.

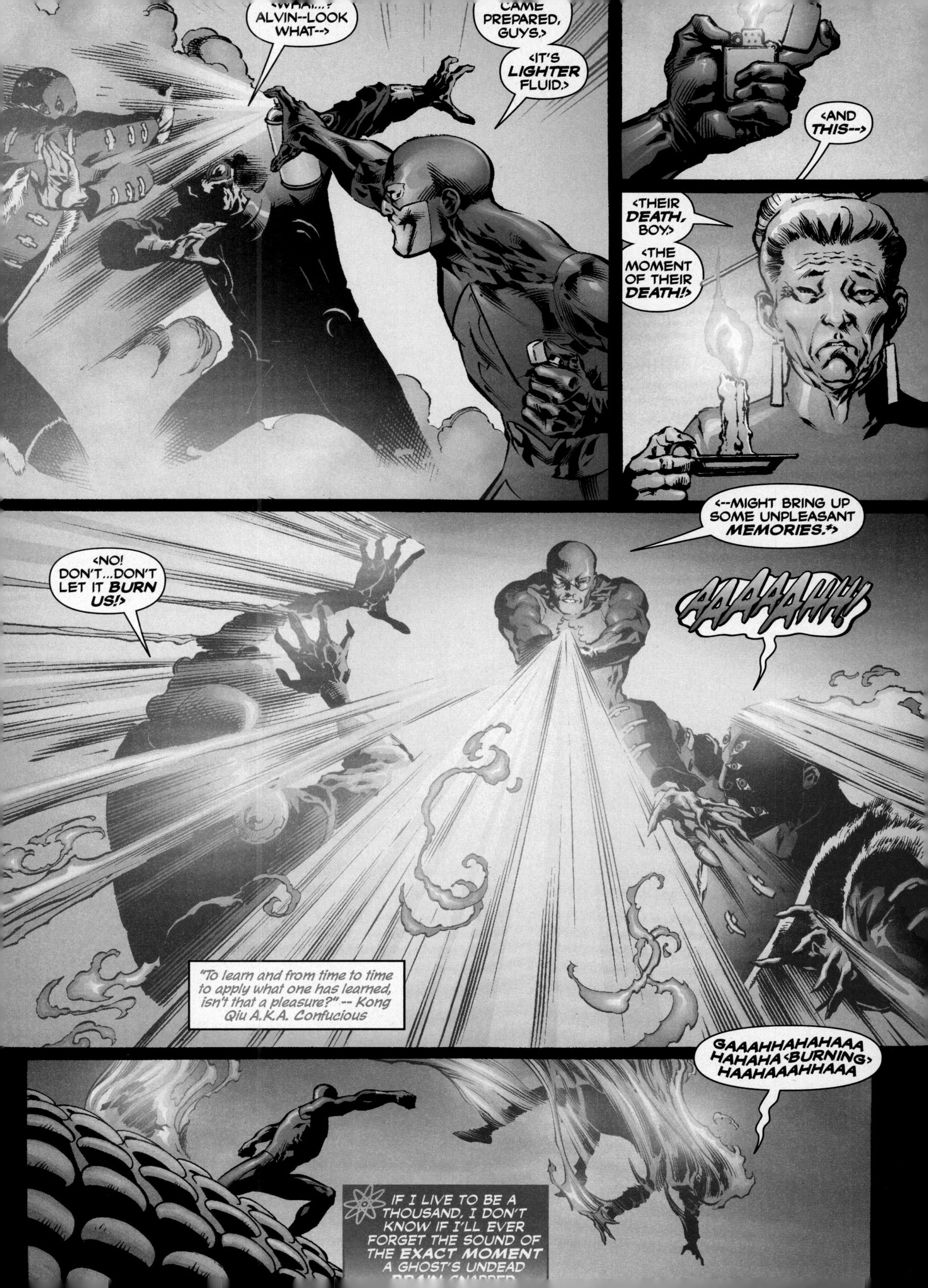
ALVIN--LOOK WHAT-->
CAME PREPARED, GUYS.>
<IT'S LIGHTER FLUID.>
<AND THIS-->
<THEIR DEATH, BOY.>
<THE MOMENT OF THEIR DEATH!>
<--MIGHT BRING UP SOME UNPLEASANT MEMORIES.*>
<NO! DON'T...DON'T LET IT BURN US!>
AAAAAHH!
"To learn and from time to time to apply what one has learned, isn't that a pleasure?" -- Kong Qiu A.K.A. Confucious
GAAAHHAHAHAAA HAHAHA <BURNING> HAAHAAAHHAAA
IF I LIVE TO BE A THOUSAND, I DON'T KNOW IF I'LL EVER FORGET THE SOUND OF THE EXACT MOMENT A GHOST'S UNDEAD

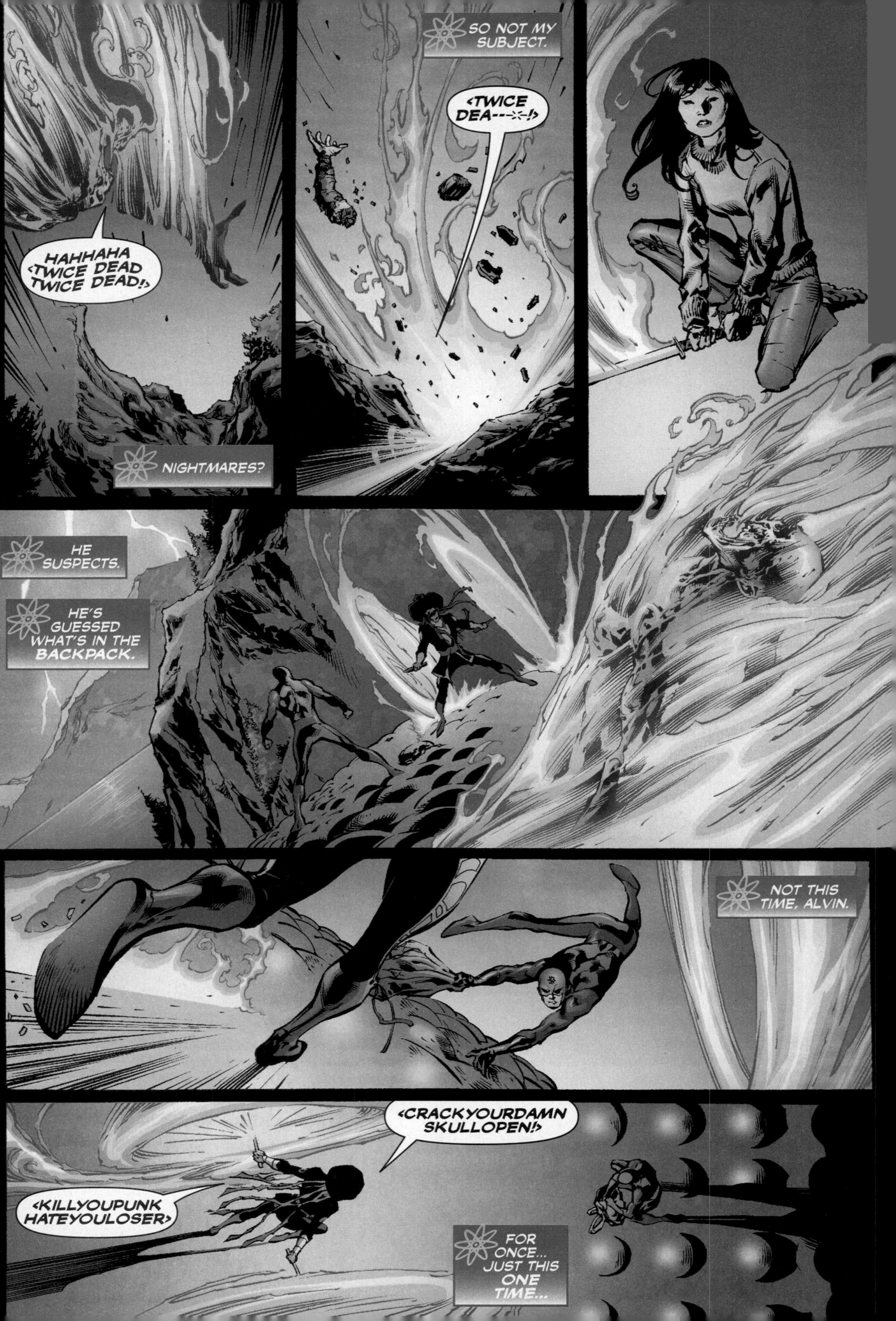
HAHHAHA <TWICE DEAD TWICE DEAD!>
NIGHTMARES?
SO NOT MY SUBJECT.
<TWICE DEA---!>
HE SUSPECTS.
HE'S GUESSED WHAT'S IN THE BACKPACK.
NOT THIS TIME, ALVIN.
<CRACKYOURDAMN SKULLOPEN!>
<KILLYOUPUNK HATEYOULOSER>
FOR ONCE... JUST THIS ONE TIME...

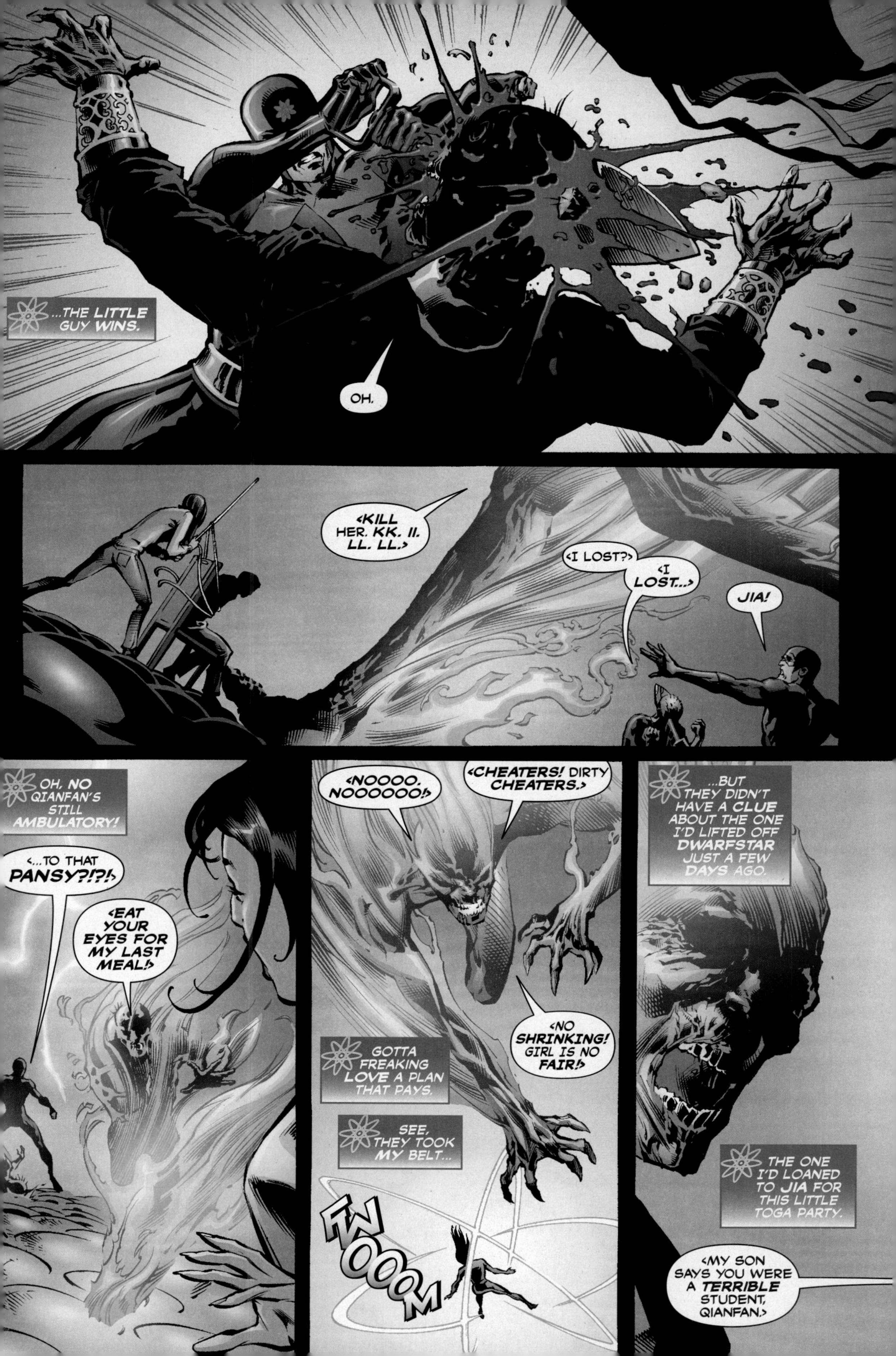
...THE LITTLE GUY WINS.
OH.
<KILL HER. KK. II. LL. LL.>
<I LOST?>
<I LOST...>
JIA!
OH, NO QIANFAN'S STILL AMBULATORY!
<...TO THAT PANSY?!?!>
<EAT YOUR EYES FOR MY LAST MEAL!>
<NOOOO. NOOOOOO!>
<CHEATERS! DIRTY CHEATERS.>
<NO SHRINKING! GIRL IS NO FAIR!>
GOTTA FREAKING LOVE A PLAN THAT PAYS.
SEE, THEY TOOK MY BELT...
FWOOOM
...BUT THEY DIDN'T HAVE A CLUE ABOUT THE ONE I'D LIFTED OFF DWARFSTAR JUST A FEW DAYS AGO.
THE ONE I'D LOANED TO JIA FOR THIS LITTLE TOGA PARTY.
<MY SON SAYS YOU WERE A TERRIBLE STUDENT, QIANFAN.>

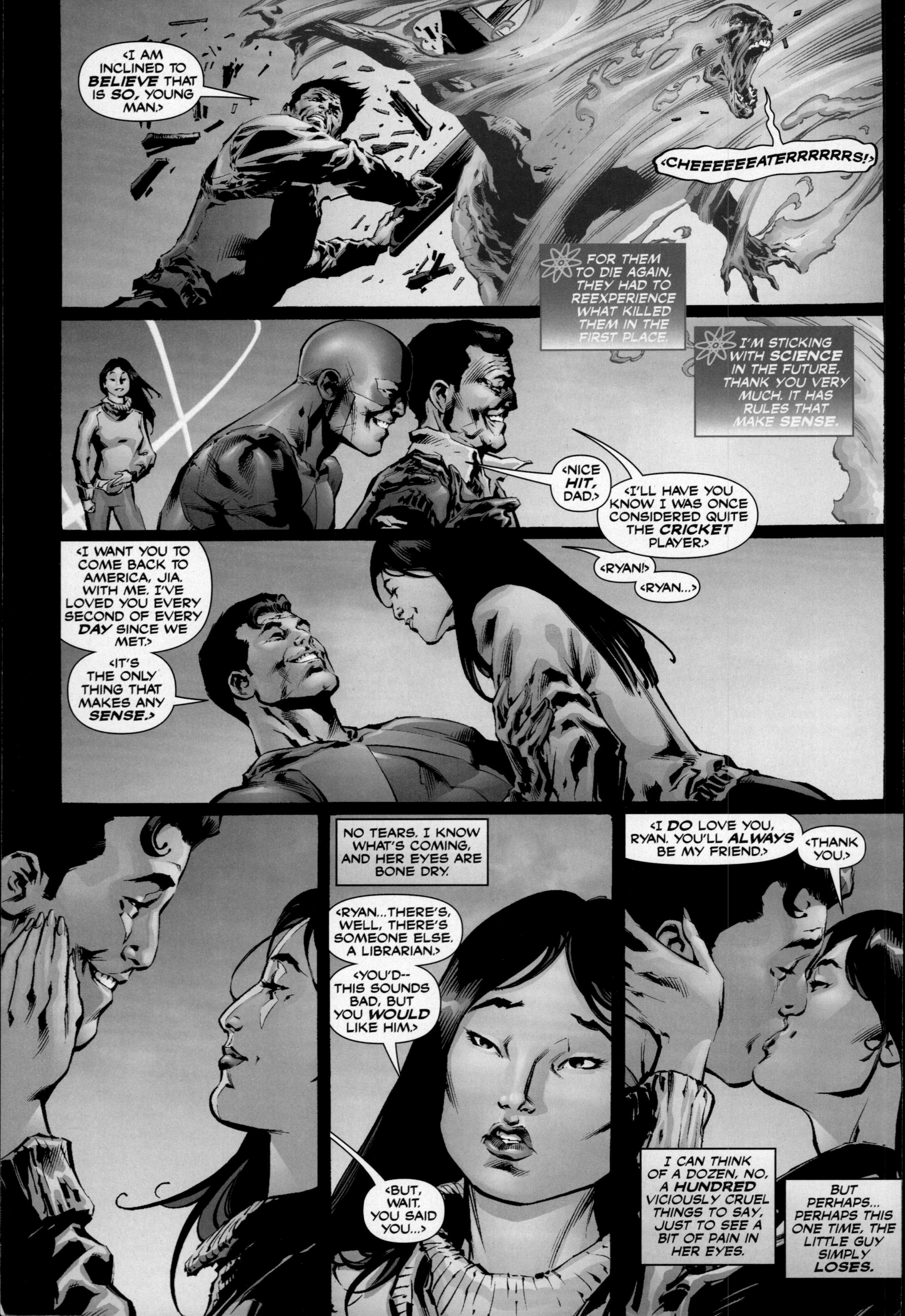

‹I AM INCLINED TO BELIEVE THAT IS SO, YOUNG MAN.›
‹CHEEEEEEATERRRRRRS!›
FOR THEM TO DIE AGAIN, THEY HAD TO REEXPERIENCE WHAT KILLED THEM IN THE FIRST PLACE.
I'M STICKING WITH SCIENCE IN THE FUTURE, THANK YOU VERY MUCH. IT HAS RULES THAT MAKE SENSE.
‹NICE HIT, DAD.›
‹I'LL HAVE YOU KNOW I WAS ONCE CONSIDERED QUITE THE CRICKET PLAYER.›
‹I WANT YOU TO COME BACK TO AMERICA, JIA. WITH ME. I'VE LOVED YOU EVERY SECOND OF EVERY DAY SINCE WE MET.›
‹IT'S THE ONLY THING THAT MAKES ANY SENSE.›
‹RYAN!›
‹RYAN...›
NO TEARS. I KNOW WHAT'S COMING, AND HER EYES ARE BONE DRY.
‹RYAN...THERE'S, WELL, THERE'S SOMEONE ELSE. A LIBRARIAN.›
‹YOU'D-- THIS SOUNDS BAD, BUT YOU WOULD LIKE HIM.›
‹BUT, WAIT. YOU SAID YOU...›
‹I DO LOVE YOU, RYAN. YOU'LL ALWAYS BE MY FRIEND.›
‹THANK YOU.›
I CAN THINK OF A DOZEN, NO, A HUNDRED VICIOUSLY CRUEL THINGS TO SAY, JUST TO SEE A BIT OF PAIN IN HER EYES.
BUT PERHAPS... PERHAPS THIS ONE TIME, THE LITTLE GUY SIMPLY LOSES.

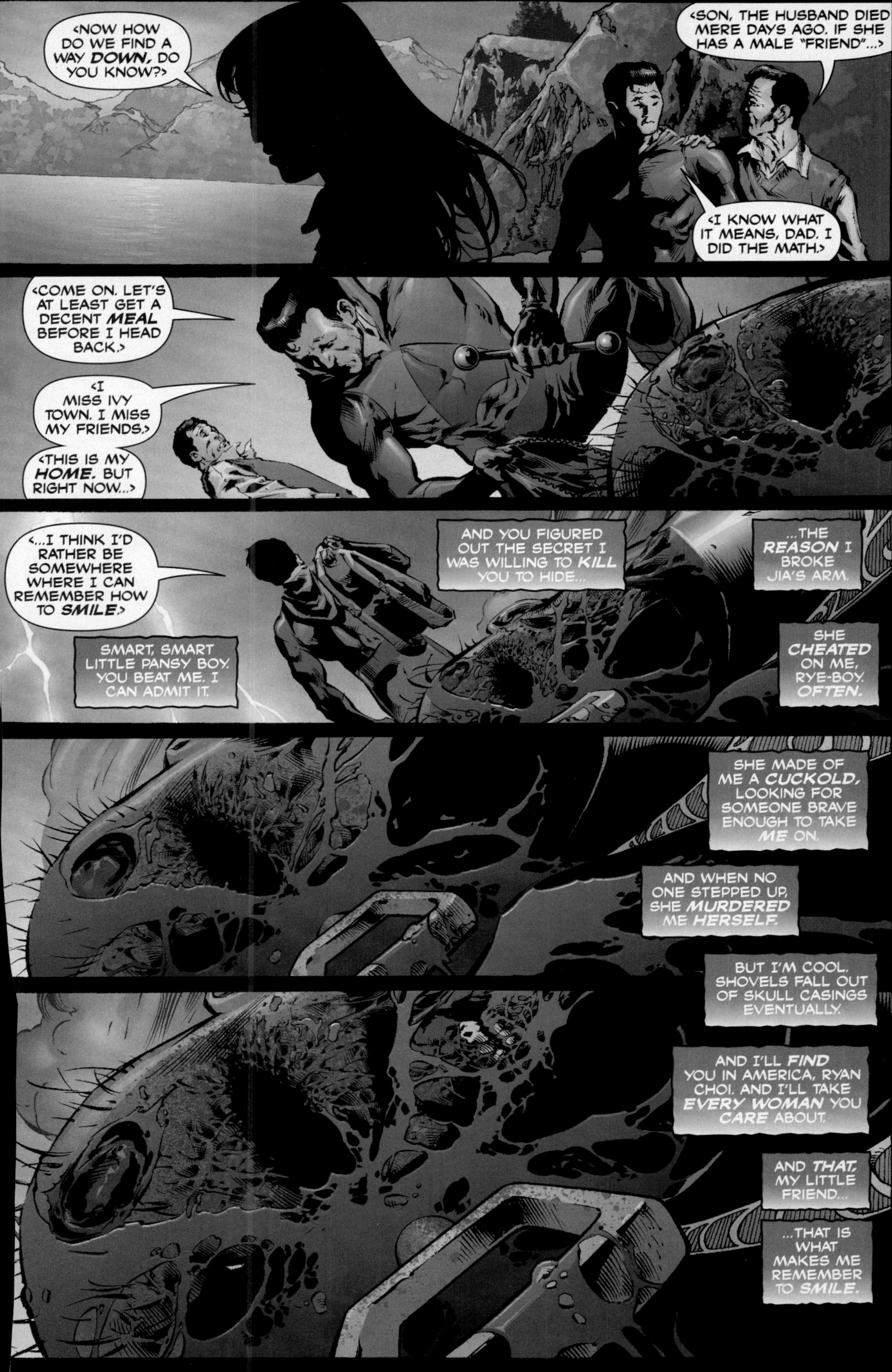

<NOW HOW DO WE FIND A WAY DOWN, DO YOU KNOW?>
<SON, THE HUSBAND DIED MERE DAYS AGO. IF SHE HAS A MALE "FRIEND"...>
<I KNOW WHAT IT MEANS, DAD. I DID THE MATH.>
<COME ON. LET'S AT LEAST GET A DECENT MEAL BEFORE I HEAD BACK.>
<I MISS IVY TOWN. I MISS MY FRIENDS.>
<THIS IS MY HOME. BUT RIGHT NOW...>
<...I THINK I'D RATHER BE SOMEWHERE WHERE I CAN REMEMBER HOW TO SMILE.>
SMART, SMART LITTLE PANSY BOY. YOU BEAT ME. I CAN ADMIT IT.
AND YOU FIGURED OUT THE SECRET I WAS WILLING TO KILL YOU TO HIDE...
...THE REASON I BROKE JIA'S ARM.
SHE CHEATED ON ME, RYE-BOY. OFTEN.
SHE MADE OF ME A CUCKOLD, LOOKING FOR SOMEONE BRAVE ENOUGH TO TAKE ME ON.
AND WHEN NO ONE STEPPED UP, SHE MURDERED ME HERSELF.
BUT I'M COOL. SHOVELS FALL OUT OF SKULL CASINGS EVENTUALLY.
AND I'LL FIND YOU IN AMERICA, RYAN CHOI. AND I'LL TAKE EVERY WOMAN YOU CARE ABOUT.
AND THAT, MY LITTLE FRIEND...
...THAT IS WHAT MAKES ME REMEMBER TO SMILE.

READ MORE ADVENTURES OF YOUR FAVORITE HEROES IN THESE COLLECTIONS FROM DC COMICS:

KINGDOM COME

THE GREATEST SUPER-HERO EPIC OF TOMORROW!
ELSEWORLDS
KINGDOM COME
Mark WAID Alex ROSS

Mark Waid and **Alex Ross** deliver a grim tale of youth versus experience, tradition versus change and what defines a hero. KINGDOM COME is a riveting story pitting the old guard — Superman, Batman, Wonder Woman and their peers — against a new uncompromising generation.

WINNER OF FIVE EISNER AND HARVEY AWARDS, INCLUDING BEST LIMITED SERIES AND BEST ARTIST

IDENTITY CRISIS

NEW YORK TIMES BEST-SELLING AUTHOR OF THE ZERO GAME
BRAD MELTZER
RAGS MORALES MICHAEL BAIR
IDENTITY CRISIS
Introduction by JOSS WHEDON, creator of BUFFY THE VAMPIRE SLAYER and FIREFLY
"The IDENTITY CRISIS mystery involves the biggest DC heroes... and uses all of Mr. Meltzer's skills as a thriller novelist." — The New York Times

BRAD MELTZER
RAGS MORALES
MICHAEL BAIR

CRISIS ON INFINITE EARTHS

CRISIS
ON INFINITE EARTHS
MARV WOLFMAN & GEORGE PÉREZ

MARV WOLFMAN
GEORGE PÉREZ

DC: THE NEW FRONTIER VOLUME 1

DC: The New Frontier
VOLUME ONE
BY DARWYN COOKE WITH DAVE STEWART

DARWYN COOKE
DAVE STEWART

SEARCH THE GRAPHIC NOVELS SECTION OF
www.DCCOMICS.com
FOR ART AND INFORMATION ON ALL OF OUR BOOKS

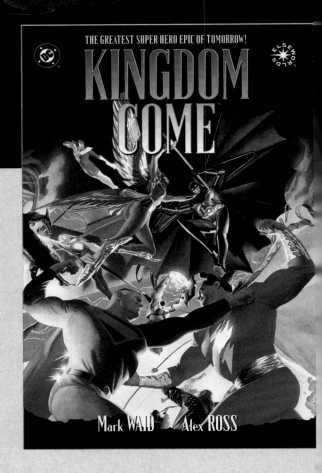

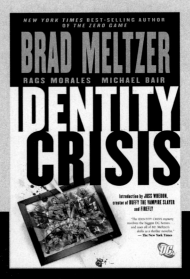

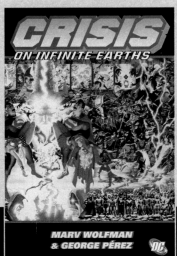

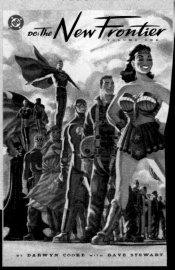